TO AFRICA & BEYOND

TO AFRICA & BEYOND

*Walking Through the Storms of
Life with a Thankful Heart*

Joseph Meyers

authorHOUSE®

AuthorHouse™ LLC
1663 Liberty Drive
Bloomington, IN 47403
www.authorhouse.com
Phone: 1-800-839-8640

PastorJoseph7Ruth@wordpress.com

Published by AuthorHouse   03/27/2014

ISBN: 978-1-4918-7102-7 (sc)
ISBN: 978-1-4918-7103-4 (e)

This book is printed on acid-free paper.

Scripture quotations marked NKJV are from the Holy Bible, King James Version (Authorized Version). First published in 1611. Quoted from the NKJV Classic Reference Bible, Copyright © 1983 by The Zondervan Corporation.

Scripture quotations marked (NLT) are taken from the Holy Bible, New Living Translation, copyright © 1996, 2004, 2007 by Tyndale House Foundation. Used by permission of Tyndale House Publishers, Inc., Carol Stream, Illinois 60188. All rights reserved.

TABLE OF CONTENTS

DEDICATION

Dedicated posthumously to my dear wife, Ruth Helen Taylor-Meyers, the Love of my life, who shared most of these experiences with me, in fact who was an essential part of many of the events herein described. How I wish she could have lived to help me write this book! But without consulting me and without my prior agreement, the Sovereign Lord God of all that exists called her home to be with Him! Ruth's Coronation Day (crowned with Eternal Life) came on July 17, 2011 and I have been required to finish my pilgrimage on this earth without my Covenant Companion. Of course, subsequent to her Home-going I realized the importance of my joyful submission to God's Wise & Merciful Sovereignty! Only when I have joined Ruth in Heaven's Glorious Land will I understand the purposes of my Heavenly Father in what He allowed.

Secondly, this Book is dedicated to my daughter, Lani Rochelle Pitofsky (a successful administrator at the VA Hospital in Seattle and a woman with an intellect like a steel trap and a work ethic beyond reproach) as well as her irrepressible husband, Peter, who is Mr. Sunshine, and who makes it his life's work to bring humor, laughs and happiness to everyone he meets.

Thirdly, this book is dedicated to my awesomely wonderful two Sisters, Norma Jean Boggs who gave me a wonderful Brother in-law, Mr. Tom Boggs, as well as Juanita Ruth Sawyer who gave me another wonderful Brother in-law, Mr. Charlie Sawyer. By the way, the French way of addressing in-laws is like: "Beautiful Mother for Mother In-law or "Handsome Brother" for Brother In-law or "Beautiful Sister" for Sister In-law. Do you think we Americans could learn something by this?

Fourth, this Book is dedicated to the prolific (like bunny rabbits) "Taylor Clan", Ruth's Family who so lovingly and graciously has continued to include me as part of "The Family"! To Paul Taylor who is like a Brother to me; to Esther, Ruth's Sister (and mine). To Tim Taylor, the youngest of eight of Ruth's Brothers who's Faith which resulted in Healing from three stage-four cancers has inspired the entire Taylor Family (of which I am a part). I love all 100 + of you!

Last, but most of all, this Book is dedicated in humility and thankfulness to my wonderful Adonai (Lord, Absolute Ruler, Final Authority and Savior (Deliverer, Conqueror), Jesus Christ . . . and to Yahweh/Jehovah (Self-Existent One, Source of Life or Life-Giver), with His multiple names and titles given as a Gift to the Human Race by Him Who loved us so much that He gave His Only Begotten Son to be a Redemptive Sacrifice so as to redeem us from under the power of the Evil One. To Elohim (Mighty, Strong, Strength of a Wild Ox), Jehovah-Jireh (the Lord Provides), Jehovah-rophe (Our God heals), Jehovah-nissi (God is my Banner), Jehovah-M'Kaddesh (God sanctifies [His People] or makes [His People] Holy or Righteous), Jehovah-shalom (God is our Peace)! To Him without Who we would have no life, this book is dedicated!

He is also my Heavenly Father, in Whose Arms of Love and Glorious Light I long to be! Even so, come again; come soon, I pray, Oh Bridegroom of the Church, Jesus the Christ! Lord of Lords and King of Kings!

WITH APPRECIATION

It is important to mention my deep appreciation for the help of Mrs. Linda Pagel, and her Son, Mr. David Pagel, who have so graciously given their time to critique this manuscript and develop the unique book cover! Any current mistakes or needed improvement is due to my own errors. The compliments belong to Mrs. Pagel and her Son. The same can be said regarding the invaluable encouragement and counsel of Mrs. Carol Stone. Thank you ladies! You and your husbands are wonderful friends!

FOREWORD

"What a journey!" That's what I found myself thinking as I read the manuscript of Joseph Meyers' remarkable saga of life and ministry. The Lord opened doors of opportunity for Joseph and Ruth, not only here at home, but literally around the world—from little Vader, Washington, to Africa and Viet Nam, to Alaska and Cambodia, to Chicago and Canada, and beyond. Joseph's childhood dream was to be a great healing evangelist. But God's destiny was for him to impact thousands as an international Bible preacher/teacher, and to do it with his best friend, his wife Ruth.

This autobiographical account is a study in contrasts. On the one hand it is intensely personal, but on the other hand it is profoundly spiritual. It climbs exhilarating spiritual mountaintops, and plunges into the deepest valleys. There are personal testimonies, but also biblical teachings with universal application. The transparency with which it is written is sometimes painful to read, but the lessons learned bring healing.

Even the title suggests this contrast: Walking Through the Storms of Life . . . With a Thankful Heart. Storms and thankfulness seem incompatible, but not if you walk through the storms with the Lord's help. We do not just walk into the storms, we walk through them. We don't stay perpetually in the storms, we press through to the other side of them. That's cause for thankfulness. And wherever we are, God is there. As the old song says, "Through it all, through it all, I've learned to trust in Jesus, I've learned to trust in God."

Joseph's description of the long illness and ultimate death of his son, Lance, will bring tears to your eyes. His eulogy for his beloved wife will do likewise. Painful storms; perfect peace. Unbearable grief; undeniable grace.

Joseph tells us of Ruth's love of, and adherence to, the truth. But he also is a truth-lover and truth-teller. So his revelations about his mistakes, his honesty about his "do-overs," his frustration with his inadequacies—all are told as unvarnished truth. But the truth about himself is contrasted with the truth about the God he serves. In revealing Himself in Christ, He is declared to be full of grace and truth. We not only need the truth, we need grace. That's what Jesus offers. Our foibles and failures are met with the immensity of His grace and forgiveness. Knowing that alone will help us through the storms of life.

I identified with many of the people, places, and events in this book because I go back with Joseph and Ruth about 40 years. They were interim pastors at Spanaway Assembly in Tacoma, Washington, until I became the Senior Pastor there. I was privileged to serve for a time on the board of Joseph's ministry, Church Renewal, and serve as his denominational supervisor. For a couple of years we were next door neighbors and would often take Lance and Lani to church with us when Joseph and Ruth had services elsewhere. Since then we have often been separated by miles and time, but our friendship has stayed strong.

Thanks, Joseph, for allowing us to follow you to the highest of the highs and the lowest of the lows in your life. And thank you for reminding us that in every storm one thing remains the same: God is faithful.

Warren D. Bullock
Executive Presbyter, Northwest Region
General Council of the Assemblies of God

FOREWORD

Foreword for *Walking Through the Storms of Life . . . With a Thankful Heart* by Joseph Meyers

Don Detrick, D.Min., Associate Network Leader, Northwest Ministry of the Assemblies of God, Adjunct Professor, Northwest University and Assemblies of God Theological Seminary;

Author: *Growing Disciples Organically: The Jesus Method of Spiritual Formation*

My wife and I recently spent a few days at a Seaside, Oregon beachfront inn. Winter storms often blow in from the Pacific, and one such February storm blasted our small second story room during a particular night of our stay. The wind howled down the chimney and literally shook the windows, floor, and walls, occasionally awakening us from sleep. Having spent eight years of our lives not far from there, we were not particularly frightened by the intensity of the storm, and I awoke early the next morning with anticipation. Gone were the clouds and wind, and a blue sky welcomed me as I strode down to the beach, camera in hand.

Beachcombing and photos would occupy me for the next several hours as the combination of wind and high tides had coughed up onto the sands a plethora of treasures from the deep. The hope of discovering some valuable or unique object motivated my search. Although rare these days, old Japanese glass fishing net floats were sometimes found on days like this, even rarer were old bottles, some adrift at sea for years. I held onto a hope that I might even find an old bottle with a message inside—perhaps some sailor's last love letter before perishing years ago as his vessel sank during a storm similar to what we'd experienced the night before.

But it was not to be. My treasures that morning were the photos I was able to take, and a few seashells and sand dollars my young granddaughters might add to their collection. However the thought of finding a message in a bottle is intriguing, and motivated an internet search of the topic.

The Guinness Book of Records actually keeps track of old messages found in bottles. And the oldest one on record is a message in a bottle found in April 2012 by a Scottish skipper on the North Sea that had floated around for 98 years before he fished it out of the water. Oddly enough, the bottle discovered by Andrew Leaper was only about 9 miles from where it had originally been released on June 10, 1914 by Captain C. Hunter Brown of the Glasgow School of Navigation. He had released this bottle along with 1,899 others that day in an attempt to map the currents of the North Sea. And the message was still intact: "Please state when and where this bottle was found, and then put it in the nearest post office."

One would expect more information, more drama, more romance, more . . . *something* from such a discovery! But the Guinness Book of Records does not embellish the facts—sometimes a message in a bottle, even one that has drifted about for nearly a century, can be quite boring and offer little information to help today's traveler navigate the chilly waters of life.

The truth is, we often set off on the journey of life in anticipation of a great adventure, only to discover more disappointments than excitement along the road. The wise traveler, however, learns from both excitement and disappointment, recording lessons learned along the way. Those who go before us, such as Captain C. Hunter Brown of the Glasgow School of Navigation, may well invest much effort in mapping the currents, and helping others make discoveries and avoid the obstacles that will enable them to finish the journey successfully.

Like Captain Brown, my good friend Joseph Meyers has provided this book as a roadmap for the great adventure of life that lies before each of us. Joseph's journey has taken him around the world and through experiences many of us will never face. From humble beginnings, he has accomplished much during his lifetime as a student, teacher, pastor, and missionary. He has led many to Christ, and diligently taught the Word of God. From the mundane to the miraculous, through dust, dirt, and danger, he has navigated through the most challenging storms by keeping his heart set on the North Star of the soul, a vision of the Lord that cannot be diminished by clouds, currents, or catastrophes.

In this book you will discover priceless pages from the diary of a pilgrim, one who has carefully documented his journey, providing us access to lessons that are best learned from others who have gone on before. Joseph's steadfast faith and insight into biblical truth will add light to the dark and shadowy places of your soul. His conviction that God is good and will provide a way through the storm will provide nourishment to feed your soul when you are hungry for a word of hope to sustain you along the way. His determination to see the good and utilize the power of the Holy Spirit will be a well of water to quench your thirst for encouragement when your plate is full but your cup is empty. And his gentle reminders to live at all times with a grateful heart will be keys to unlock the doors of your prison of fear and release you to move toward your divine destiny.

I don't know what you might be facing. Each of us faces different storms and at different places and times, but we can be certain that storms will come. It is best to be prepared. *Walking Through the Storms of Life . . . With a Thankful Heart* will help you do that very thing. Better than a message in a bottle, the messages contained in these pages will be true treasures, to help you overcome life's storms and stay on course.

Don Detrick, D.Min.
Associate Network Leader, Northwest
Ministry of the Assemblies of God
Adjunct Professor, Northwest University and
Assemblies of God Theological Seminary
Author: *Growing Disciples Organically: The
Jesus Method of Spiritual Formation*
Feb 23, 2014 North Bend, WA

Introduction

Key concepts & Biblical Guidance
for Daily and Global Living

This is a book about lessons learned in the crucible of Life's Storms, and the attitudes needed in successfully facing those storms. The necessary attitudes are these:

1. A Sense of adventure and expectation for Divine Providence, protection and favor rather than an attitude of dread, fear or self-pity; knowing God loves you! God is a Good God and the Devil is a bad devil. Please don't get that confused or mixed up!

2. An Expectation of Providential & miraculous Guidance through each Storm;

3. An Expectation of God's Miraculous Provision through the Storms of life coupled with a daily practice of faith filled praying and intercession before God for your own needs and the needs of others;

4. A willingness to engage frequently, if not constantly, in self-examination[1] for the purpose of understanding the wisdom needed for each day;

   a. the reason(s) why I am where I now find myself, needed

---

[1]   Ezra 10:10-19; Psalm 26:2; Lamentations 3:38-48; I Corinthians 11:28-32; II Corinthians 13:5; Galatians 6:4 (Amplified Bible) "But let every person carefully scrutinize *and* examine *and* test his own conduct *and* his own work. He can then have the personal satisfaction *and* joy of doing something commendable {in itself alone} without [resorting to] boastful comparison with his neighbor."

course corrections (if any), intense consideration of the consequences that will come from the choices I make each day.

b.   Speaking of choices, one should always remember that choices normally have cumulative consequences for people and circumstances. Each choice either builds or increases strength, knowledge and wisdom; or is destructive, detractive and weakening of future opportunities and fulfillment of purposes.

4.   Remember that Life has meaning!

a.   God created each of us to have Significance, Purpose and Meaning to our life.

(1) If these seem to be missing from our life, such a negative perception (feeling insignificant and without purpose or meaning in our life) is either an expression of impatience or misunderstanding of where we are in the process of God's purposes being accomplished in one's life.

(2) or, an indication that we are out of the Will of God altogether, off the right path and needing to repent and return to where we are expected to be in our relationship with God so that purpose and meaning can return.

(3) If the first be true, then an attitude adjustment with the help & guidance of the Holy Spirit is all that is needed;

(4) But if the second is true (we are out of the will of God) then a serious and maybe even prolonged period of self-examination and repentance is required to help us make the course correction in our life that is needed.

(5) Remember, God HAS gifted you with purpose and meaning for your life!

b.   The things that happen to each of us (circumstances that arise) have reason (Divine or Satanic Purpose) behind them. (Book of Job, chapters 1 & 2)!

(1) Has God revealed to you something about the meaning and purpose of your life?

    (a) If not, it will be extremely important for one to spend a period of time in prayer, the devotional personalized reading of God's Word, and active seeking of counsel from tried and tested Spiritual Leaders whose integrity and heart after God are beyond question.

    (b) If you have some sense of God's Will for your life, then maybe it is time to contemplate on the admonition of some unknown Saint, "Never doubt in the Dark what God has revealed to you in the Light."

(2) To discourage us from the direction we are presently headed in life so that God can get us back on track toward fulfilling the purpose for which He created us.

(3) To encourage us in the direction we are headed (a little bit of, "Well done! Thou good and faithful servant!" message from our Creator).

(4) To help us make small or large course corrections in our life.

(5) To encourage us to fulfill obligations and Covenant Relationships in a way that establishes more firmly the element of integrity connected to our Life Message. Faithfulness to your spouse & family! Don't break promises!

(6) Does your life have a Message, and do you know what that Message is?

    (a) Noah had a life message. See if you can figure it out!

(b) Abraham had a life message. See if you can figure it out!

(c) Moses had a life message. See if you can figure it out!

(d) Joshua had a life message. See if you can figure it out!

(e) Joseph had a life message. See if you can figure it out!

(f) John the Baptist had a life message. See if you can figure it out!

(g) None of these men could have done what the others did. The timing and the Call of God only fit their life on the earth at the time they lived.

(h) God has equipped each of us for the time and culture in which we live and He expects us to fulfill His purposes that are unique to our personal abilities, interests and God-given potential (Grace-giftings).

(i) Realize that no one that has ever lived in human history could have done what God has asked you to accomplish with your Life Message and Purpose— only you can do that! [2]

(j) You may right now be an alcoholic or drug addict

---

[2] Ezekiel 3:16-21; 33:2-9; Isaiah 52:8; Acts 20:28-31; Revelation 11:3-13; Matthew 10:1; Acts 19:15; First Corinthians 12:4-11, 27-31; The reign of Cyrus over Babylon was prophesied by Isaiah around 620 B.C. or 130 years before Cyrus lived in 750 B.C.; and Cyrus did what God said he would do during the ministry of Jeremiah, Haggai and Zechariah. Only one man could have made the prophecy and only one man could have fulfilled it. Not Noah or Abraham or Moses could have accomplished what Isaiah or Cyrus accomplished. So it is with each of us. We each have our God-appointed task to do for Him during a specific period of time in human history. Do you know the details and purposes of your task, or the personal giftings and abilities God expects you to use to accomplish your task in God's Kingdom?

or have been molested or told you were trash and would never amount to anything.

(k) God did not create you to spend your whole life suffering as a victim!

(l) When life hands you a lemon, make lemonade with it, as my wife and I did, in taking the ashes of our Son's wasted body into high school gymnasiums and women's prisons or youth detention centers to warn and equip other youth. So also you can take the ashes of your life and do something great with them that will benefit many other people!

(m) Find out through study and counseling with Godly people what God's purposes are for your life. Get rid of self-pity! Tell yourself, "I am strong! My life is like a Treasure of Gold hidden in a field! I will find the Treasure God has buried within me and I will use that Treasure to help others, and for the Glory of God." Just do it!

Chapter One

The Storm of Unintended Consequences birthed out of Foolish Choices

The Storm

It was a warm, sunny day, that day so very many years ago, as I walked along a California beach with my Father. We had progressed down the beach; just enjoying being together, the tide was out, but starting to come back in. Then we came finally to a place where there were tall cliffs on one side and the ocean on the other. Dad suggested that we climb the tallest of the cliffs which, as I remember, must have been all of 50 to 100 feet in height.

Dad was an experienced mountain climber, not in any technical sense, but he had grown up in the Tetons of Wyoming and had done a lot of climbing in those mountains. I remember clearly that both of us were dressed lightly as would be normal in the warmth of a Spring or Summer day in central California. I had on a pair of tennis shoes, slacks and shirt. Dad was similarly dressed.

As we began our assent up that sheer cliff there were, at first, ample finger and toe holds that made the climb relatively easy. Dad climbed first and so was above me on the cliff. That had to be a "God-thing" as we would later discover. On the way up, I once looked down and noticed that the tide was coming in and the rocks below were beginning to be surrounded by water. What began to cause a little concern was that the closer to the top of the rock cliff we came, the fewer were the opportunities to grasp something or put the ends of my tennis shoes onto a small protrusion in the cliff.

Dad finally reached the top and pulled himself up and over to safety, and onto the flat ground above. By that time I had reached a point where, because I was so much shorter than my Father, I could no longer find toe-holds or finger-holds with which to continue my assent. I was stuck on that sheer, perpendicular cliff and unable to ascend or descend. In the meantime, we had been so focused on the climb, which had turned out to be far more dangerous and risky than I'm sure my Father had already anticipated that we had failed to notice the changing weather and the decent of evening shadows. The wind had come up, the weather was changing and our position on that cliff was extremely precarious, especially for me. It began to look as if maybe a rain storm was blowing in from the sea. As my situation slowly dawned on me, I felt the first pangs of fear. The palms of my hands became sweaty and my knees felt unsteady. So the psychological as well as physical danger was suddenly being compounded.

As Dad sized up my (our) situation he laid down flat on the top of the cliff, wrapped his legs around a strong looking bush, and began to lower his torso down over the edge of the cliff in my direction. He then extended one hand down to me and asked me to grasp his hand. I let go with of my hold on that cliff with one hand, and reached up to him. The tips of our middle fingers touched, but Dad was unable to grasp my hand so as to pull me to safety. In a calm, reassuring voice that spoke of confidence I doubt he felt, he informed me that since we were miles away from any Park Ranger station or a telephone or any other form of help, we were going to need to solve this problem between the two of us.

He then outlined his plan of action. Even though I was pressed flat against that perpendicular cliff and holding on for dear life, I was to force my body out away from the cliff in a way that would allow me to bend my knees as best I could, then letting go of my hand-holds on the cliff shoot one hand up toward him as I jumped. He promised to catch that hand and pull me to safety. It was our only hope! Dad must have realized that, especially with the storm coming in and the possibility of rain, I would not be able to remain on the cliff long enough for him to go for help and return in time to rescue me. So this was it! We had only one try. If he missed my hand or I somehow failed to perform the jump/reach scenario correctly so that he could grasp my hand and pull me to safety, I would surely fall to my death on the rocks some 50 plus feet below.

I cannot possibly do an adequate job of describing the psychological storm within my mind, emotions and will power that day on the cliff. My sweaty palms and weak, shaky knees against the cold stone of that cliff were only external evidences of the internal struggle with fear washing over me. I wished for a different set of choices but there were none.

How did I get into this position? What had started out to be a fun time with my Father on a warm, balmy California day had turned into a hellish, life-threatening nightmare! Regrets, second guessing and wishes for a chance to back up and redo our choices of that day would solve nothing. I'm sure Dad must have been going through a similar emotional storm that early spring day as he looked downward at his Son whose life clung precariously to quickly diminishing options in a seemingly impossible situation. How would he face his wife (my Mother) if this ended badly? How could he ever forgive himself for getting the two of us into this predicament?

I knew I could not hang onto the small safety and comfort of finger and toe holds. Time, fear and the incoming change of weather all dictated a leap of faith or a terrible fall that would surely end in the breaking of every bone in my body or, maybe, a merciful and sudden death on the rocks below. I wanted to live! Obedience and trust in my Father were my only choices if I hoped to have the opportunity for health and life.

Results Coming out of the Storm

My knees bent, my hand shot up toward my Father's hand. I am alive and well today as a testimony to God's Grace and help, as well as the stubborn Will-power of my Father who now, with only half of his body on top of the cliff and the top part of his torso hanging downward on the side of the cliff, had the herculean task of pulling the dead weight of my body up over the top of that cliff to safety.

I remember so very clearly Dad's words to me after I was safely on top with him, "Son, we won't tell your Mother about this, will we?" It was many years later before Mom found out about that wonderful day on the cliff when God taught my Father and myself lessons about commitment, obedience, trust, faith, perseverance, hope and the need to think & plan carefully before making hasty choices!

There would be another day, years later, a day of deep discouragement and bitterness of soul when I would re-learn the lessons of boyhood by means of a supernatural visitation from God, coupled with the words, "Son, down the road (of life) you will need to know that I know where you are!" But that is another story. Actually, the times I would need to remember those words and the fact that God was very much aware of my location and need and, by implication, that I would be sheltered and cared for within His Love for me; these are multiple stories to be shared. The first two are separated by from 10 to 13 years (from the time I was somewhere between 6 to 12 years of age (1949 to 1955) all the way to 1966 when I was about 23 years of age, from a child jumping with trust to catch my Dad's hand to a grown man, married and feeling that God was not treating me right because I was having to work too hard to pay for my Bible College training instead of spending enough time with my lovely, beautiful Bride, a gift from God); all because of the work & study requirements.

And then too, times much later on in life, out in Africa, looking down the barrels of guns pointed at my head or deadly snakes threatening my life or angry witch doctors also wanting to take my life. At each point, needing to know that my Heavenly Father knew where I was and by implication was in control of my circumstances, allowing what was happening within the confines of His Sovereign, disciplining (training), loving and merciful Will! There is always the temptation, when events or circumstances in life are not to our liking to want to choose to quit in disgust, saying, "This is not for me!" And then make choices under the stress of disappointment, or frustration, or self-pity or anger that will alter our lives and, as a consequence, cause us to miss the very best that God has planned for us!

I can say now, in 2014, at 70 years of age, that there were many times I was tempted to "throw in the towel" and make life altering choices because I was exhausted, disgusted, filled with self-pity, or angry. There was one period of my life, after we came to the end of our missionary career that I literally laid on my bed and prayed over a period of months that God would take my life. Depression and a sense of failure and self-pity had set in and it was only because of the love of my precious wife, the friendship of Pastor Fulton Buntain in Tacoma, Washington and the tender patience of my Heavenly Father that I was able to survive that season of my life. Physical and emotional fatigue is a great catalyst that the Enemy of our Souls can use against us in an effort to cause us to miss out on God's highest destiny for our individual lives. This is true for each of us! God has a unique destiny for each person, just like each snow flake is unique or each flower or each part of His awesome Creation is unique. And we should each remember the promise given by the Holy Spirit through His Prophet, Jeremiah.[3] And then again there is the assurance of Psalm 139:16-18 (New Living Translation), that each moment and day of our lives is planned by God before we are born.

> For I know the plans I have for you," says the LORD. "They are plans for good and not for disaster, to give you a future and a hope. **12** In those days when you pray, I will listen. **13** If you look for me wholeheartedly, you will find me.
>
> <u>Psalm 139:16-18—NLT</u>
>
> You saw me before I was born. Every day of my life was recorded in your book. Every moment was laid out before a single day had passed. How precious are your thoughts about me, O God. They cannot be numbered!

But there is a price to pay for experiencing God's best in our lives! And that is also what this book is all about! It is about the price Ruth and I paid to experience God's best in our lives, and how we learned to live with thankful hearts and positive attitudes even while we suffered, continuing daily to pay the price necessary for success, and obedience to God. Part of that price being the long hours of study, learning, travel, teaching, hard work, the disappointments, personal betrayals even by those we served and loved. Often there was work that required me to be awake and faithful to my responsibilities 16 to 18 hours out of each day. There was language study in France from 8 AM to 11 PM five days a week with only 9 months to learn the language. In Africa, dangerous trips into the jungle to visit our churches, rescuing persecuted African

---

[3]   Jeremiah 29:11-14: New Living Translation ®, copyright © 1996, 2004 by Tyndale Charitable Trust. Copied from the PC Study Bible Software Electronic Data Base.

Christians from certain death even as we risked our own lives, or long hours of work at the Bible School in order to train African pastors. Even standing guard, with my 12 gauge shotgun, over the students at the Bible School while they slept at night so as to insure they would not be murdered in their sleep because of the crime wave by hardened criminals & murderers set free from jail by the President of the country. That story, and so much more, is also in this book!

If I had quit, or made different choices instead of letting God direct my life and make some important choices for me, I would not be where I am today with a life history that has taken me all across West Africa, Europe and Southeast Asia. I have students that I have trained living and ministering in Ivory Coast, Ghana, Togo, Benin, and Senegal, and indeed, so I am told, throughout West Africa. I have had many, many adventures in the Jungles of West Africa, in Thailand, Cambodia, Vietnam, and across northern India up into the Himalayan Mountains, all the way to the ancient Kingdom of Sikkim [4] just south of Nepal, and was part of a team of 13 people that traveled with Micah Smith north of Hanoi to open an orphanage near the border with China. I got very sick on that trip and one of the team members later told me that he didn't expect me to survive.

---

[4]   Sikkim (/'sɪkɪm/; also known as Shikim or Su Khyim) is a landlocked Indian state located in the Himalayan Mountains. The state borders Nepal to the west, China's Tibet Autonomous Region to the north and east, and Bhutan to the east. The Indian state of West Bengal lies to the south. [With 610,577 inhabitants as of the 2011 census, Sikkim is the least populous state in India and the second-smallest state after Goa in total area, covering approximately 7,096 km2 (2,740 sq mi). Sikkim is nonetheless geographically diverse due to its location in the Himalayas; the climate ranges from subtropical to high alpine, and Kangchenjunga, the world's third-highest peak, is located on Sikkim's border with Nepal. Sikkim is a popular tourist destination, owing to its culture, scenery and biodiversity. It also has the only open land border between India and China. Sikkim's capital and largest city is Gangtok.

I was with another team of men when we were arrested in Nagaland (northeastern India) and then were freed the next day, allowing us to teach and share with pastors in that region. I also met men and women on that trip who had been beaten and left for dead, and had suffered greatly for their faith in Christ.

In Vietnam we met with 90 plus members of the Underground Church to encourage men and women and children, all of whom had spent years in jail, suffering greatly for their Faith in Christ. Walking through the streets of Hanoi was a thrilling, beautiful and wonderful experience and I saw it as part of my reward for walking in obedience to the Lord. My visit to the Hanoi Hilton, where John McCain and so many others of our Vietnam Veterans were held prisoner, suffering horrific torture while there, was an eye opening experience! I saw the instruments of torture that were on display, but seriously doubt that the two guillotines present at the time I was there, were used during the Vietnam War. As I understand it, those were used by the French against their own North Vietnamese prisoners before the USA even got into the war. If one believes the Vietnamese account, the cruelty of the French created much bitterness toward the white man & Western Civilization and were a large part of the reason our American soldiers met such resistance.

Being part of a team that took two truck-loads of supplies down steep dirt jungle roads slippery with mud and with high cliffs on one side and 1,000 foot drop offs on the other was both dangerous, and challenged our trust in God. But we persisted into the refugee camp and prepared to give needed supplies to new refugees from the Karen (pronounced: "kuh-wren") Tribe that would arrive shortly out of the Burmese jungle and into the northern Thailand jungle Refugee Camp. They would be virtual captives, not allowed by the Thai government to assimilate into Thai culture but forced to spend the rest of their lives in that Refugee Camp where only people like us who brought supplies to them plus United Nations trucks that came from time to time would keep them from starving to death. I was told that the Burmese Army regulars were a short distance away from the camp and that all that guaranteed our safety were the Karen Freedom Fighters. Periodically they would cross the border to attack that camp. I met and visited with people who had lost arms and legs to the land mines planted by the savagery of the Burmese soldiers. All of that provided eye-opening, gut wrenching adventures that a person could never arrange for with a travel agency no matter how much money you paid them. But God had quite evidently seen into my heart and seen my love of high adventure as well as my love for Him and desire to help others, and to make my life count for Eternity. So He put together all those parts and pieces to give me a life that has been extraordinary almost beyond description.

The capstone of all these experiences was, for me, seeing 10,000 people come to Christ in one three night meeting in Abidjan, Ivory Coast. The story of that meeting and the miracles of healing, and deliverance of Witch Doctors from demonic possession is also in this book. I was there and privileged to be a first hand witness to it all! Nothing could be more exciting or more gratifying than the experience of those three nights!

Preaching, after we returned from Africa, in churches across the USA, Alaska and British Columbia provided free travel to some of the most beautiful and historic places in North America! We were continual tourists even as we taught seminars in the churches, encouraged congregations and pastors and held school assemblies, telling our son's story and teaching in the public school system, youth detention centers and women's prisons from Alaska to California. We taught on AIDS and sexual abstinence until marriage; and also on the fact that choices have consequences. Better to think about consequences before you make choices! (As to our subject matter in such secular institutions, sometimes it is easier to get forgiveness than to receive permission.) Pretty nice! And all expenses paid!

These antidotes and much more are what this book is about. And the rest of what is contained in this book is how to learn to walk in obedience to God while maintaining a thankful heart in the midst of difficult and painful circumstances, the testing of the very fiber of one's inward character and commitment to Jesus Christ.

Unanswered questions: Why, while I was faithfully serving God in Africa, was my Son, back home in southern California, beaten and raped for two years and infected with AIDS? Why was a missionary acquaintance beaten to death in the Congo and his body fed to crocodiles? Why didn't God heal my wife of vascular dementia (not enough oxygenated blood getting to her brain)? Why did my wife die of a brain hemorrhage while we were planning our retirement? Why couldn't we at least have had another year so as to reach our 50th Wedding Anniversary? Why did I lose my only grandchild to an abortionist's knife and my only Son to AIDS? In these matters and so much more, I have no certain answers. But in all these matters I await entrance into Heaven to get the answers!

This I do know, that God is compassionate, perfect in love, and faithful. This too I know that He doesn't always rescue us from the consequences of bad choices in our own lives. And often we must suffer consequences due to the wrong choices of those we love, and have to express that love with patience and forgiveness when we feel most like ringing their rebellious necks! Someday, we will understand! Life is not fair! And that is true because we live in a broken world, a world broken by sin and selfishness, by rebellion, hatred, bitterness and resentment. God is a good God and the Devil is a bad Devil! God created a perfect earth and placed perfect humans on the earth with intelligence far above the smartest of the people that now live. It was Satan that introduced hatred, competition, selfishness, jealously and divisiveness. The world is broken partially because of what Satan did and partially because of what Lucifer inspired humans to do.

But too many people get that mixed up and turned upside down, thus losing out on the best things in life because of the confusion of unanswered questions, bitterness toward God and other people, self-pity that destroys faith, and the refusal to forgive those who hurt us. The rain falls on the just and the unjust, on Christians and non-Christians alike! The Bible declares that all Believers must pass through suffering in order to enter the Kingdom of God. If the reader will study the Scriptures in the footnote below [5] they should come to understand why suffering is necessary for our entrance into the Kingdom of God. Suffering is necessary to discipline the soul (emotional life, thought life and personal priorities) of each individual.

Attitudes of a Child—Attitudes of a Champion

One other Biblical teaching that is crucial to joy filled Christian living in the middle of unanswered questions due to suffering is the following.

Matthew 18:3-4—New Living Translation
3 Then Jesus said, "I tell you the truth, unless you turn from your sins and become like little children, you will never get into the Kingdom of Heaven. **4** So anyone who becomes as humble as this little child is the greatest in the Kingdom of Heaven.

One of the characteristics of little children (sure wish they could keep this through their teen years!) is that of humble and unquestioning trust in their parents. One of the things Jesus is teaching here is that

---

[5] Acts 14:22; Matthew 10:38; 16:24; Luke 22:28-29; 24:26; II Timothy 1:8; 2:11-12; Hebrews 2:9; John 12:25-26; 16:1-2, 33; Romans 8:17; I Peter 4:12-13; Revelation 2:10

in order not to lose our faith in God, we need to develop that same loving, obedient and unquestioning trust in our Heavenly Father as a young child has in its earthly parents. That position will be like a wall of protection against bitterness, cynicism, rebellion or yielding to the temptation to lose our faith in our Heavenly Father and drop out of church, become cynical about other Christians or simply give up and quit trying! Children don't require their parents to prove or explain everything, they simply love their Mom and Dad so much they trust them and take what they say at face value.

This preparation to become a Champion in God's Kingdom, thus gaining a Glory filled entrance into Heaven & Eternity is somewhat like the suffering of a man preparing his mind and body to climb the Matterhorn in the Swiss Alps, or the football, basketball or soccer team preparing to play like champions! One has to be teachable and trainable, have an open mind and learn to take instructions without angry argument or resentment. Some people are too stubborn or opinionated, too captivated by sinful and self-centered desires, too lazy, too unwilling to make the necessary sacrifices, too lacking in focus to be able, through training and practice and with a teachable spirit, reach the heights of success. And consequently unable to become a champion, an expert, and a success (however they define success). The attitudes of a champion are also necessary to being able to consider the possible truth of things you do not currently accept as fact, and is also crucial to realizing God's perfect plan in your life! One should not be so opinionated that they are unteachable. If a person is unteachable they WILL FAIL to realize God's best in their life and will find themselves settling for less than what God intended for them! However one should pick with great care whomever they accept to be their mentor and teacher!

There is much to give up and much to trim away from one's lifestyle in order to be successful at any great achievement in this life, and so it is, likewise, in preparation for entrance into the Kingdom of God or to achieve God's destiny in one's life. There are no guarantees except the guarantee of the faithfulness and love of God! The guarantee comes with LIFE after death, and eternity in Heaven with our Blessed Savior who also suffered and died on earth as the supreme sacrifice, paying the penalty that should have been ours for our hearts of sin and rebellion. To receive Eternal Life is the greatest gift of all, and if God never answers one other prayer, the answer to our prayers for forgiveness and salvation should be enough to establish thankfulness in our hearts! Let Jesus be the center of your joy, and all your expectations! Surrender your own desires in life to the sovereignty of His desires for your life. You'll only turn out to be a winner, a champion if you will do that!

The Scripture gives part of the answer in James 1:2-4 (New Living Translation)

> [2] Dear brothers and sisters,* when troubles come your way, consider it an opportunity for great joy. [3] For you know that when your faith is tested, your endurance has a chance to grow. [4] So let it grow, for when your endurance is fully developed, you will be perfect and complete, needing nothing.

This is true in learning to be a better football player or mountain climber, participant in the Olympics, musician, fifth degree black belt in karate, or champion in any other of life skills. It is true also in learning to be your best for God and letting him help you realize your highest potential in this life and preparation to shine like the brightness of a star lit sky or even as one single star itself throughout Eternity.

> ## Daniel 12:2-4—NLT [6]
> [2] Many of those whose bodies lie dead and buried will rise up, some to everlasting life and some to shame and everlasting disgrace. [3] Those that are wise will shine as bright as the sky, and those who lead many to righteousness will shine like the stars forever. [4]

Biblical Illustrations of Foolish Choices & Unintended Consequences

<u>Peter bar Jonas and Judas Iscariot</u>

There were two men who betrayed Jesus just prior to His Crucifixion. One was Judas Iscariot and the other was soon to be, Apostle Peter. Each had differing motivations for their actions, but each made foolish choices proceeding outward from the motivations of their hearts, foolish choices with unforeseen and unintended consequences. Before engaging in a brief discussion of the two men, we need to make a couple observations. First, it is vitally important to engage our "inner person" with a critical, candid and honest analysis of our own heart motivations before making decisions, and that is true for all decisions both great and small. For sometimes what seems to be a small, inconsequential choice can actually set in motion events that present the possibility of further choices which we would never have had available to us if we had not made the first choice. These sequential choices can move us inexorably toward larger, life-changing choices and unintended consequences which may result in personal ruin or personal fulfillment depending on the spiritual and psychological character of those choices. And the long range unintended consequences can be glued, in our future, to people

---

[6] Holy Bible, New Living Translation ®, copyright © 1996, 2004 by Tyndale Charitable Trust. Accessed in the PC Study Bible Data System on December 13, 2013. All rights reserved.

whom we love but who suffer or enjoy the consequences of choices we made years before the loved-ones came into our life.

Secondly, unless one has a clear and undoubted directive from the Holy Spirit of God regarding one's choices, it is always best to refrain from making important choices too hastily, instead one should live in a prayerful attitude of "not my will, Lord Jesus, but yours be done in my life". It is always the highest form of faith and wisdom to pray that prayer, mean it, and live out the daily practical implications of that heart commitment to Trust and Obedience toward our Heavenly Father. The urge to "take matters in one's own hands" as well as the urgings of impatience, fear or too high a regard for one's own opinions can be almost irresistible in moments of crisis and high stress. But such attitudes can, and often do, lead to terrible consequences both in the short and long term development of the course of one's life.

Most Bible Scholars agree that the heart motivations of Judas, prior to his betrayal of Jesus came from a desire to force Jesus to make different choices. Jesus was talking about crucifixion, but Judas, who was convinced that Jesus was actually the long awaited Messiah spoken of by most of the Old Testament Prophets, wanted Jesus to start performing the necessary miracles through which the Roman Empire would ultimately be overthrown. The ultimate goals of Jesus and of Judas were at polar opposites. Jesus, who had come to earth as God's Perfect Sacrificial Lamb, intended to offer His own Body as the supreme sacrifice by which all men would be able to receive forgiveness, pardon, and justification and, ultimately, total Transformation. The transformation would empower each human being to become Sons/ Daughters of God, joining the Family of God, becoming the Bride of Christ and made Holy through the shed blood of Jesus! This, in turn, would qualify them to spend eternity in Heaven with God their Heavenly Father and Jesus, their Heavenly Bridegroom.

But the goals of Judas were earthbound and focused on the immediate overthrow of the Roman Empire, a goal totally foreign to what was in the Heart and Mind of Jesus. Judas had correctly identified Jesus as the Messiah, but tragically misunderstood the Plan and Purposes of God, as well as God's Prophetic Calendar. Someday, Jesus will overthrow all Powers, governments and Empires. [7] But first, it was imperative that He free the human race from the legal hold Lucifer held over us due to the legal transaction in the Garden of Eden at least four thousand years earlier. Adam, being the Federal Head of the Human Race had the legal right to decide under whose authority the Human Race would exist.

To be sure, Judas probably did not understand all the legal ramifications of his disobedience that day, but the dynamics of it all are clearly explained in Scripture. [8] Also it is imperative that we live in obedience to God. It is not necessary for us to understand God's decisions, or what He allows in our life. "Trust and obey" like a child are the key concepts!

When will we poor, fallen creatures ever learn that God loves us and that He also never makes a mistake? Why? Because He is Omniscient, Omnipotent, Omnipresent and thus has no need for our help in directing the affairs of Heaven, Eternity or Salvation History here on earth!

---

[7] I Corinthians 15:21-28; Ephesians 1:19-23; Colossians 1:15-20; Hebrews 2:5-9;

[8] Romans 5:14; 6:16; John 8:34; II Peter 2:19; I Corinthians 15:22, 45-49; Genesis 2:17; I Timothy 2:13-14—this passage makes it clear that Eve fell into transgression because she was deceived—but Adam, as the Federal Head of the Human race deliberately chose to join Eve in her transgression although he was not deceived. Adam chose Eve, God's gift to him, over God, the Giver of the gift and thereby sold us into slavery to Lucifer, who had transformed himself into the bodily presentation of a serpent. And that is why the Serpent, throughout Scripture is a type or symbol of Satan (Lucifer, the Devil).

Chapter Two

Storms that Confirm the Direction of a Person's Heart

Not all life's storms are concerned with the temporal, like physical health, injuries to the body through accidents while driving an automobile or performing one's duties at work. Those storms mainly impact life here on earth, with no lasting spiritual or even psychological consequences. Those things are normal to all human life as we live out our days in this Broken World! But it is the storms of one's heart that have the potential to be the most damaging, with consequences that set the tone for one's life on earth and, ultimately, one's eternal destiny. The storms of the heart also have the potential to strengthen one's spiritual and psychological life and thereby actually be the catalyst for blessing, success and much happiness.[9]

Examples of this latter truth could be for instance, an early romantic "heart-throb" that comes to an end. Especially in early teen years or even early adulthood, these can be psychologically painful. But then, if one is willing to be obedient to the guidelines found in God's Word as well as wise counsel from parents, pastors, other spiritual leaders or several good books on various aspects of love and marriage, God arranges the entrance of "THE ONE" that He intends to be our life's companion; i.e., the person that will most bless our life with love, wisdom and balance. In this case, one looks back at the early pain and realizes that our psychological and spiritual struggle were a necessary precursors to

---

[9]   See Spurgeon's Devotional notes for the AM of November 9, 10, 11 & 12

the later exuberance of having found one's soul-mate, the choice blessed by God for our Life's Companion in the pilgrimage of adult life.

Like Tropical Storms and Hurricanes, the storms of one's heart most often start with small winds that blow. These could be winds of repeated disappointments beginning in childhood, feelings of inadequacy or unfairness or bitterness or psychological pain from the actions of others or one's own ill-advised choices.

It may take months or even years for this kind of storm to gather strength and eventually develop a destructive force. [10]

And so I have tried to relate the storms in my own life so that, in spite of the fact that I have been privileged to live such an extraordinary life, one filled with adventure and personal fulfillment and the sure knowledge that God has consistently and miraculously intervened in my life and given me 70 plus years to live out my pilgrimage when so many others have suffered and died or just plain suffered incredibly, that

---

[10] In Greek, the word for "spirit" is also the word for "wind". The Bible speaks of various human attitudes as being "a spirit of ...." and teaches that winds of various emotions and/or thoughts can impact our life for good or for evil. What we dwell on (thinking habits) in our minds are like winds that blow through our human psyche and create character and personal identity (Mt. 15:19-20; James 1:13-15); the same is true about emotions we cultivate that become habits concerning the way we deal with life. These mental and emotional winds have overwhelming power over the kinds of decisions we make (the way we exercise our free will); and those decisions send our lives in directions of good or evil. In short, we can be, if we are not careful, our own worst enemy! Or we can be good to ourselves by simply walking in surrendered trust and obedience to God, our Creator. The Bible is our owner's manual for the successful operation of our lives, and the choice is ours as to whether we will make decisions on the basis of what is in the Owner's Manual. From how we handle finances, to our sex life, to our marriage and parenting skills, to how we get along with people in the business world. It is all there, if we will just read and absorb what has been written. Some manufacturers tell me that most people don't read the owner's manual for their car or appliances in the home and pay higher than normal maintenance and repair bills as a consequence. So it is in our spiritual, psychological and relational lives!

you would not think that my many blessings have kept me from great pain, many tears, and horrible disappointments. I have not been exempt from these, but I have been privileged to see clearly the sustaining Hand of God underneath my life and failures and weaknesses. And that God has sovereignly chosen to preserve me in the middle of my many adversities. I know this, too! That it has been not only the sovereign mercy and grace of God in my life, but my own choices, as I lived in obedience to what the Bible Teaches, that have helped me escape from the destruction of Satan in my life.

There is much I have to cherish in my memories of Mom and Dad, and for which I sincerely honor them! Mom and Dad were both Godly people, and we were in church every time the church doors were open which usually meant four times a week. Dad was a hard worker, a good provider of the family and had an awesome intellect. His main profession was that of a school teacher. I remember when Dad got his M.A. from San Jose State University with a Major in Math and a Minor in Physical Science. I remember how he struggled to master calculus which was a requirement of his graduate studies. But he was also a jack-of-all-trades as a carpenter, mason, electrician and mechanic and good at whatever he set his hands or mind to accomplish. Dad was also an accomplished poet, song writer and biblical scholar. It is a shame he never got published because I have read most of what he wrote and it is all worthy, in my estimation, of publication.

My earliest memories of Mother are of myself sitting at her feet after she would call me to her with the words, "Okay, Joseph, it is time to do your memory-work." That call meant reviewing all the Bible verses and chapters I had already memorized and adding new verses or a new chapter to what I already knew by heart. In fact, while I was still in grade school I knew the entire Life of Christ by memory, thanks to my Mother's diligence in making sure I had the Word of God growing in my heart and mind. I was also required to spend one hour per day practicing the piano and, later on, 30 minutes per day learning to play the violin. Due largely to my Mother's influence I learned to love the Word of God like few children ever do. I remember quoting Scripture on the Ralph Sanders radio broadcast in Seattle, Washington and doing so for a solid 30 minutes without stopping or hesitating. Later, at the age of 12, I would preach my first sermon on the back of a hay wagon just outside Lubbock, Texas.

But Dad had one outstanding fault that negatively marked my life. To this day, at age 70, I sometimes have dreams in which Dad's "fault" is very pronounced and frightening. I have to wake up and pray that God will help me turn loose of this and that forgiveness will dominate my mind and emotions.

Mother also had at least one outstanding fault that stood out to me and would eventually cause me some problem in the early years of my marriage to Ruth, until I realized that Ruth was really nothing like my Mother, and not guilty of the fault for which I had thought she was a lot like my Mother. How stupid, faultfinding and unfair can we humans be?

One lesson to be learned here is that the more one focuses on the faults of another person the more one becomes just like that person! "As a man thinks in his heart, so is he", the Bible says. So if I think frequently of the faults of others, how can I do any less than become guilty of the same fault? And I do remember the day that Ruth said to me, "You are just like your Father!" I went to our bedroom and wept in bitter realization and repentance of the truth of that statement! I later did some heart-felt apologizing to my wife whom I had so unjustly accused of a certain fault!

It is not without reason that the Bible declares the human heart (will, emotions and intellect) to be deceitful above all things.[11] And then adds the rhetorical question, "Who can know it?" The New Living

---

[11]   Jeremiah 17:9

Translations puts it this way, "Who really knows how bad it is?" Or, from the Message Bible, comes the idea that the human heart is "a puzzle that no one can figure out". Last I checked, we are all born with a human heart, which means that we are in trouble from the start. The Prophet/ King, David, affirms [12] that we are all "born in sin"; i.e., conceived and born with a depraved heart; i.e., a depraved set of emotions, thoughts and priorities; with the sin nature already firmly installed within us. Until we surrender to the Lordship of Christ, until we make that choice, we are lost, walking in darkness and not capable of living any other way. We are born in rebellion against all authority (especially God's authority or control in our lives). David begs God to create within him a clean heart! [13] Even after the New Birth experience we continue to struggle (as an old Indian once put it) with the internal war between the white dog (good side to our nature; what is right, proper, pure & wise) and the black dog (evil side to our nature; selfishness & lust). "Which one will win?", the old Indian was asked. He answered, "Whichever dog you feed the most!"

The storm, for me, would come later during my Teen years when I struggled with self-will and rebellion! There is always an issue that the Enemy of our Soul brings onto our path of life. For me it was quite normal and innocent. Girls! And was I ever girl-crazy! Pretty normal stuff for a young lad just entering puberty! But Mom and Dad were good parents and very strict (although I didn't always appreciate it) especially when it came to rules about my boyish romantic inclinations. But that was a storm that would come later and threaten to ship-wreck my future.

By the way, as I write this paragraph I have my laptop computer tuned in to sky wire. discovery.com and am getting ready to watch Nik Wallenda, of the world famous "Flying Wallenda Family" walk across

---

[12]   Psalm 51:5-7, 10

[13]   Ibid.

the Grand Canyon on a steel wire that is only two inches across (less than the width of my i-phone) and stretched 1,500 feet high, up above the canyon floor to walk about ¼ mile across the Grand Canyon in Arizona. Nik Wallenda seems to be very calm as he gets ready to start this historic journey, as are his Mother and Father and closest family and friends. So how does one get to the point where they are calmly confident in the performance of an extra-ordinary feat? This almost seems like "old hat" to them all because of the previous training that is life long and constant. They are Champions! And you, dear reader, can also be a Champion in the arena of life God has chosen for you! Focus and self-discipline, as well as faith in God and a certain self-confidence that comes from endless hours of training are necessary if one is to fully realize their God-ordained purpose and destiny in life!

Lesson to learn: Both well-defined goals and a lot of hard work can confirm the direction of one's heart; but so also, can laziness and an absence of goals, along with a misunderstanding of one' own unique & God-given destiny. Anyone who doesn't know what God's gifting to them personally is, or what God's unique call upon his or her life is, just hasn't spent enough time in serious thinking and praying. Watching TV, daydreaming or self-pity won't help anyone live a fulfilling life! Think! Self-examine! Admit mistakes! Take advice! Study! Work hard! With those guidelines, anyone can realize the dreams that God has placed in their heart!

I grew up in a very strict German/Jewish home. From before I started grade school I was required to spend one hour each day memorizing Scripture. My Mother, who was in charge of that part of my upbringing, was totally convinced of the value of Scripture memorization as a means to protect against sin and to establish the bent or direction of a person's heart. [14] She was also convinced that I needed discipline and structure in my life, even as a young grade-school age child. I grew up learning to make my days and minutes count. Yes, I was allowed to be a child and there were moments of play and childish daydreams. I do remember some psychological pain because Mom and Dad didn't have the best or most quiet relationship. But basically, life was good and life was safe, as it should be for children.

As one of the last of the "boy preachers" of the 1950s, I began my ministry at the age of twelve years old. Already, at that young age, my greatest dream was to become a "world-wide Healing Evangelist", as I used to term it. My heroes were men like T.L. Osborne, Jack Coe, A.A. Allen, William Branham and Oral Roberts. I wanted, more than anything in my life, to be just like them and to travel the world, pray for the sick, and see miracles of healing (blind eyes opened, deaf ears unstopped, and the lame healed & made to walk). Even as I write this, I feel that old passion for a "healing ministry" arising in my heart. I had witnessed such miracles in the meetings of the men just mentioned and thought there could be no greater Calling, no finer, more exciting and fulfilling life than to pattern my life after those great Men of God. Of course, in the immaturity of my boyhood dreams I had no realization of the very human foibles even preachers that I perceived to be "great men of God" would have in their own personal lives. But the retrospect of passing years demonstrates that the Favor of God was indeed upon me because He was shaping my heart [15], and protecting me not only from evil from without, but from the evil of my own foolishness of heart when immaturity and destructive passions came to the forefront.

---

[14]   Job 22:22; Psalm 1:2; 37:31; 40:8; 119:97; Prov. 2:1-13; Isaiah 51:7; Jeremiah 15:16; Colossians 3:16

[15]   Ezra 6:22; 7:21, 24-26; Proverbs 16:1, 7, 9; 21:1; John 19:11; Psalm 105:25; 106:46; Daniel 4:35; Acts 7:9-10

Mom and Dad had received appointment as missionary-candidates with the Pentecostal Church of God (Joplin, Missouri) and were slated to go to Africa. This had been one of Dad's dreams of many years. We traveled from church to church across the United States for more than a year as Dad presented his vision of ministry in that far away "Dark Continent". My folks had adopted a Baby Brother for me before we began to travel. But I do remember having as one of my chores the task of hanging his diapers on a line outside in sub-zero weather in Kansas and Missouri when the diapers would freeze stiff and hard as a piece of wood as I lifted them from the warm basket to the clothes line. A matter of seconds and they were frozen stiff!

Later, the next fall, outside of Houston, Texas I would find myself on the back of a horse-drawn wagon enjoying a hayride with a local youth group on Halloween night. I don't remember exactly how this all came about, but I do remember beginning to share Biblical Truth coupled with warnings about the possible evil consequences of self-centered rather than God-centered choices. I spoke about what the promises of God could do with each of their lives if they would only yield their Will and hearts to Him. I don't remember what my theme was or how I presented it, but I do remember that we stopped, as did the horse drawn wagon behind us, after pulling in close so everyone could hear what I had to say. There was a powerful anointing from the Holy Spirit upon us all; kids were crying and praying and committing their lives to Christ. It was a powerful evening and only Eternity will reveal what the Holy Spirit accomplished that night that was catalysts in helping those young people make life-changing decisions.

I do remember also that I began preaching "double-headers" every night with Dad as he continued his itineration in an effort to raise his funds for our eventual ministry in Africa. But Dad was not successful in his bid to go to Africa with the PC of G. We returned home to California and Dad returned to his career as a Grade School Teacher in Santa Rita,

California and then in Gonzales. It must have been shortly after our return from Dad's effort to go to Africa that we attended a Pentecostal Church of God Camp Meeting in Gilroy, California where I met T.L. Osborne's Son, [16] Tommy Jr. Tommy Jr. also had a Thompson Chain Reference Bible and we spent hours studying and preparing sermon notes. Somehow, Tommy and I were asked to preach at the afternoon Youth Services. I remember that the crowd shouted "Amen" and "Praise the Lord" at just about everything we said. And I had to shout loudly in order to be heard over the commotion. It was there I developed a style of preaching that was reminiscent of the old-time camp meeting speakers of the 19th Century.

We were attending the "Pink Church" in Salinas, California at the time of my encounter with Tommy Osborne Jr and the Gilroy Pentecostal Church of God Camp Meeting. While living on Mae Avenue in Salinas my folks and I became acquainted with a lady who lived about two blocks from us and was known as a very Godly woman. I forget the woman's name but I do remember that I was attracted to her zeal for God. Eventually, with my parent's permission, I began preaching at various Pentecostal Church of God churches throughout Northern California. I would play my violin and preach and pray for the sick. During summer months we even held "brush-harbor" meetings, where a framework was set up with wooden poles and then covered over with tree branches and leaves. A small platform would be erected, the Meeting was advertised.

---

[16]   T.L. Osborne was one of several "healing evangelists" that traveled the world back in the 1940s and 1950s and experienced powerful anointing from God in their lives to cause the blind to see and cripples to walk. I have attended meetings as a boy in my pre-teen years where goiters dropped off of different parts of people's necks or other parts of their bodies; legs were lengthened in front of our eyes so that the length of a person's two legs matched. Cripples threw down their crutches or got up out of wheel chairs to walk like any normal person. T.L. Osborne was one of these healing evangelists, like Oral Roberts, Jack Coe, A.A. Allen and William Branham.

I was the featured Evangelist. These were the years of my early teens and I traveled over a large area of Northern California, from Salinas to Gilroy or Watsonville all the way over to Modesto and the surrounding areas. The offerings, I believe, were kept by this lady who used them to pay the expenses of the meetings plus her own personal travel expenses. I didn't care anything about the financial aspect, I was simply thrilled to be doing what I best loved to do—travel and preach as the featured evangelist wherever we went. Souls were saved and sick bodies healed by the power of God and that was all I cared about! To my young mind this was all the beginning of the fulfillment of my dream to become a "world-wide healing evangelist". And, it was during this time that a gentleman approached my Father with a proposal that I travel with him and preach healing and evangelistic crusades. He would supply the big tent to house the meetings, do the advertising and cover all other costs. I would do the preaching and the praying. To my boyish mind this was the beginning of the realization of my dream to become an international healing evangelist. But with the wisdom God gave him, Dad refused to allow me to travel with the man, and I am now thankful for Dad's decision (although I certainly wasn't at the time). I surely would have had a different direction in my life had Dad not made that decision. Obedience to my father helped position my life so that I could later meet and marry Ruth and go on to earn a post graduate degree in Bible & Theology and enjoy a lifelong ministry in the Assemblies of God. Here is a perfect example of why God expects children to obey their parents!

Every summer I would work to earn enough money to pay my way to Youth Camp which was held in the Redwoods of Northern California. These were fun times when kids played shuffle board, ping pong, basketball and baseball as well as going for walks in the forest. But they were also spiritually serious times when kids would rededicate their lives to Christ and clean up whatever sins were in their lives. It helped us stay on track in our walk with God from year to year. But I remember one fifteen year old boy, whose Father was a pastor and the kid was bitter toward his Dad, the Church and God. In fact he seriously believed that he had committed the unpardonable sin (Matthew 12:32) and had no reliable hope of ever going to Heaven when he died. His name was Jim. Jim claimed to have no feelings of love for God or his parents or anyone else. He said that the only reason he was there was to see the girls. I asked him to "go to the altar" at the end of a service and kneel before God for just five minutes while I knelt beside him and prayed. He agreed, but by the last night of the week of Camp he had still not kept his word to me. After my own time of prayer at the altar, one of the kids told me that Jim was down at the hamburger stand getting a snack. For being just 15 years old Jim was an extremely tall young man, over six feet tall. I have always been short for my age. I rushed down to where Jim was about to buy something to eat and reached up to grab him by the front of his shirt. I said, "Jim, you promised me to go to the altar to pray for just five minutes. Now you are going if I have to knock you down and drag you!" It was a ridiculous thing for me to say, and Jim could have swatted me away like a fly. But he saw my desperation and decided to honor his promise. We went back up to the Tabernacle and I knelt down on the sawdust floor beside Jim and began to pray. Jim remained stony faced with his eyes wide open. Apparently determined to fulfill his promise to me and then leave.

As I began to pray, a deep groaning rose up from within me which years later I would connect with the Bible reference found in Romans 8:26-27. [17] At the time I didn't understand the spiritual dynamics of

---

[17] Romans 8:26-27—Amplified Bible "So too the [Holy] Spirit comes to our aid *and* bears us up in our weakness; for we do not know what prayer to offer *nor* how to offer it worthily as we ought, but the Spirit Himself goes to meet our supplication *and* pleads in our behalf with unspeakable yearnings *and* groanings too deep for utterance. And He Who searches the hearts of men knows what is in the mind of the [Holy] Spirit [what His intent is], because the Spirit intercedes *and* pleads [before God] in behalf of the saints according to *and* in harmony with God's will."

what was happening in my soul/spirit. All I could think to say was, "Oh God!" That was it. My eyes were tight shut and I repeated, "Oh God" over and over again. Jim had promised to stay only five minutes. But when I opened my eyes some time later and glanced at my watch I realized that several hours had passed. It was now after 1 AM in the morning. My throat hurt, my voice was hoarse and my stomach muscles ached. I glanced to my left. Jim was still there, eyes wide open, but I noticed one solitary tear trickling down his face. I went back to groaning and repeating my two word prayer. But somehow, I knew that a great spiritual & psychological victory was being won. I don't remember how much longer we continued there, but I do remember that the spiritual bondage in Jim's mind and emotions was broken and that he was able to surrender his heart to Jesus Christ, knowing that God loved him and forgave him. He was gloriously saved that night! Sins forgiven and freed from bitterness and hatred for God and his parents. I have wondered through the years about what happened to Jim. But I know this, that night he was set free to serve God, and I had given birth in the realm of the spirit world to a spiritual son!

But to every Chosen Vessel of the Lord will come the testing of the mettle, strength, quality of the inner character. That "inner character" must be tested in order to establish the priorities of the heart. My test would be in the person of a young high school girl, tall and shapely. I called this teenage heartthrob, "my Indian Princess". If I remember correctly, her nationality was from 25% to 50% Cherokee. To me, she was very physically attractive. Of course, to a teenage boy with high testosterone levels, is there anything more important than physical attraction? When my parents realized that, once we got off of the school bus each afternoon, "My Indian Princess" and I were walking to her house where we could have plenty of time alone, my folks forbade me to walk with her to her house after school. A parental commandment I chose to ignore. Furthermore, I would walk the two blocks from our home to hers each morning before school where we were again alone in the house for a short period of time. Somehow, the Spirit of God with Whom I also spent much time alone protected me (us) from the most serious of mistakes. My heart was so passionate for God in those days of psychological and hormonal vulnerability that I just could not bring myself to take full advantage of the opportunities "my Indian Princess" gave me to satisfy my carnal desires for her. By a combination of God's Protecting Grace and the choices of my Spirit-controlled Conscience I remained a virgin until the day of my marriage in 1962 to the most beautiful, wonderful and godly woman I have ever met, Miss Ruth Helen Taylor.

A year or so after "my Indian Princess" and I finally broke up, she was "found with child", an event that most certainly was no "Immaculate Conception". My parents later told me that my name came up as the possible father; but those suspicions were determined to be unfounded, and even the "Indian Princess" testified that I had always been a Gentleman and shown the utmost restraint, treating her always with respect.

After "my Indian Princess" and I broke up, I continued to be as "girl crazy" as ever. These were the youthful storms that could have destroyed my walk with God and put a black mark on my future. And so the point is that "the passions of the heart whether sexual in nature or simply addictive, like overwhelming desires for alcohol, drugs, ungodly friendships or an inordinate fixation on entertainment and "good times" are storms of the heart that can shipwreck a life. I am so thankful for the help of the Holy Spirit through this difficult time.

It should be remembered, however, that the Holy Spirit will not force Himself or act to overpower a person's "free will", and so it is the true bent of the tree of one's inner character, and how each of us handle those stormy passions of life that blow through the sails of one's soulish nature (will, emotions and intellect) that most often make the difference between a life well lived, or a life that has suffered one shipwreck after another. These internal storms of emotional and mental upheaval, coupled with personal priorities and spiritual value systems will have almost overwhelming and determinative impact on whether or not one ever fulfills their God-ordained destiny. And that God-planned, God-ordained destiny is the reason for which each of us are created!

Cold air storms and hot air storms, when they collide, cause what meteorologists term, severe weather. Severe weather comes in different forms, like tornados, cyclones, hurricanes. Internal storms of rebellion come in the forms of self-centeredness, lust in any form, or stubbornness. And these when colliding with the internal storm of wrong priorities or confused values often results even bigger or more severe storms of life. It was at this point (before LaVina and I broke up) that I made a decision which could have altered the entire course of my life. My passion for this "Indian Princess" coupled with my desire to get out from under my folk's authority led to a confusion of priorities and values. It was at the end of my Junior year in high school that I learned some states would issue marriage licenses to 17 year old teenagers. I reasoned that if I joined the national guard and agreed to go to boot camp after my Senior year, I would then sign up to become a chaplain in the army, fulfill my dream of serving God and still marry the girl of my youthful dreams in spite of my parent's disapproval and advice to the contrary. What I was willing to sacrifice was the Biblical injunction to "honor your father and mother" as well as what had been my childhood dream of becoming a "world-wide" healing evangelist. Somehow I convinced myself that God would be pleased with all this; or, at least, I would be serving Him maybe to a lesser degree of obedience but could have the girl I wanted all at the same time. I never did become a world-wide healing evangelist, but that isn't the real issue. The real issue was the stormy winds of rebellion that blew so strongly through my heart during those days, coupled with my willingness to make compromises over what I really did believe was God's Will for my life.

I will never know what LaVina would have been like as a wife and companion in the ministry, but from the perspective of age, and after 49 years of marriage, I recognize that my teenage hormonal attraction didn't hold a candle to the wonderful woman God finally gave me. And I am convinced that Ruth Helen Taylor (Meyers) has far outshined as a Wife, Mother, Lover and Companion in the Ministry anything that my original heart-throb could possibly have been. LaVina had already lost her virginity and sometimes felt pulled to the other guy who contacted her from time to time, while Ruth had "kept herself" for the man she would marry. I never had to worry about the faithfulness of her heart. Ruth's sense of ethics, integrity and purity before God has been stellar and rock solid. She has been a wonderful companion along life's stormy road and I would have lost a great deal if I had continued down the path my heart was taking me for those few brief months while infatuated with "the Indian Princess". I will always be thankful for God's providential protection and mercy over the instabilities of my heart during those days.

One truth I need to mention, just in passing and from the perspective of years of pastoral counseling. When a young man robs a girl of her virginity he destroys something within her, a feeling of self-worth and control over her own destiny. From that time forward, she will be more vulnerable to temptation, especially at times when she is unhappy with the man to whom she is married. Pre-marital sex sets both males and females up for further bad choices later on in life! Don't go down that road! Girls, tell that guy, "no!" no matter how much he promises you or sweet-talks you. And for the hormone driven young men, don't be some first class, self-centered jerk that leads you to rob girls of their strength of character because of your selfish desires to satisfy your lust.

And even if she wants sex with you, do yourself and her, a favor and tell her, "no!" You'll be a stronger, better, and in years to come, happier man for having done that.

A second issue is that God had His own plan for my life, a plan that was prophesied during that period of time by an Episcopal Pastor, who just happened to pick me up from alongside the road as I was hitchhiking home from preaching one of my meetings! I doubt that he even realized that he was being used of the Holy Spirit to pinpoint my God-ordained destiny at the time of his "prophecy" or that what he had done was to prophesy. He probably didn't even believe that such things were possible after the age of the Apostles. I'll never know. The Episcopal pastor would later tell my Father that I was destined to become a Bible Teacher. This was a statement that did not please me at all because I wanted to travel the world and become a healing evangelist like my boyhood heroes. I was offended by what the Episcopal pastor said, but events later in life would prove him to be accurate.

I have, in fact, over the years, become a sort of "international Bible Teacher" (ministry in Africa, Europe, Southeast Asia and Canada, as well as the United States.)

I need to add that usually my Father took me by car to do my preaching. But that was on the condition that he could "tear my sermon apart" from beginning to end on the way home after the meeting. I agreed. And it was then that I learned how to handle constructive criticism. I knew my Dad loved me and that any criticism offered was not to wound me but to help me.

But another storm would also come. Really it wasn't so bad, because I had regained some degree of equilibrium in my emotional and thought life. My heart was fixed on fulfilling what I knew to be God's Call upon my life. But the storm would bring me unexpectedly to a crossroad, and a decision would need to be made rather quickly. I had gone ahead and joined the California Army National Guard, but down in my heart

I knew beyond any shadow of a doubt that this was not the direction I would take my life. It was just a fun little side trip that fulfilled some of my instincts for adventure, an instinct for adventure that is still with me today.

Some months before joining the California National Guard with the promise I would go on six months active duty on my 18th birthday, I had preached a Youth Revival Meeting for a pastor by the name of Don Landers. Pastor Landers and his family had since accepted a pastorate on the Island of Oahu, Hawaii and felt a desire to contact me prior to my 18th birthday with an invitation to come to Hawaii that summer. He would arrange for me to preach about six weeks of meetings and/or do some Summer Daily Vacation Bible School efforts for children. Once again God was asking me to make a decision on what direction I would go with my life. I would need to apply for an honorable discharge from the National Guard without having fulfilled any of my obligations to them.

The choice was a "no brainer" in my mind! I would apply for an honorable discharge from the California National Guard and, if it were granted, would proceed to Hawaii that summer. In the meantime, having received my letter with the decision to accept his invitation, Pastor Landers contacted, without my knowledge, some friends of his who were pastoring a small church in central California and recommended they invite me to come preach a meeting for them. In the meantime, the Honorable Discharge from the California National Guard arrived. And everything was in place for me to receive another lesson on how important even the smallest of choices can be for the fulfillment of our life's destiny! For who should be at that little church in San Ardo, California but the young lady, a Bible College graduate, who was living with the pastor and her husband and working in the church, and would within a little more than a year's time become my wife and companion for 49 years, that's Who!

Neither of us could have known what would be the results of my single little decision, at the ripe old age of 17, to resign from the Army National Guard and go preach in Hawaii that summer. That young lady, Ruth Helen Taylor (she was Taylor-made to be a Meyers!) would someday become a much sought after Bible Teacher in churches across the USA, Alaska and Canada! She would outshine my own ministry in some ways but would also spend ten years with me in West Africa where she would work with me at the Institut Théologique et Pastoral in Daloa, Ivory Coast. She would be the School Nurse, Head Librarian, Bookstore Manager, Professor of Christian Education plus Professor of Women's Health Issues, and Professor of French Grammar. After our years in West Africa she would travel with me for twelve years as an itinerant Seminar Speaker. Ruth would write and self-publish six seminars complete with Study Guides (still available today). But I digress . . . . So allow me to regroup.

I went to San Ardo and preached that week of meetings. I remember walking into the pastor's home and seeing Ruth lying on the couch. Typical male, my eyes roamed over her form and the thought went through my mind, "I could never be interested in a skinny thing like that." Before I left at the end of the week I was wildly "in love" with that skinny thing (infatuated, a victim of puppy love?) and remarked to the pastor's husband that, "If I don't marry Ruth it won't be because I didn't try." Before saying goodbye I had pressured a promise out of Ruth to exchange letters if I would write to her. I believe my first letter to her was within a couple days after I returned to my parents place in San Jose, California.

I went to Hawaii that summer to hold six weeks of meetings in the churches, as well as conducting a Daily Vacation Bible School for children at the Assembly of God church in Aiea where the Bloom Sisters were pastors. I also remember preaching at churches in Kane'ohé and Hale'iwa where Don Landers and his wife pastored. There were three other weeks of meetings in other cities on the Island of Oahu but I do not remember their names. I do remember eating "two finger poi" and other Hawaiian dishes.

After six weeks in Hawaii I flew back in to the Los Angeles International Airport (LAX) and was met by Ruth. While in Hawaii I had shown Ruth's picture to everyone I could get to show an interest and proclaimed, this is the girl I am going to marry. Most people exclaimed about how lucky I was to be marrying such a beautiful young woman. Of course that only encouraged my infatuation with her. I use the word, "infatuation" because from the experience of years I have come to the conclusion that mature love can only be learned; it has more to do with a commitment of mind than an emotional response. Of course, both are important and necessary.

Ruth had agreed to meet me at the airport in Los Angeles but I had neglected to mention the time difference between Hawaii and Los Angeles when I had given her the time of my arrival. Consequently she had to wait an extra hour and was somewhat worried about it all. In my youthful exuberance and preoccupation with my own emotions I "popped the question" on the drive north on Highway 101 toward San Ardo. Ruth's response was that although she thought I was a nice guy and certainly dedicated to the Lord and His Work, she did not know me well enough to give me an answer. Of course, I told her to take all the time she would need.

I believe it was the next day or the day after that we drove together approximately 100 miles north and west to Big Sur (located on the coast a few miles south of Monterey, California). There we sat and dangled our feet in a forest stream at Big Sur State Park and just got acquainted. By the end of the day Ruth laid her head on my shoulder and started to softly cry. I asked her why she was crying and she said, "I'm starting to fall (for you)." I don't remember where we went to eat on the way back south to San Ardo. In fact, my head and heart were so much in the clouds that I probably didn't have much appetite for anything except holding hands with this beautiful young woman who was in the process of giving her heart to a man almost four years her junior. I was a high school graduate and she had already graduated from college (Bethany Bible College in Santa Cruz). But we shared a common Call from God to spend our lives in Africa.

Contrary to the way courtship is practiced in today's world, we didn't spend our time "making out". In fact, I'm not sure we even kissed each other one time that afternoon. Instead we talked about our goals in life and shared information about our respective families. Ruth had seven living brothers and a sister. One brother who was my namesake (Joseph) had died at birth and a sister, Grace, had died of kidney disease at age sixteen. Ruth's father was a deacon in the church she attended in the north end of Tacoma, Washington where she had grown up. Ruth remarked that now her Mother would finally get her Joseph back.

My Father was a school teacher. Ruth's Father was a painter who only worked six months out of the year. Ruth had grown up in a family so poor that sometimes all the ten children (before her Sister's death) had to eat was bread and gravy for supper and maybe a peanut butter and jam sandwich for lunch. Ruth had left home in Tacoma to attend Bethany Bible College in Santa Cruz, California where she would also do house cleaning and the work of a nanny with small children in private homes, thus working her way through school, graduating with a three year diploma in Christian Education and Foreign Missions. She had grown up in a large two story home which I would latter refer to as, "the barn" (mostly because it looked like one). The ten kids liked to play baseball out on North Visscher Street where they lived.

I had grown up in central California, living for the longest time in Salinas, but moving for my Senior year in high school to San Jose so that my Father could complete his studies at San Jose State. There were four children in my family. I had an adopted brother, Harley Daniel, eleven years my junior plus two sisters, Norma Jean and Juanita Ruth. I remember the loving, relationship of mutual respect that always existed between us siblings. My younger sister still likes to tease me about making her play "cowboys and Indians" and yet refusing to "play dolls" with her. My Father graduated from San Jose State with an M.A. in Math and minor in Physical Science. Ruth's Dad barely knew how to read and write because he had been forced to drop out of school as a grade school kid in order to help support his family.

Ruth and I, both, had kept our virginity and were determined to do so until we were married. [18] I would learn, years later, that Ruth had received six formal proposals of marriage while attending Bethany. In each case, the deciding factor was that none of her suitors professed a Call from God to be a missionary in Africa. Ruth was determined not to marry anyone who did not share that with her. In fact, there was a tall handsome young man whom she loved and wanted to marry. Don had a beautiful singing voice and the two of them sang duets together. However, although they were engaged to be married and Ruth was hoping that Don would feel the "Call" to go to Africa, it just was not to be, and so she suffered the necessary heart break and severed their relationship. Guess what? This short little German Jew would ace out all those handsome studs and end up with the prize! And what a prize she was! Awesome Wife, awesome Lover, wise Counselor to me and perfect Mother to our children! Ruth (aka, Pepper, China Doll, and Sweet Leilani) and I would spend ten years as Assemblies of God missionaries in the Ivory Coast (Cote d'Ivoire) of West Africa. She was a wonderful wife, and, as far as I was concerned, I was the luckiest, most God-blessed man in the world!

---

[18] Hebrews 12:16; 13:4; First Corinthians 6:9; 7:2-5; Ephesians 5:5; Colossians 3:5-6; Revelation 22:15; Genesis 1:27-28; 2:24; Leviticus 21:13-15; Proverbs 5:15-23; Titus 1:6

Ruth was my "Sweet Leilani" (Sweet "Flower of Heaven", in the Hawaiian language) and we were married on July 7, 1962, that is the seventh month and the seventh day of the month. I sure wasn't about to wait until 1977 so as to have all sevens in our anniversary date. Seven, in the Bible is the number of perfection and I was convinced that my Bride was perfect! At least she was perfect for me! Our wedding took place at the University Place Assembly of God church in Tacoma, Washington and all of Ruth's 7 living Brothers and her one living Sister were present along with both our parents and all the in-laws (and outlaws). We drove that night as far as a motel near Olympia and then continued the next day to our honeymoon cabin on the shores of Lake Cushman, about 15 miles from Olympia, Washington. When we arrived at the motel near Olympia that night I remember the owner of the motel holding up the keys to our room with a big smirk on his face. I tried to look as dignified as possible as I took those keys.

The first serious storm that came to my life after Ruth and I were married was after we had moved from Portland, Oregon where I attended first, Cascade College (taking the first two years of core classes required in most colleges), and then Portland State University for one year, switching my major to Foreign Languages (Spanish & French). During this time, Ruth obtained a job at Montgomery Wards' Department store as a time-keeper in their human resources department. She earned more money than did I, pulling in the grand sum of $1.47 per hour while I worked at Forest Lanes Bowling Alley earning $1.43 per hour. So between the two of us we earned $2.90 per hour. Our rent was $90 per month and we budgeted $10 per week for groceries. I think gas for the car ran about 25 cents per gallon. We were faithful to pay our tithes to the church which amounted to about $46 per month (10% of the $464 total gross income per month). My duties at the bowling alley were to vacuum the concourse area and clean each of the seating areas of the 48 bowling lanes, clean the nine restrooms and two restaurants and a large dining area used for major events and do it all in six hours of time nightly. After getting off work in the middle of the night I would hurry home to catch 4 to 6 hours sleep, take Ruth to her job each morning and then hurry downtown to the campus of Portland State University (known then simply as "Portland State") where I was pursuing a major in Foreign Languages with a minor in World History. I believe Ruth rode the bus home each evening except in the dead of winter when I would again drive across town to get her and bring her home. It was a grueling schedule for both of us.

I remember, as I would drive across Portland, having to slap my face in order to stay awake until I got home. I also remember falling asleep in the middle of tests in either French or Spanish, often confusing the two languages. I worked nights, first at Emmanuel Hospital and then for a Janitorial company I remember, while attending Portland State that I would take 5 minute "cat naps" in between classes. In those days, my internal clock worked with precision to the second. I would sit down in the middle of the hall ways, fall fast asleep, to wake up exactly 5 minutes later and continue down the hallway to my next class. I was proud of the fact that I could do that, and tested my timing over and over again.

We later moved to San Jose, California in 1965. Ruth got a job as an apartment manager on Pamela Avenue in San Jose for which we received free rent in payment for her services and I found employment working for Pacific Finance Loans, 15 N. Market Street, San Jose (funny I should remember that address after 40 years!). It was while working for PF (Pacific Finance Loans) that the storm came.

My job title was that of "Bill Collector" which included that of a Repo Man and Skip Tracer plus representative of the company in all Small Claims matters where people had a job but simply were not making payments on their loans with PF. Some of these were contractual loans when people had purchased furniture on credit from a local Furniture Store or an automobile from a local car dealer. Another part of my job was to run credit checks on people and then submit the loan to our office manager for his final decision as to whether we would "buy the paper" (finance the deal) or not. When people fell behind with their payments my job was to work with them to help them catch up or refinance into a regular loan with the furniture or automobile as collateral. If a loan became 60 to 90 days or more delinquent and it was obvious that our credit decision was a bad decision, my task would be to take a truck and some workers, go out to the home and repossess the furniture. Sometimes, people would skip town or purposefully neglect to give us their new address, and so would hide from us. That was when I put on the hat of a Skip Tracer and did my best to find them. I remember once, using an alias name and pretending to be a long lost friend, I traced a man to Mexico City and the actual barber shop where he was getting a haircut. I became pretty good at all the aspects of my job and won several awards as well as a promotion to "Collection Manager". But once, when I went out to repossess a house full of new furniture, I encountered a room full of men in the living room, each had a wine bottle or can of beer and who picked up a club or knife as they formed a circle around me. The owner then stepped into the circle of men and asked me, "What was it you said you came here for?" My reply, "I just want to go back to the office." He said, "I think that would be a good idea!" But I was so angry and feeling humiliated by the time I got back to the office that I asked my boss to let him call for assistance from the Sheriff's Office. That suggestion was denied with the words, "We'll just cross this off as a bad debt, and swallow it." Wise boss!

Frequently I went "chasing" in the evening after regular work hours. "Chasing" meant going out to people's homes and talking to them about their past due payments. When this happened, my new Bride sat home alone in the evening while my work day continued. Ruth was such a patient and supportive wife during this time, but bitterness and the sense that God was not treating me fairly by not providing so I didn't have to work so hard began to mount in my heart and spirit. I would have preferred being home making love to my new Bride than chasing "flakes" and "dead beats" as we used to call them.

These long hours at work caused me to reassess what I was doing, and so I dropped to a part time position as "Bill Collector" (forgoing my recent promotion to Collection Manager). This was a difficult decision at the time because I was excited about my new title and responsibilities at work plus the increase in salary ($800 per month), but I also knew that, in order to fulfill the Call of God on my life that I would need to return to my academic preparations, attending Bethany Bible College where I would eventually earn a Bachelor of Science Degree in Biblical Literature, with a minor in Foreign Missions studies. So I changed my focus and began taking a full academic load while continuing to work part time for Pacific Finance Loans. About this time, I bought a "Honda 305" which was a large road bike for that time (1960s). I paid $350 for the bike. It would probably be worth thousands now. A few of my friends called me "the motor cycle riding preacher" as I began commuting daily across the Santa Cruz Mountains, from San Jose to Scotts Valley. But still the bitterness and self-pity were rising in my soul and instead of enjoying this time, I was doing a lot of internal complaining, most of it aimed at God. I wanted to be with my new bride but my work and academic load made very little room for romance or relationship building. The situation reminds me, from the perspective of time and spiritual understanding of the ways of God, of the Scripture in Deuteronomy 8:2-5 which says that God allowed the Israelites to wander in the wilderness for 40 years, allowed them to hunger, the then also supplied food from heaven in the form of manna (a small coriander like seed it had the taste of pastry and was prepared with oil); furthermore the Bible says that their clothes and shoes did not wear out or their feet swell. [19] In spite of God's miraculous provision for them, the Israelites grumbled and found fault all during the 40 years of wilderness wandering, which in itself came about because of disobedience to God after several months of travel when they were finally ready to enter The Promised Land? [20]

My own grumbling against the Lord was no different than what the Children of Israel had done during their travels in the wilderness. So God, in His Mercy, did not take my Divine Destiny away from me but did teach me a very severe lesson.

And so it happened! . . . . God showed up in a startling and amazing way and the lesson began! My Manager had asked me to go to Palo Alto, north of San Jose but south of San Francisco, located on the Nimitz Freeway (Interstate I-5) to repossess a man's Cadillac. The man had tried to hide from us and was refusing to pay for the car. So one of my colleagues in the office drove me to Palo Alto to the address where, as the Skip Tracer, I had found him. When we arrived I picked the lock on the garage door and, since I had no keys, went in to hot-wire the Cadillac. In the meantime, my colleague headed back to the office and left me to drive the Cadillac back alone. As I drove on to the Nimitz Freeway (at that time, two lanes going in each direction with a grass meridian between the two directions of traffic), I began my habit of grumbling to the Lord about how hard I was working to be obedient to His Call on my life for Ministry and Missionary work in Africa, and how little God was doing to help me. In my mind He was almost like a slave driver and I told Him so!

Suddenly, I felt a presence in the back seat of the car! My first reaction was one of fear because I thought maybe the owner of the

---

[19]   Exodus 16:14-36; Numbers 11:7-9; Deuteronomy 8:3, 16; Joshua 5:12; Psalm 78:24-25; Hebrews 9:4;

[20]   Numbers 13:26-33; 14:1-25; Deuteronomy 1:26-45; I Chronicles 11:23;

Cadillac had somehow sneaked into the back seat and would presently do some terrible violence to my person. I looked in the rear view mirror but saw no one, then turned my head as best I could to see who it was in the back seat. There was no one that I could see. As my attention returned to the flow of traffic in front of me I was horrified to see that all lanes of traffic were stopped dead still on the freeway! I was traveling at exactly 55 miles per hour and seconds away from rear-ending the traffic in my lane. I instinctively braked and I pushed hard. My foot went clear to the floor board! I had no breaks! In those days most cars had a hand break for the emergency. I jerked that emergency break and it pulled out easily. I had no regular breaks, and no emergency break! The next thought that went through my mind was that I was going to die or be severely injured, with no idea of how many other people would be injured because of my lack of attentive driving. I thought, "This is Home Going time. God, my Father, is fed up with my moaning and complaining and He is taking me out of here. So I headed the Cadillac into the grassy meridian toward a concrete column which supported an overpass. I headed straight for that, thinking that at least, this way, no one else would get hurt, but I did expect to die within the next couple seconds. To my amazement the car came to a dead stop just inches from that concrete column. (Remember, I had no brakes)! I was shaken! As I bowed my head over the steering wheel and tried to regain my composure, the voice of my Heavenly Father, spoke very loud and firmly in my head. He said, "Son, I did this!" I replied, "Lord, you did this?" "Yes", the Father replied. He continued, "Down the road (of life?) you are going to need to know that I know where you are!" End of conversation! The Presence I had felt left the car and I was alone. I wish I could have seen into the Spirit world about that time! But this wasn't a time for seeing God or Angels or having a wonderful religious experience. It was meant to be a moment of severe correction to my grumbling and an act of God's Mercy to me; a lesson in Faith and Trust, in both the Love and Sovereignty of the God I claimed to serve! I drove the Cadillac back onto the Freeway and nursed it back to the office at 5 to 10 miles per hour. And yes, there have been many times since that day that I was reminded that God knows where I am! If He is all powerful (Omnipotent), if He has all knowledge (Omniscient) of every detail of every person's life, and is everywhere present all at the same time (omnipresent over His Creation) and thus never loses contact with any of us, then we really have nothing for which to worry.

It was during this time of stress and emotional upheaval that God chose to bless us, and especially to answer the cry of my wife's heart for a child. We had been married for more than four years and had been unable to have a child as a result of our union. Ruth would cry out to me and to God to give her a child. I was certainly more than willing to do my part, and reflected that we were both having a lot of fun trying to make it happen, but the rest was really up to our Creator. Finally we decided to adopt. I don't remember how we found out about an attorney in San Francisco who handled private adoptions. We set up an appointment to see him and were asked to answer a list of questions about ourselves and our preferences, our ability to raise and support a child both psychologically and financially. All we wanted was a child and we didn't care about the gender or race. Eventually, we received that long awaited phone call stating that a child would soon be born and that we could adopt it as our own after the birth and establishing that the baby was in good health. But the infant died at birth and we were back where we started. Ruth was mourning the loss of "her baby" when another call came a few weeks later from our attorney's office, this time with more information than the previous opportunity.

A certain young, very petite Irish girl by the name of Mary would be giving birth to a baby boy. But she wanted to meet and question the prospective parents before deciding to release "her Son" to us for adoption. We were hesitant, but our attorney advised that we grant her wish or risk falling into disfavor with her from the start of the process. We arranged to take her to lunch and visit with her for a couple hours. Mary was particularly thrilled about our plans to pastor churches and eventually go to Africa as missionaries. Mary had grown up in a Catholic orphanage in Ireland and knew that no baby born "out of wedlock" could ever be a Catholic Priest or Nun. When we told her that such was not the case in Protestant churches she became quite excited and said, "To think, my Son could grow up to be a Priest!"

Mary had gotten together with a big tall Swede studying to become an attorney, but his Father had warned him that if he married before he finished his studies that he (the Father) would not finish paying for his Son's studies. Consequently he told Mary that he could not marry her until after his studies were completed. I remarked to Ruth after we left that lunch interview with Mary, "Wow! She is such a pretty package maybe we could get another baby from her later on." I was only kidding but Ruth did not think very highly of such a crazy idea, even if I was kidding. Ruth and I said to Mary during our conversation that if she should decide to keep her baby that such was her right to do so, but that we would deeply appreciate it if she make that decision before the baby was born, that once we held him in our arms it would be too traumatic to be required to give him back to Mary, his birth Mother. Mary assured us that her decision was firm and that there was no danger of a change of mind or heart.

Later, Mary gave birth to a robust baby boy that would become our Son. She asked to see the baby after he was born but was told that it was against the rules for her to see the baby she had signed over for adoption. Furthermore, the nurses or doctor would not give her any information about her baby's health. Mary was upset when we went in to tell her goodbye and thank her for trusting us with her baby. When she explained that she only wanted to see him and make sure he was healthy we went to the nurses and insisted that Mary be allowed to see her baby. Reluctantly, the medical staff complied with our wishes. And we then walked out of that hospital with our brand new baby Son of two days of age. Ruth started to cry once we got in the car and started driving away with our Son. Being a male, I didn't understand and asked her, "Well what are you crying for now?" Her rely, "Because I'm so happy!" I just shook my head at the unpredictability of female emotions (from an inexperienced male perspective) and rejoiced with her at how God had blessed us with this precious little life.

We then settled on the campus of Bethany Bible College and obtained a job as caretakers of the grounds of Pacific Mission Villa there in Scotts Valley (near Santa Cruz), California. This was home to foreign missionaries returned on furlough to raise funds for their next term of overseas service. The campus of the college (BBC), as well as Pacific Mission Villa, is situated in the beautiful redwood forests of Northern California, just eight miles out of Santa Cruz. I again found employment to augment our income and worked as Night Manager at the local Shell Gas Station. The days were long and nights at the Shell Gas Station seemed even longer. I was fortunate to average six hours of sleep per 24 hour period. Often, that just didn't happen and I needed to function on 4 hours nightly sleep! I remember trying to study Greek at around 10 to 11 PM only to wake up in the middle of the night still seated at the kitchen table.

Chapter Three

Perseverance in the Storms that Come during Active Ministry

Storm One—Chapter Three
First Pastorate: Bethel Assembly of God, Yakima Washington

The year was 1969 and I was graduating from Bethany Bible College in Santa Cruz, California. Ruth and I were Caretakers for Pacific Mission Villa overlooking the beautiful Bethany [21] campus. As I neared graduation day I realized that we would need a different place to live and that the position of Caretaker of Pacific Mission Villa, which afforded us free housing in payment for our services, would be given to a different student since I was graduating. I began to send out resumes to churches in Northern California as well as other states, including Washington State.

An invitation to "present my ministry" came from Bethel [22] Assembly of God in Yakima, Washington. The church paid for my plane fare from San Jose, CA to Yakima, WA. I was warmly greeted at the airport by a

---

[21] The Biblical Bethany is located on the east side of the Mount of Olives and about 1.7 miles from Jerusalem. The word, "Bethany" is from an Aramaic root meaning "date house". Apparently date trees were planted and dates were grown in that area.

[22] The Biblical Bethel is located about 12 miles north of Jerusalem and on the other side of the valley from Ai. Bethel means, "House of God". "Beth" is house and "El" is the Hebrew word for God.

Mr. Don Law and his wife and spent that Saturday night with them and their two boys. Early Sunday morning I went into the living room to study and pray. All was quiet and my hosts and their two boys seemed still sound asleep. I flipped a switch that I expected to turn on a light; instead the fire alarms went off (heard even by the neighbors next door). My hosts rushed into the living room and headed toward their sons' bedroom, shouting as they went, "Fire! Fire!" It was almost comical for I was also shouting, "No! No! as I stood there in the middle of the living room. I knew what had happened. I had unwittingly set off the fire alarm system. Naturally, the alarms had sent them into panic mode and all they could think about was getting their two sons out of the house. The panic was based mainly on the fact that they had close friends who had lost their children when their own home burned to the ground.

Later that morning, Don Law introduced me to the congregation with these words, "Well our pulpit candidate sure knows how to stir up a lot of excitement before he even presents his ministry!" After preaching that morning I flew back to California and was met at the airport by my wife, Ruth. The congregation voted on me a few days later and the Board called me to say that I had not been elected; that the congregation was too divided because I had been picked by the Board to candidate. They offered to appoint me as the pastor and I later called them back, after discussing the matter with Ruth, and accepted their invitation. Ruth wasn't so sure we had made the right decision because she immediately recognized that we would be walking into a divided church and would probably have a rough time gaining the confidence of the faction that had voted against us.

As I remember it, I had a long conversation with the Board over the phone about their relationship with at least half the congregation who had no trust in their integrity or wisdom. I don't believe they had explained matters to me in advance, but am not sure. The Board's relationship with the previous pastor had deteriorated to the point that they had no confidence in him or his preaching. But half of the congregation loved the previous pastor, Rev. Jim Hicks, and appreciated his ministry. Jim was a simple, country preacher who loved his people and ministered faithfully to their needs during the week as well as on Sundays. The Board Members didn't like his countrified preaching and manners and wanted a more modern and urbane preacher. They had quite a "laundry list" of complaints against him, most of it just knit-picking at his preaching style and content. They had finally pressured him so greatly that he resigned, but remained in town because of the home he owned in Yakima.

And so it was into that situation that Ruth and I moved to Yakima and rented a home out on Prasch Avenue. I would soon learn more details from the Board about their feelings toward their former pastor, none of which seemed legitimate to me, but then I was a newcomer and so didn't really feel qualified to form any hard and fast opinions at that point. I began a program of visiting in the homes of the congregants and listening to their concerns (and bitterness and anger). We would pray together and I would search for ways to help each person move forward in love and forgiveness so as to take full advantage of the new realities (like it or not, they had a new pastor and the church needed to move forward). I also visited with the former pastor and his wife so as to learn from him his side of the story. I was doing my best not to take sides, but the fact that the Official Board had, against the will of the majority of the congregation, pressured Reverend Hicks into resigning was a fact hard for me to justify. I began, in spite of myself, to feel that the main problem in the Church was the Official Board and that they had been high handed and insensitive to Christian ethics as well as the feelings of the people they were supposed to serve.

It was during this time that my Son, Lance David, had asked his Mother this question, "Doesn't Daddy love us anymore?" Ruth was surprised at such a question coming from a little four year old boy concerning his daddy and so asked Lance why he had asked such a question. His response, "Because Daddy is never home." Ruth wanted to reassure him as best she could that I did indeed still love them. So she answered his question by saying that the reason I was gone so much was because I was trying to help the people in the church serve Jesus as they should. She then asked a question that she thought would be the clincher and satisfy our little son. "You wouldn't want the people to go to hell would you?" Lance's response, with all the bitterness of soul a little four year old could have that was missing his daddy, "Yes, let them go to hell! I want my daddy!" Ruth was shocked at his reply and relayed Lance's words to me that evening when I finally got home. I should have been more sensitive to my little son's needs!

Six months into our ministry as the pastors of Bethel Assembly of God the Board asked for my resignation. Their complaint? I was too short of stature to be a good leader. Amazing! But that was a wake-up call for me. If these men were that shallow in their thinking and priorities as to focus on my physical stature or, what was more probably the case, too hypocritical in their judgments to want to work through the problems concerning my leadership style or naiveté because of my inexperience as a pastor then I knew I wouldn't be able to work with them. What I really suspected was the case was that when they appointed me they thought I would be easy to control and were finding out that such was not the case. Without even hesitating, although the request for my resignation came as a surprise, I replied, "Brethren, I feel that you are entirely in God's Will to ask for my resignation. Not that I am going to resign, but your action tonight brings into clear focus in my mind where the real problem is causing the division and injured feelings in the congregation. The problem is this Board!" With that, I explained that what I would do is call for a special election. I promised the Board that if I lost that vote, I would immediately resign and furthermore said that the Sectional Presbyter would be called in to conduct the business meeting. Furthermore, I would make it clear that the vote would be to either retain me as pastor or the Official Board as Deacons. The party (I or the Board) that lost the election would consequently be dismissed from office. The next day I called my Presbyter and spiritual pastor, Rev. Leland Gross, and explained to him what the Board had said and what had been my response.

The Church By-laws were carefully followed in setting up the special election and I worked closely with my Presbyter to make sure he was satisfied with the way I was handling this crisis. On the appointed evening, the election was conducted by Rev. Leland Gross. I carried the election and the Board was dismissed. At that point, about 50% of the congregation resigned their membership and left the church. From that standpoint, it was impossible to feel any sense of victory or to rejoice. However, the same thing would have happened if the Board had been reaffirmed and I had lost. It is just that the identity of people leaving and/or staying would have been different. So now, I would preach to half the number of folks that I had previously minister to when we first arrived as their new pastors.

Within the next six months there was a growing desire on the part of those who had stayed to once again have their old pastor return. I was sympathetic to their feelings. So called Rev. Hicks and asked him to conduct a two week "revival meeting" for us. He and his wife would play the piano and sing and he would preach. At the end of the two weeks, I resigned and the pulpit was once again open. Another business meeting was called for, and Rev. Jim Hicks was elected and back in the pulpit. So now, Ruth and I were without income and I went to work for a Finance Company in town. We had to move from the nice home we had rented into a smaller home closer into town in order to afford to pay the rent.

I began immediately to seek a new pastorate and to contact open churches in the District. I had, during this time, also moved up from Licensed to Ordained Minister in the Assemblies of God.

Ruth and I, when we got married, had agreed that we would seek appointment as Assemblies of God missionaries to some country in Africa. But one of the requirements for that to happen was two years of successful pastoral experience. At that moment the "successful" part of that requirement didn't seem to be developing very well for us. At least that is the way we were feeling about current developments. I had acted with integrity and, I believed, sensitivity to the leading of the Holy Spirit. Years later when we did apply for missionary candidate status and met with the Foreign Missions Board I brought up the subject of some of what I considered to be our "failures" in pastoral experience over the years. The response of the Board was, "We are not really concerned with all that. You were only "sharpening your spiritual tools" (translation: "developing better people skills, as well as how to solve church problems") and, in the process, learning valuable lessons that will be needed in cross-cultural situations on the mission field." And that was the end of that subject. Internally, I think Ruth and I both breathed a sigh of relief.

Storm Two—Chapter Three
Second Pastorate: Vader Community
Church, Vader, Washington

And so, after several months of waiting for God to show us His Will for our next step forward toward missionary appointment we did receive an invitation to present our ministry at the Vader Community Assembly of God church in a small town listed in one book entitled "The Ghost Towns of Washington". Vader was, at the time we went there to be their new pastors, a town of 350 population made up mostly of misplaced "tar heels" as the people from North Carolina are called. But this would prove to be one of the happiest times we would have of the several churches we served. These are lovely, friendly people and the church grew from about 25 to 30 in attendance as high as around 150. That meant that more than one third of the town attended our services. I enjoyed preaching to these folks and visiting in their homes. They were simple country folks but a joy to be with.

The men in the congregation were avid deer and elk hunters and from where Vader is located the wilderness is less than 15 miles away.

The church parsonage was an older home with cracks in the walls large enough to allow the wind to blow through the home. The Master Bedroom was small, not really a Master Bedroom in the truest sense of the word and the door to our room was a blanket that did blow sideways when bad weather moved in. Moss covered the roof and we had to put pots and pans out to catch the leaks whenever it rained. Our salary at the church was $75 per week plus parsonage and utilities. People did bring us groceries from time to time. One dear lady used to bring us a cow tongue or cow brains from time to time, and always in a bucket of blood. I had eaten cow tongue as a boy growing up and also enjoyed cow brains with scrambled eggs. So this was a flash back to my childhood. Not so with Ruth, and I must admit it was something of an adjustment for her. We always enjoyed the venison or elk meat the hunters in the church would bring us. Fish was a different story! Ruth never did like fish but would force herself to eat what was provided. I love fish and was elected by my wife to prepare the slimy, smelly fish (as Ruth described it) for cooking. Ruth just had a hard time with even the smell of those "stinky" fish, and I used to tease her about that.

It was during this time that we adopted our second child. Lani Rochelle came into our home at the ripe old age of nine weeks. We went to Pomeroy, Washington and the adoption was handled there through the Welfare Department. Apparently, a local girl, daughter of a prominent family in the area, had gotten pregnant. Family pressure would not allow her to keep her child and so Ruth and I were blessed with this precious little "bundle of joy".

A rather humorous event during our stay in Pomeroy happened in the following manner. A Social Worker had brought the baby to us to care for during the day with the idea that she would return in the evening to get the baby and give us an opportunity to "sleep on it" overnight before making our final decision as to whether this child was who we wanted. But Lance, during the day, had already made up his mind that this was his baby sister and no one was going to take her away from him. So when the Social worker came that evening to pick up Lance's baby sister he began to cry and then get frustrated and angry. Ruth tried to explain to Lance that she Social Worker needed to take his Baby Sister back overnight so as to get more food and diapers for her and get her ready to travel with us the next day. But Lance saw the Social Worker only as the person that was taking away his Baby Sister and so he went over and kicked the lady in the shins. We, of course, were embarrassed and apologetic. She assured us that Lance's behavior was normal for a small child that really didn't understand what was going on. We, for our part, had already made up our mind that this little girl was who we wanted, but the system works like the system works when dealing with the government and there was no choice being offered us.

The next morning the Social Worker arrived at the door with Lance's Baby Sister, fresh formula and diapers and all we needed to care for her until we could get to a store to buy our own things. Of course, we had already been preparing for this event and had a new crib set up to receive this precious little child whom we already loved.

Lani Episodes!

One antidote about Lani gives substantial insight into her personality right from infancy. Her bedroom was right across the hall from where Ruth and I slept. Lani would shake the sides of her crib until the screws worked loose and then she would methodically unscrew the screws until the side of the crib would fall, crashing, to the floor after which she would proceed to crawl out of the bed onto the top of the dresser next to her bed. The room was so small that there was nowhere else to put the dresser. Once she got on top of the dresser she would try to lower herself down to the floor, but was afraid of falling and so could never quite bring herself to let go the top of the dresser. At that point she would start to cry. Now this scenario repeated itself almost every night. Ruth and I would be sound asleep, then rudely awakened by the crashing of the crib side to the floor. At first we would go running in to the room to find out what all the racket was about. Of course there was the expected parental admonishment, "No, no! Don't do that." But Lani was a strong willed baby from the start! A beautiful child whom we doted on and loved dearly, even the "strong willed" part. And our commands not to do certain things seemed to feed her determination to do them! It didn't take more than a time or two to figure out the whole scenario. So we would wait until we heard Lani's cries for help. Finally, one time, Ruth got her camera before she went into the room. "Oh, so you like hanging from the top of the dresser, do you?" she said. "Let's see how long you can hold on" followed by a series of pictures taken before Ruth lovingly rescued her one more time from her own choices. Even if Lani had fallen, she would not have been hurt, and we knew that. Of course she would have screamed and cried as if she was dying. But we were careful parents and would not have allowed her to get seriously hurt.

Lani Episode Two

I remember once when I was up on the roof of the parsonage trying to see what I could do about the leaks around the chimney. The roof had a rather steep slant to it and I remember hearing this tiny voice, "Hi, Daddy!" as I turned to see Lani on the top step of the ladder, peering at her daddy with a cherry smile and greeting. "Oh, hi, Sweetheart," I replied as my heart sunk to my shoes! "Did you come to see your Daddy?" I queried with a cheerfulness that contradicted the fear I actually felt for my daughter's safety. I did not realize then that these two early episodes were only warm-up events for more serious challenges to her personal, psychological and spiritual safety that would come during her adolescence. I walked with an outward calm I did not feel down the slant of the roof to where my daughter was on the top rung of the ladder. Gently picked her up and held her close to my chest as I came down the ladder to safety.

Lani Episode Three

A couple other episodes that happened when she was little: once she climbed up on a chair that was propped against a cherry tree in our yard. From there she accidently kicked the chair over as she proceeded to climb the tree. She was only about three years old at the time and just at that age when a child likes to exert its new found will and abilities. And Lani, like her Father, has a spirit of adventure that can get her into trouble if she is not careful. It showed up in those early years. Ruth heard some crying and screaming out in the yard and rushed out to find Lani hanging on for dear life to the trunk of the tree. Her little chest was scratched and bleeding and Lani was scared (a rare moment in her young life). So Ruth rescued her one more time, took her back into the house to clean her up and put soothing medicine on her "owies".

On one other occasion this adventurous child of ours decided to sun bathe out in the middle of the street. Ruth suddenly heard the honking of horns and ran out the front door to find Lani down the street about a block away, laying on her back and basking in the sun. The driver of the car had seen her in time to drive around her instead of over her and was honking to get her Mother's attention. He had no idea whose child this was. He just wanted to get someone's attention. Fortunately, we lived in a small town of 350 people and so heavy traffic was not a problem. At three years old, Lani seemed totally oblivious to the danger into which she had placed herself when she left the house to go sunbathe on the street or climb a tree. Believe me, Ruth was an excellent, watchful and careful Mother but Lani was "hard to keep up with".

Lani Episode Four

It was always hard to keep this fearless child corralled and safe! But that fearless part of her emotional makeup would pay off years later when, as a young teenager living in West Africa, she would need to kill a deadly snake that had gotten into the girls shower room at the boarding school where she was living. All the other girls in the shower room were paralyzed with fear and screaming. But not my daughter! She would say, "Well get something and kill the silly thing!" at which she added action to her words, rushed to where there was a broom in the next room, came back into the shower room and beat the snake to death. That was some feat because most of the snakes were not only deadly but moved faster than a human could move.

Another time (and this was also in West Africa) Lani was swimming in the city swimming pool and did not see a deadly snake swimming right toward her. Fortunately the life guard saw the snake and was able to kill it before it reached Lani. Lani probably would have grabbed the snake, bit its head off and threw its body out of the pool! Not really! I wish! Actually she would have undoubtedly died a horrible and painful death had the snake reached her, but God was gracious and spared her life by means of the life guard!

Before writing the next section I need to express great thankfulness to God for His hand upon my daughter's life! At age 43, Lani has turned out to be a very responsible and sensible middle aged woman. She is a top notch administrator at the VA Hospital in Seattle, Washington. She recently has been recognized through the VA hierarchy on a national level, and been promoted to a job that reaches across the whole Veterans Administration system. I am proud of her and the way she has turned her life around. She is almost universally admired and respected by her colleagues as well as her bosses. Some months ago when she was promoted out of her department it took three people to replace her, and with this last promotion they are still bewailing the great loss of her presence in the department! The expressions are frequently, "How can we replace the hole left that Lani used to fill for us, but is no longer there to carry the workload." So I have a Father's thankful and proud heart for what my wonderful daughter has become!

Family Issues & Insights (Part One)
Insight #1: Biblical & Secular Culture

Marriage and parenting are never easy. Those who truly learn to love in a self-sacrificing unselfish manner will surely learn also, to endure pain. Emotional pain, mental pain, psychological pain! Sleepless nights, depression and discouragement go hand in hand with the most wonderful and joyful of emotional highs that come with finding your one true Love and holding the noisy little bundles of joy that come later with the fruit of your Love. Marriage is awesome! Raising and playing with children and providing for their needs are also awesome responsibilities & joys. Picnics! Trips to the park, fishing, camping, playing monopoly or wrestling on the living room floor with pets and children are all wonderful experiences that hopefully will be long remembered so as to balance out the emergency trips to the hospital coupled with the anxiety of not knowing whether your wife or your child will survive. Hopefully the camping trips to Yosemite or other national parks or, in the case of our family, the museums and castles and cable car rides from mountain top to mountain top somewhere in Europe, or souvenirs from some tourist trap, will balance out to some degree the bad stuff during the teen and young adult years with the kids that inevitably also come.

And so some of the issues I wish to address in this section come out of personal experience, times when my mind & emotions have been pierced by the knife points of these issues and I have suffered greatly.

The rebellious, mouthy teenager has never been a teenager before and is desperately trying to sort out the emotions and events of their own lives, events even that can come without the parent's knowledge because the child is too embarrassed or fearful to confide in the parent. But their parent has also never been a parent before, at least has never before been a parent of that particular child with their particular set of problems complicated by their own unique personality, and so that season of life is happily, or sometimes painfully or tragically new to both parent and child.

My wife and I taught marriage seminars later in life and then had to go home and continue living out the implications of our own teachings in practical terms with each other. Occasionally, but not too often, one of us would say to the other, "What was it you taught earlier this evening?" So here are some issues that have my own life experiences as a background . . . .

Cultural Influences

The first issue is culture. Are you surprised? But we live in an historical setting in which there is a cultural war raging between Christian parents and teachers in the secular education field; even a war between Christian parents and a burdensome, intrusive federal and state government which has taken to themselves the right to interfere with and even counteract the teaching or standards of conduct children receive in the home. For many different reasons there is a breakdown in our families caused mainly by the struggle between the home and an increasingly godless society or intrusive government.

I remember teaching on the subject of Family Values at the Institut Théologique et Pastoral in Daloa, West Africa. The subject of husband/wife relationships came up. One African student pastor asked, "Can I whip my wife when she misbehaves or is disrespectful?" That question is so African! When I replied in the negative, he pressed the matter by asking, "Can't I at least pull her ear?" Again, I replied negatively. I also remember when my African night guard (who lived on the same property with Ruth and I in Daloa) said to me, "Pastor, I could never treat my wife the way you treat your wife." I was surprised! "Why, Moussa?", I asked. He answered without hesitation. "Because if I did, she would get mouthy and bossy and take the place over. I would lose control of the household." This conversation was expressed in the French language in which I am fluent! Moussa continued, "I treat my wife like a child half the time, whipping her as I would a child, and like an (adult) woman, being romantic with her, the other half". That too is an expression of African culture! This will be repulsive to the American mind, as it should be! But to the West African way of thinking, it is perfectly acceptable. I have personally witnessed (out of my second story apartment window in Daloa) the beating, in the African courtyard below, of women by their husbands. Interference in such an event would be dangerous to life & limb, certainly inadvisable or impossible. So in light of this example, would my reader agree that culture should not be allowed to establish concepts of right and wrong?

An expression of Mossi culture is that if a man has a son and there is only one bed in the home, the man and his son sleep in the bed. The wife and the daughter sleep on the dirt floor where rats and mice and other varmints can chew on them during the night. I could tell you stories about that one! I could also describe many beautiful aspects of Mossi culture.

As a Christian lady, a Godly woman, my wife never would have thought it acceptable to go topless to some beach in West Africa or France or Italy and lay out in the sun along with other men and women even though such activity is acceptable in those cultures. She was too much of a lady and had too much respect for herself and the God she served and the husband she loved to even consider such a thing. She understood clearly the difference between righteous and holy patterns of behavior in contrast to that which is an expression of human decadence. She once said to me, after we had watched on television a group of women who claimed to be Christian strippers, "The first thing God did for Adam and Eve after their sin was to put clothes on them!" Ruth also understood that a Godly, righteous woman will dress in such a way as to call attention to her face rather than any other part of her body; and also that being clothed with Godly character, sweetness and humility are attitudes of more value than physical beauty or expensive clothes.[23]

As a Christian man, hopefully a Godly man, I never would have considered taking a whip to my wife in an effort to correct her just because we were living in West Africa where it is culturally acceptable to treat one's wife in that manner. Culture should not, and in God's eyes

---

[23] I Peter 3:2-5; 5:4; Titus 2:2-5, 11-15; I Timothy 2:9-10; Isaiah 61:10; 28:5-6; Proverbs 1:8-9; 4:7-9; 16:31;

does not, establish good & evil, right and wrong! People who use culture to justify lifestyle set a trap for their own soul, misery for their entire family, and disaster for one's eternal destiny!

In fact, a woman might be beautiful or a man handsome until they open their mouth. A good question for each of us, "What comes out of my mouth? A sewer of curses, vulgarity, impatience, anger, bitterness, hatred . . . or a Godly character of love, kindness, graciousness, forgiveness, respectfulness and encouragement?"

Do I need to be specific? The "F" word, the "S" word or expressions like "crap" or "pissed" are words out of the sewer of a decadent culture and should not be part of the vocabulary of a person who claims to be a Follower of Jesus Christ. It should not be acceptable to be professional and refined at work or church, but talk and act at home or among one's friends like you just crawled out of the city sewer.

Choose your friends carefully. Refuse the culture of the American sewer. Opt for friendships with people who know how to keep it clean even when they are upset or angry; better yet, who are guided by Biblical values! You will eventually be like your friends, so choose them carefully! I have seen this happen within my own extended family where people gradually deteriorate into the image of the friendships they have cultivated. The only reason to have undesirable friends is so you can influence them, rather than allowing them to influence you. Jesus did eat and drink with the riff raff of society but He always influenced or changed them. They never were allowed to influence or change Him. Remember when Judas wanted to change Jesus' priorities? Eventually Judas hung himself because he was on the wrong side of the purposes of God. Jesus never allowed anyone from the wrong side of God's Will to influence His life.

So what is my point? Simply this, that culture (any culture, from anywhere in the world) does not establish right and wrong, good and evil; these do not change from culture to culture, but come from objective (not subjective) truth found only in God's Word. Jesus said, "If you love me, keep (Greek, "obey & guard as precious") my commandments."[24] Cultural relativity, (as far as Truth or good & evil are concerned), is a lie aimed at dulling our senses about what God intended human culture to resemble! Sorry, secular anthropologists, but to a great degree you got it all wrong!

With a graduate degree in cross-cultural communications, I recognize that there are many beautiful parts to every culture and I could name many of them. In these cases it is not a matter of right and wrong, just differences. And the missionary or any international traveler needs the ability to recognize where principles of good and evil enter the picture (and this is where one needs a knowledge of Biblical Principles & Teaching) or where cultural norms are just a matter of a different way of viewing life. In West Africa it is an insult of the highest order to hand someone something with your left hand. And, out of their societal setting, there are valid reasons for that cultural norm.

The Thai culture is one of the most beautiful cultures I have ever witnessed, and I have witnessed many. The Thai people are so very gracious and thoughtful of others. Many cultures are polite, even respectful. But the Thai people add graciousness to their politeness and respectfulness. They honor their parents, each other and the guests in their country and they do it with such humility and graciousness that you could almost want to stay there the rest of your life.

God created variety in human culture (meaning of Cosmos or "world") and, the Bible teaches that He decorated planet earth with the human race expressed through many colorful and beautiful cultures. However, input from the Bible, Source of all final authority, is needed

---

[24] John 14:15; I John 2:4-5; Hebrew word, "shamar" from Exodus 15:26 has similar meaning; i.e., ("hedge about with thorns in order to protect and attend to without exterior intrusion or damage")

Joseph Meyers

to further explain where we are going with this. In the New Testament First Epistle of Saint John, chapter two, verse 15 the Holy Spirit tells us, to "love not the world (human culture), neither the things (makeup or parts of human culture) in the world".

Cosmos (Greek, Kosmos [25]) is here translated "world" and has a variety of very similar meanings and translations. Primarily it can be translated, "culture". Let's look at them:

(1) It means "decoration". In non-biblical or secular Greek, especially in the writings of Homer and Plato, it was sometimes used to refer to the way a woman decorated herself with clothing and cosmetics; i.e., the culture of her attire! [26]

(2) That which is well assembled; arrangement or a building (again, Homer and Plato)

(3) "Cosmos (kosmos) is used often in the sense of order." The way anything is put together. So what is the cosmos of your life, your heart desires? Church, Bible Reading, prayer, friendships with Godly people or a party life-style with drinking, carousing, vulgar language and sex outside of marriage? How is your life, entertainment (books you read, movies you watch) and goals put together? What is the arrangement of your thought life, your desires and preoccupations? [27]

(4) The inhabited world; the culture and society of men & women through which the world is decorated. [28]

(5) The abode of men or the context of history; it can refer to

---

[25] Strong's Greek Dictionary, NT:2889 see: First John 2:15

[26] Kittel, "Theological Dictionary of New Testament Words" (TDNT); "Kosmos"

[27] Ibid. Example: Genesis 6:5: "every intent of the thoughts of his heart was only evil continually".

[28] Ibid.

the order in which rowers of boats assemble for battle, or as a political term, referring to government rules & regulations which bind together the citizens of a city-state.[29]

(6) In a number of Scriptures the word, kosmos, has the meaning of, "the totality of human interpersonal relationships (society). [30]

(7) "Human culture has fallen into conflict with God but God acted to bring redemption and reconciliation to those who are willing to stop fighting with Him and surrender to His Kingdom of Love and Righteousness." [31] In God's plan of salvation God stands opposite the world of culture. Sin and death had entered humanity and invaded human culture. God's prophets and even Jesus, the Son of God, came into the world of culture to change it! Jesus was born in Bethlehem not for the purpose of redeeming planet earth, but to purchase with His Blood the redemption price for human individuals and cultures sold under sin to Lucifer. "Christ eventually departs from the world (human culture) and leaves behind those who are His to conduct their

---

[29] Theological Dictionary of the New Testament. Copyright © 1972-1989 By Wm. B. Eerdmans Publishing Co. All rights reserved.)

[30] If the reader will put the word "culture" in the place of "world" in each of these passages you will understand more clearly the real message or meaning of what is written. These Scriptures are not talking about planet earth and the dirt upon which we walk; they are talking about the culture of men and nations. Mark 8:36; 16:14; Luke 4:5; 9:25; 12:30; Matthew 4:8; 5:14; 6:32; 13:38; 16:26; 26:13; Romans 1:8; 3:19; 4:13; (in this context, see Genesis 18:18; 22:17 where it is not planet earth that God promises to bless but the Godly people and culture that would come out of the body of Abraham); I Corinthians 4:13; II Corinthians 1:12; Colossians 1:6; I Timothy 3:16; I Peter 5:9; II Peter 3:6; I John 2:2; 3:1, 13; Romans 11:12, 15; especially apparent in John 1:10, 29; 6:33, 51; 12:19; 14:17, 19; 16:20; 17:21;

[31] Exegetical Dictionary of the New Testament © 1990 by William B. Eerdmans Publishing Company. Insert "culture" for the word, "world": See also: John 1:9; 3:19; 12:46; 13:1; 16:28; 17:11; Romans 5:12f; I John 4:1, 3; II John 7; II Corinthians 1:12; James 1:27; 4:4; II Peter 1:4; I John 2:17; 5:4-5.

lives in constant conflict with the nature of the kosmos (human culture)". [32]

(8) All of the above are confirmed by <u>Strong's Hebrew/Greek Definitions</u> as well as the <u>Exegetical Dictionary of New Testament Words</u> [33]; the <u>Louw & Nida Greek-English Lexicon of the New Testament</u>: which defines, Kosmos, as referring to the world system, world's standards, or that which is associated with secular society; the above is also confirmed by <u>Thayer's Greek Lexicon</u> and W.E. Vine's <u>Expository Dictionary of New Testament Words</u>.

God, the Holy Spirit, goes on to say in the Inspired Word that if anyone loves the world, (human culture) the love of God, our Father in Heaven, is not in that person. So if God created and decorated His world with human culture, why would He warn us not to love human culture saying that to do so would be evidence that the love of God is not in us? The simple answer is that human culture has been infected by demonic spirits, beginning in the Garden of Eden, and has consequently deteriorated to the point of almost total depravity and decadence. One may not like that answer, but our likes and dislikes cannot be allowed to define Truth.

Dear reader, have you noticed the details of the fabric of American culture that are changing? Consequently, there is a struggle taking place in families, towns, counties, states and the federal government seeking to

---

[32] Ibid., read all of John 17 but particularly verses 4, 6, 9, 11-18, 21, 23-25 reading "culture" where you see the word, "world". Notice in v.4 the word, "earth" which is a different Greek word speaking of the dirt we walk on and making my point that "earth" (Greek, GE [ghay], dirt) is different than "world" (Gr., [kosmos] or "culture")

[33] Exegetical Dictionary of the New Testament © 1990 by William B. Eerdmans Publishing Company. All rights reserved.)

totally transform what it means to be an American. Political Correctness, a Woman's right to Choose (choose what? Choose to murder unborn infants?), Gay Rights; all these things are at the forefront of the struggle and in direct defiance of the commandments of our Creator. According to God's Word, if we love this culture to the point of accepting and participating in its evil, then the love of Father God is not in us and our soul is bound for Hell. One cannot defend or protect what God has condemned and hope when your spirit leaves your body at death to spend eternity in His Presence. Jesus came to establish a righteous culture on earth.[34] When He said that He had come that we might have Life and have it more abundantly, He was recognizing that "God's Life in the human heart" to a great extent no longer existed on this earth. All that remained on the earth once full of the Life of God was human existence controlled by Evil (Evil that separates human life from a quality of Life that lives for Eternity!) Jesus came to reestablish the connection between God and His creation. God had already started over several times but now, through Jesus the Christ (the Anointed or Chosen One) it is God's plan to start over one final time. [35]

John 15:19—"If you were of the (culture) the (culture) would love its own. Yet because you are not of the (culture), but I chose you out of the (culture), therefore the (culture) hates you." (In every instance the Greek word, "kosmos" is used and means "culture".)

Romans 12:2—"And do not be conformed to this culture (Greek, kosmos), but be transformed by the renewing of your mind, that you may prove what is that good and acceptable and perfect will of God."

---

[34] Genesis 22:18; Ezra 9:2; Malachi 2:14-15; John 15:1-3; Romans 9:3-5; Galatians 3:16, 28-29;

[35] Gen. 6:5-8; 12:1-3; Deut. 8:1-20; John 3:16-17; Matt. 18:11; I Tim. 2:5-6; II Peter 3:13; Rev. 21:1-4

Ephesians 2:2-3—". . . in which you once walked according to the course of this culture (Greek, kosmos), according to the prince of the power of the air, the spirit who now works in the sons of disobedience . . ."[36]

James 4:4-6—". . . Don't you realize that friendship with the culture (Greek, kosmos) makes you an enemy of God? I say it again: If you want to be a friend of the (culture), you make yourself an enemy of God. What do you think the Scriptures mean when they say that the spirit God has placed within us is filled with envy? But he gives us even more grace to stand against such evil desires. As the Scriptures say, God opposes the proud but favors the humble." [37]

And there are many, many such references all of which use the word, "kosmos", with the meaning of "culture". It is a spiritual, cosmic cultural war in which we are engaged! Ultimately, this war is between God and Lucifer. And we humans are their servants doing their bidding. Whose servant are you? On which side are you?

Storm Three—Chapter Three
Years Wasted: A Disastrous Interlude Between Pastorates And God's Will for our lives.

"To every action there is an opposite and equal reaction" this is known as Newton's Third Law of Motion. But I would like to suggest that there are motions of the human psyche, of attitudes and thoughts. People often change because of pressure being brought to bear upon their own sense of what is acceptable behavior. Such was the case near

---

[36] So right here in Ephesians 2:2-3 is confirmation that the source of cultural decadence is Satanic presence within people's lives.

[37] Holy Bible, New Living Translation ®, copyright © 1996, 2004 by Tyndale Charitable Trust. Used by permission of Tyndale House Publishers. All rights reserved.

the end of our 30 month pastorate in Vader, Washington. Our time there was, for the most part, enjoyable. We loved the people in the congregation and they loved us. Ruth was particularly close to a number of the young married women in the church and able to help them with problems in their marriages. Some of those young women were married to men who had never really committed their lives to serving the Lord Jesus Christ. In fact they often seemed more committed to hunting, fishing or taking care of livestock than they were to their own wives, let alone God! Mainly self-centered men who were too busy being macho tough guys or sports fans than they were to building solid marriages or become spiritual leaders in the church or their wife, learning how to be good fathers and good examples (spiritually and psychologically) to their children.

I found myself falling into the same trap, though I knew better. But my preoccupation was what it had always been; i.e., that of being a good pastor and a good preacher. In the process of long hours of study or counseling others or administrative duties for the church I was leaving Ruth and the children to fend for themselves. Even on family night if there was an emergency call by someone in crisis I would drop my time with the family and try to help the person in crisis. Again, Lance did not have a father who spent enough time with him teaching him how to play ball or do other manly things that would help him be acceptable to other boys his age. Lance was an artistic type and really not interested in sports. Well, his father (me) was a bookish, academic type and usually one of the last to be chosen, when I was a boy, when teams were picked for some event at school. I did go out for track in junior high and wrestling in high school. So I wasn't completely alienated from a sports mentality, but Lance seemed to have no interest in sports of any kind. He was very artistic and had a great sense of humor. But, in retrospect, I should have insisted that he and I at least practice throwing and catching a ball and maybe get a couple other boys to practice a little football or basketball at somewhere fairly private so that Lance could have taken time to at least develop some abilities along those lines. Or even just take Lance hiking in the woods or hunting at deer season. We just never did it, and that was my failure, not my Son's.

So finally, after hearing much complaining from my wife about me not taking enough time with the family, I solved the problem (I thought) by resigning from pastoring the church. We ended up moving to Tacoma to live with Ruth's Mother in the large house in which Ruth grew up as a child. The problem was, however, I still had not learned to relax and just play with my family. I did get a job in Kent, WA fabricating beverage cans of all sorts. I don't remember the name of the company but it was hard work and I profited from the physical exercise.

In my spare time I worked hard with some friends of mine to set up a non-profit corporation that would supposedly attract investors and that we would use fees from our efforts to send money overseas to missionary endeavors around the world. The name of our corporation was World Missions Investment Enterprizes. We were able to get IRS clearance and had a corporate attorney who donated his time helping us with legal issues. But ours was a "pipe dream" that never came to fruition because we were not trained or accredited investment brokers. The idea, while being an expression of our hearts of a desire to help finance various missionary projects around the world, was doomed to failure from the start, simply because we did not have the expertise needed to make it work.

So once again, I had gotten myself involved in activities that took me away from my wife and children. I did get my license to sell insurance with a company by the name of Preferred Risk Insurance and was qualified to sell life, health and auto insurance. But that also was not even close to the training I needed for the fulfillment of the WMIE (World Missions Investment Enterprises) dream.

But Ruth had finally gotten fed up with my promises to take more time with the family and we began to have some serious relationship problems as a result. This turned out to be a difficult time for our family, mainly due to my preoccupation with other priorities. Looking back on things now, I am absolutely amazed that my precious wife was as patient with me as she was.

It was during this time also that our Son began to have real problems at school. We first noticed the problem when he began coming home crying and saying that he hated school and that he never wanted to go back to school. He and his sister would both make a beeline for the bathroom when they got home. Neither one of them would use the school restrooms. I don't remember now what that was all about but I do remember that Lance's teacher was making fun of him in front of his classmates. The problem, it seems, was that Lance was not masculine enough to suit the teacher, who himself was a little on the effeminate side. And then, at least once, the teacher threw a basketball with extreme force at Lance's face. Lance was not able to catch the ball and it hit him in the face. Lance wet his pants on the way home from school that day and vowed never to return to the school. When Ruth and Lance saw how upset I was toward Lance's teacher they begged me not to arrange a meeting with him and the School Principal. Instead, Ruth went and met with them. I have since regretted going along with that decision, but agreed to it because of pressure from my wife and son. Lance didn't want me to make a "big deal" out of it at the school and Ruth was afraid I would be too angry to handle the situation properly. I do believe that some situations call for something more than a calm gentlemanly conversation. There is a time for a Father to stand up in protection of his wife and/or children and do so in a way that a clear line of boundary is drawn. What I had thought of doing was picking up a basketball and taking it to my meeting with the teacher and School Principal with the purpose of testing how good Lance's somewhat effeminate teacher was at catching a ball thrown unexpectedly at his face, and then also demanding that the teacher be fired. Maybe it was for the best that Ruth went. The teacher later admitted that his reasoning for throwing the ball in Lance's face was because Lance reminded him of himself. He claimed that he was only trying to help our Son overcome a lack of ability in the area of sports activities. Humiliating a boy in front of his classmates is not the way to help him and to this day I regret not taking that basketball to the meeting I should have arranged and attended!

I also recognize that the real problem behind all this was that I was not spending enough time with my Son and was not insisting that he learn to catch a ball and do a minimum of a few sports oriented activities. I should have worked with Lance in these areas in the privacy of our home and yard so that he was better prepared to relate to other boys who were good at sports. The underlying fault was mine! I was never in general "good at sports" myself as a boy. But I had gone out for track and set a school record in Junior High for the 50 yard dash. Later I would turn out for wrestling but suffered a neck injury and was not allowed by my parents to continue. At least I had tried and I should have helped my Son do the same. Also, part of my hang-up was the way my father had pressured me to learn automobile mechanics and carpentry when I preferred to learn violin and piano and become a "boy preacher" and to travel and speak in churches throughout northern California where we lived. I spent hours memorizing Scripture and practicing the piano but had no interest in the things my Father had wanted to teach me. Consequently, I was reluctant to pressure my own Son in the area of sports activities.

Storm Four—Chapter Three
Completion of Graduate Studies, Chief Baker and Chest Pains

After a short time of 18 months pastoring the First Assembly of God church in Ellensburg, Washington we realized that we were approaching the age limit (36 years of age) for being able to apply for Foreign Missions Appointment. And so, in the Spring of 1976 we decided to resign from our pastorate in Ellensburg and move to Springfield, Missouri where I would attend the Assemblies of God Graduate School (now Assemblies of God Theological Seminary) for the purpose of earning an M.A. Degree with a double major in Biblical Literature and Cross Cultural Communications, and, at the same time, applying for Missionary Candidate Status.

Ruth and I had decided to resign our pastorate and just strike out on faith to move to Springfield, Missouri. For the non-Christian that term "strike out on faith" might be hard to understand. It simply means that one is determined that God will supernaturally honor a choice we have made in obedience to His Will, and will override any negative circumstances that seem to dictate a more "reasonable" course of action, one that acts according to facts as they are in the physical universe, rather than believing that some supernatural power (like the Biblical God) will intervene to rescue us from what some would say was a foolish action. We had no money saved and not even enough to rent the U-Haul trailer to get us out of town. We started selling as much of our furniture and unneeded belongings as possible. I even sold a 30-30 rifle Ruth and bought me for one of my birthdays. We were serious about "clearing the decks" to make this transition from Ellensburg, Washington to Springfield, Missouri then back to the West Coast to spend two years itinerating among the churches in a fundraising effort so that we could then move to Albertville, France and the Centre Missionaire where we would learn the French language.

And then God gave us favor with the congregation in a special way. People started bringing both monetary gifts as well as items we could sell in our yard sale. I remember that one family brought us silver pieces like trays, coffee pot and other items. By the time all this was finished, we had enough money to not just get out of town but to pay gas and lodging expenses across the country and then survive financially for six weeks as we worked to get settled in our new location (Springfield, Missouri). Actually, we camped at KOA camp spots and cooked over a Coleman kerosene stove all the way across the country. It was fun! And we had a great time with the kids. The children enjoyed living in a tent and sleeping on camping cots more than we did. And then, we also lived in that same tent for about two weeks while I looked for work and a place for us to live. Ruth finally got a job managing an apartment complex, for which we received free rent with utilities paid. So we and Lucky, our pet miniature poodle, and Carrot, our orange cat, all moved in. This turned out to be a blessing from the Lord! One thing I remember is that most of our tenants were college age kids. Lance and Lani enjoyed going "dumpster diving" whenever a group of students moved out of the apartments. Many games and other prizes were brought by the kids into our apartment. One game was called "Stock Market" and provided hours of family time and enjoyment for us.

We slowly began to get settled in to a family routine and I (Joseph) was able to get registered for the Fall Semester as well as landing a job working for a Seventh Day Adventist Health Foods Bakery where a couple thousand loaves of bread was produced every night. It was hot (due mostly because of the large ovens where the loaves of bread were baked). I don't remember what the hourly wage was, but it was a job that provided for my family. I gradually worked my way up until I became the Chief Baker, responsible for getting thousands of loaves of bread ready for the store shelves or shipment to customers by the next morning.

As Fall classes began at the Seminary, I found myself carrying a full academic load of 9 to 12 credit hours and working full time to support my wife and two children. What suffered here was what always suffered over the years, family life and sleep. I seldom got more than 4 to 5 hours sleep per night (I considered myself lucky to ever get six hours sleep). And that was broken up by two hours sleep in the middle of the day and two hours' sleep at night. My work day at the bakery started around 5 or 6 PM each evening and would last until whenever the job was done, usually around 3 or 4 AM. Then it was home to bed and up and in attendance for my first class by 7 AM. My efforts would eventually earn me an M.A. Degree with a double major in Biblical Literature and Cross-cultural Communications. The latter academic major was vitally important because I would not only be ministering to Muslims in West Africa, but because the Ivory Coast (as it was known then) contains 64 tribes speaking 64 different languages with several hundred Dialects among those 64 languages.

Once a week I was on my feet working, or on my derrière (backside) studying, for at least thirty hours without a break. But there were times now and then when we had brief moments of "family time". The kids loved the board games we played, but most of all they loved it when I took them in the car down to the paved corner vacant lot in the middle of winter. There I would start driving across the lot and then hit the brakes real hard. That would, of course, set the car spinning in circles across the frozen surface of the vacant lot. For a few seconds the car was out of control and we spun around and around. But I was always careful to measure the speed as opposed to the braking action and the kids would scream with delight. We didn't take Ruth with us when we played that way, and she sure wasn't comfortable with "her kids" doing what we were doing. But we did it anyway like three rebellious children, and had a blast! I was probably the biggest kid of all. Then it was back to the apartment and more tame activities in which Ruth could participate.

What she did like most was when the two of us were alone at night. Then she had my full attention and we could just focus on each other's thoughts, concerns & companionship. But that only happened once a week on Sunday nights.

Also, during this time I had been appointed by the Seminary Administration to the post of what was equivalent to "Student Body President" and met once a month with my student advisors to respond to concerns or information coming to us from Delmar Guynes, President of the Seminary, or to plan Student Body Functions or communicate with the administration about student concerns. I think my official title was Chairman of the Student Advisory Council.

My intense schedule began to take its toll on my physical body and people began to notice the way I would shuffle down the aisles going from one classroom to another, or on my way to a meeting of some kind, or to the library to study and write. I had no idea that anyone was paying any attention to me and my condition at all. I do remember having chest pains and wondering if I would survive, or die of a heart attack. But, quite frankly, I didn't care. I was beginning to get despondent. But also, I figured that if God had really called Ruth and I to go to Africa He would somehow see me through my crisis of failing strength and daily chest pains. I don't remember saying anything to Ruth because I didn't want her to worry. I just kept going to work and trying to get my end of the year papers written. At stake was the M.A. degree for which I had worked and sacrificed so much.

And then it came, a letter in the mail which included a one thousand dollar check from the department of Foreign Missions of the Assemblies of God. The comment was that they would like me to quit work, finish my papers and complete requirements for graduation, doing so without the strain of working to support my family. Ruth and I were both amazed and so very thankful. We had no idea until sometime later that my fatigue and physical struggles had been noticed. Surely God had intervened for us.

So very typically for us humans, one of the thoughts that went through my mind was, "Okay, so when I have graduated and have used up the one thousand dollars on living expenses, how in the world will I pay for our way back out to the West Coast so we can begin itineration among the churches with the purpose of raising our monthly and cash budgets prior to leaving for language studies in France?" I should never have had that thought. Wasn't God demonstrating once again that He could and would provide for each step along the way as long as we walked the pilgrim path of trust and obedience to His plan for our lives?!

Storm Five—Chapter Three
Language Studies in France & Switzerland

After 18 months of itineration throughout much of the United States we were finally able to raise our budget of more than $4,000 in monthly support plus about $25,000 cash to help with special African projects to unreached people groups or feeding the hungry in famine stricken parts of Africa or construction projects. I don't remember all the details of what was in the budget, except we also needed funds to pay for our children's schooling, as well as our own language studies first in Albertville, France and later in St. Legiér, Switzerland where I attended a Swiss Bible College. It was there I took Bible and Theology courses, so that I could master the French vocabulary needed for my own later teaching ministry in those areas.

The way this is all done is that missionary candidates travel from church to church, mostly in the part of the USA in which they live, but they can go to the churches across the country in which they are invited. They have up to 24 months to raise their entire budget plus their current living expenses as they travel. This is considered to be the next to the

---

final step necessary to confirm the Call of God upon their lives to be Missionary ambassadors for Christ in the country for which they have been authorized by the Assemblies of God to work. Once this has been accomplished, there is one more step in the confirmation process and that is the ability to learn a foreign language (where that is necessary) in which they must communicate the Good News of the Biblical Message of God's Love. Failure in either one of these last two steps would be a disqualifier for Foreign Missions service. But, with a lot of hard work and sleepless nights, we were successful!

Even now, more than thirty years later, I am able to think in French when conversing in that language. No translation of words goes on in my head. I just know how to express the concepts I wish to communicate and do it in French without reference to the English equivalent. I sometimes even now dream in French, but not as often. The money all came in and a little more than ten years later we had retired from that season of our lives which also proved to provide building blocks for other ministries abroad. Our children, especially our daughter, were more proficient in French than were my wife and I. Lani Rochelle developed a beautiful Parisian French accent and excellent vocabulary.

When home in the USA on furlough, whenever our family would eat out at a restaurant, my daughter and I would pretend (much to the embarrassment of my Wife, Ruth, and Son, Lance David) to be foreigners. Lani would be my translator with the waitress and I would pretend not to understand English! We had a blast with that scenario! However, on the way out, after paying the bill, I would say something in perfect American English. So we had our fun! Believe me, in case you are wondering, there is a difference between the English we speak in this country and the English spoken in Great Britain or other European countries. In fact while Ruth and I studied at the Centre Missionaire in Albertville, France, our two children, Lance and Lani, attended a French public school for expatriate children. All classes (math, science, literature, were taught in French and both the teacher and the children of Ambassadors, etc., from different countries all claimed that Lance and Lani "spoke American", not English. They both returned home upset one day and asked us what language we spoke. We assured them that we speak English but explained that the vocabulary and accents of those from other countries who speak English as a first language varies from country to country. Nowhere is that more true than in England! For instance, their word for "nap" is "kip". They don't take 'naps", they take "kips"! They don't call someone on the telephone they "ring them up". The English don't drive by someone's house to "pick them up and give them a ride", they "collect them"! These are examples of differences in the way people in other countries, all speaking English, express their ideas.

Language school was hard, even for me even in spite of the fact that this was not the first time I had studied a foreign language. For Ruth, it seemed impossible and she cried her way through the nine months we studied at the Centre Missionaire in Albertville, France. So much so that at the end of our nine months of study, I was asked, in French, if Ruth and I were having marital difficulties during the year. I assured them that was not the case, but they still seemed mystified as to why Ruth did so much weeping in class every day.

Although I was still not fluent enough in French to defend Ruth adequately, the real reason was twofold, Ruth has handled much of life, and especially high pressure situations over which she has no hope of success as she thinks it should be, with tears. Secondly, and more importantly, Ruth was a perfectionist and always had been. She had little tolerance for imperfection, especially in herself. Thus, she knew that each classroom situation would box her in to certain defeat and embarrassment, simply because she knew that she could not pronounce the French words or put sentences together in a grammatically correct manner that would satisfy the teacher. No matter how many hours she studied and how hard she tried, she would be humiliated in front of the class by her standard of performance which, in her mind, would be less than what everyone else in class was doing. Everyone else's success thus became her defeat because she couldn't keep up with them. When learning a foreign language one must be able to laugh at mistakes and keep trying. Ruth just could not laugh at mistakes, especially her own.

Years later, the district denominational leadership team would beg her to appear before them, and allow them to ask her a few simple questions, the answers to which she would most certainly know, so that they could justify granting her ministerial credentials. I also begged her to become credentialed with the denomination. But Ruth knew that as soon as she sat down with these men, possibly before they asked her the first question, that she would freeze up and begin to cry. Ruth had stood in front of crowds of 500 to a thousand people and lectured from her notes and done so without a tear shed or a case of nerves exhibited. She was fine when she was teaching a lesson, but she would come apart when questioned or challenged. It became necessary in some situations for me to lay down some ground rules before Ruth started teaching. She could handle sincere questions from the audience just fine, but if anyone disapproved of her teaching at all because of her being a woman that was a problem. Or if they felt she was teaching error and would challenge her that also would pose a problem. So I would say up front that if anyone had a problem with a woman teacher or preacher or the doctrine she taught, they should discuss it privately with me before the session and I would, if I agreed with them, talk to Ruth privately. I said that Ruth taught under my authority as her husband and with my approval and if anyone had a problem with that, they probably should stay home.

After completing our studies at the Centre Missionaire in Albertville, France we moved to Pully, Switzerland (on the outskirts of Lausanne) located on the shores of Lake Geneva and about 12 kilometers from

Saint Legiér where we eventually moved to be closer to the Emmaus Bible Institute. At Emmaus I would study another nine months before moving my family again down to Marseille, France where we would board a freighter bound for Ivory Coast, West Africa.

Chapter Four

First Four-Year Term of Service in The Ivory Coast (Côte d'Ivoire) Part One

It was either the 18th or 19th of February 1981 when Ruth and I and our two children, Lance David and Lani Rochelle boarded a Freighter in Marseille, France. The ship was bound for Ivory Coast, West Africa and other ports-of-call. It would take us ten days to reach the port of Abidjan. I'm not sure what was wrong with me that day, but the large freighter we were on had just cut loose from its moorings and had not moved ten feet away from the dock when I began suffering from motion sickness, a condition that stayed with me for the next ten days and nights until the boat docked in Abidjan. So I earned the reputation on that trip of not being a very good sailor.

We ate with the Captain of the ship every day and engaged him in many interesting conversations about his experiences. He was curious about what we were doing, but we never really were able to engage him in a serious conversation about God. We sailed south across the Mediterranean Sea and after a day or two gradually turned right to go through the Straits of Gibraltar. On our left we could see at a distance certain North African cities, Algiers, capital city of Algeria, also the town of Tizi Ouzou, Oran, Mostaganem. After having passed through the Straits of Gibraltar and started down the west coastline of North Africa (country of Morocco) we passed by Casa Blanca and Rabat. As we headed south along the coastline of Africa we often saw flying fish and other sea creatures. I had always thought "flying fish" were a myth. They are not a myth! These little sea creatures actually have small wings and can fly about 100 feet before reentering the water. Porpoises were also in abundance and a joy to watch.

Countries we passed by along the way were: Spain, Algeria, Morocco, Western Sahara, Mauritania, Senegal, Guinea, Sierra Leone, and Liberia before we finally reached Ivory Coast, West Africa. At the end of the tenth day at sea we arrived in the port of Abidjan just before midnight on Saturday, February 28th. Our first day in Africa was actually Sunday, March 1, 1981.

The Captain of the Freighter had been telling us that Ivory Coast was experiencing a severe crime wave. He emphasized his point during that last meal we shared at his table that we had two choices: (1) we could leave our things in port overnight, take a taxi into town and find lodging downtown Abidjan; or, (2) stay with our things the rest of the night and probably be robbed and killed before dawn. If we chose the first option, we would be most apt to be safe but our belongings would not be there when we returned the next morning.

The reason the two options had been discussed was because the Captain had helped us send a message from the boat to Faouzi David Arzouni, one of the local Assembly of God missionaries, informing him of the anticipated time of arrival (midnight) and asking him to meet us and help get our things through customs and transported to the French AOG Guest House in Abidjan, where we would also spend the rest of the night. But we had no way of knowing whether or not our message had been received and were really nervous about the whole situation. I think the Ship's Captain was even more concerned for our safety than we were.

But, as it turned out, Faouzi did receive our message and came to meet us. However, Faouzi was delayed because of having been robbed at knife point as he entered the Abidjan seaport facility. You would have to know this feisty Lebanese, naturalized American citizen and appointed Assembly of God missionary to fully appreciate this. But he was able to fight off his attacker by wrapping his coat around his left arm and then attacking his attacker with his shoe. Faouzi then thought better of his action and threw his watch on the ground some distance away. The attacker went for the watch, giving Faouzi the opportunity to get away. He then came with his vehicle to get us and took us (and all of our baggage) to the French Guest House. We easily went through customs because the customs agent was asleep and did not respond to our efforts to awaken him. This proved to be a real blessing, not only because of the money it saved me (to bribe the customs man) but also because, in that shipment was a twelve gauge semi-automatic shot gun which would have most certainly been a problem for me when I declared it. That shotgun would play a prominent role in my efforts to protect both my wife and the students at the Bible School where we worked during our second four year term of service, but that is a story for later.

Faouzi did deliver us safe to the French Mission house which was comfortable and adequate and the grounds beautiful, but to these rookie missionaries somewhat scary because we expected to see snakes everywhere, including in our rooms, under the bed and even coming up into the toilet bowl to bite us on our bottoms. Faouzi would later admonish us that we are letting our imaginations run wild and that we didn't really have as much to fear as our overactive minds were telling us. Our daughter, Lani, insisted on sleeping with Ruth and I. And I remember her, at 8 years of age, standing up on our bed the next morning and beginning to jump up and down, saying, "Look, Momma! I'm still alive!" So true, but also true that she was covered with a total of 32 mosquito bites all over her body. Also, she required Ruth to come into the bathroom with her when she had to "go potty" just to make sure that no snake would bite her or come up through the toilet to "get her". Only once did I ever hear of a snake coming up through the sewer into a toilet bowl. But once can be deadly, and one time too many. And only once did I ever hear of a python killing a man (although, after all my years of experience in West Africa, I'm sure that happens more often than I know about). What happened was that a poor foolish man fell down in a drunken stupor and a python came along just at the right time, opened his mouth, and gradually continued crawling forward until he had swallowed the man alive. Death by suffocation didn't take long.

But things began to return to sanity for us as we became accustomed to our new surroundings. Faouzi was so very helpful in getting us moved across country to the southwest corner of Ivory Coast in the town of San Pedro.

Our first home in Africa

L to R: Lance David, Ruth Helen, Joseph, Lani Rochelle
That is wild jungle behind us in this picture: snakes & apes!

Our new home was located up on a hill about a mile from downtown and right on the edge of a sliver of Tarzan style jungle where snakes (including spitting cobras), large black bodied lizards, about 12 inches in length, with orange heads, and tons of mosquitos had easy access to us; and a tribe of apes visited our banana, papaya and mango trees in the yard, or just over the fence with irregular frequency. The apes, of course, thought the fruit and bananas belonged to them and were not happy when we harvested these items before they did.

I remember once when we had harvested the fruit off all the trees (I did not climb them but paid to have that done!). I enjoyed the papayas but liked the mangos best of all. You just can't get those fruits here in the USA that taste anything like the "real thing" out in Africa!

But, anyway, back to my story! When that tribe of apes came back a short time later they were upset (to put it mildly) that there was no fruit on "their" fruit trees. A large male ape proceeded to throw a temper tantrum (my interpretation of his motives) on top of the tin roof of our house by jumping up and down, beating his chest, and screeching forth his frustration. Of course, it could just as well have been that one of the females had rejected him.

It was necessary to keep long "snake sticks" and machetes at strategic places in and around the house, and it would be a fool hardy act of carelessness to get up in the middle of the night to use the bathroom without turning on a light and maybe even picking up a machete. Deadly green or black mambas did get into the home and, of course, had to be faced and killed. Mambas are very fast and can chase a man down at full run, bite him and kill him. If bitten by a mamba, the unfortunate victim only has about 15 to 30 minutes to live. If a vaccine is available (and we did keep one somewhere, usually with Faouzi and Linda Arzouni) it is essential to get the vaccine injected within 15 minutes of the bite. Otherwise, the chances of survival are greatly diminished. Even with a timely injection, the victim has only a 50/50 chance of survival and one will wish for death before the effects of the injection begin to take place and survival is insured. The venom attacks the nervous system and causes much pain. Hundreds, if not thousands, of Africans die every year from the venom of these snakes! They are usually only about 18 inches in length, extremely aggressive, and if you come face to face with one of these reptiles it is always a kill or be killed situation.

An article I just read on the internet describes them as from 5.9 feet (1.8 meters) long to 7.2 feet (2.2 meters) long. I have never seen them that long. Although, I do remember driving down a dirt road and seeing a snake that was taller in the exhibited coils of its body, as it traveled across the road in front of me, than the height of my automobile. That may have been a green mamba, but I doubt it. It was more likely a

Boomslang snake which is the only snake capable of chasing a prey swiftly through the trees. Other snakes are pretty much limited to the ground.

And once I stepped out of the kitchen door onto the back screened in patio to come face to face with a 5 ½ foot long black spitting cobra. I had nothing in my hands with which to protect myself. However, I knew where a six foot long stick was strategically placed on that patio and gradually backed up until I got the stick in my hands.

But I need to describe the circumstances! It was near the end of our first three years in Ivory Coast and we were preparing to put our things in storage and ship certain items home. Crates were out in the car port and near the door to the patio, where also the cobra was positioned. Several African pastors who were helping us load the crates had already climbed up on the crates out of fear of the cobra and were making a lot of noise, which was reason I had come out on the patio to see what was going on. I started toward the cobra with the long "snake stick" but the pastors warned me, that the snake would be too fast for me and would surely kill me. They encouraged me to throw my stick to them because they were practically looking down on top the snake. I followed their advice and a violent battle with the snake ensued. I could only stand down close to the snake and watch the action. Eventually the snake was killed, but not without a ferocious fight. When we returned from our furlough in the USA I had reason to return to that house, and remember seeing the blood and gore still evidenced on the patio floor.

Another memory I have was of being out in the jungle alone, on my way to preach in one of our churches. I came upon a lizard so long and large that its body extended from one side of the narrow one lane dirt road to the other. It was just lying across the road and not moving. I was intrigued and thought about getting out of my car to approach the reptile, but then thought better of it. I read years later that Komodo Monitor Lizards do not exist in West Africa, but if this was not a Monitor

I would like to know what kind of lizard it was! In fact, the picture on the internet of a Komodo dragon posted by Wikipedia looks very similar to what I saw that day on a dirt road, deep in the Ivoirian jungle somewhere east of San Pedro, Ivory Coast. I did not have my camera with me and regret not having been able to photograph what I saw. The lizard/dragon was huge! I would estimate it to be from six to ten feet in length. To my rookie missionary perspective it did not look particularly dangerous but I had read something one time that said they could be lethal with their long tails and so in retrospect, I am thankful for the caution that caused me to remain in the car. Finally the reptile moved off the road and allowed me to pass. Thoughtful of the creature, wouldn't you say?!

It was on that same trip that I saw the only live python I was privileged to view during my missionary career. I saw only the head and a short portion of its body, but enough to identify what I was seeing. I do have the skin of a 12 foot "baby" python among my mementos, but I have seen skins for sale that were 40 feet long. I remember someone telling me about seeing a python cross the school yard at the Conservative Baptist Boarding School in Bouake, Ivory Coast where Lani, and her Brother, Lance David, went to junior high and high school.

I need to mention, in case the reader may not yet have realized it, that watching TV is not a necessary past time in order to cure yourself from boredom. Nor is watching television anywhere near as interesting as just plain ole daily life on some of these Mission Fields! Daily living can satisfy the strongest most adventurous person's craving for excitement! In fact sometimes it just felt good to get home from some trip, expressing thanks to God I was still alive, in one piece and good health, then fall comfortably into an American made bed in an American made mission house with "voleur bars" (anti-thief bars) over the windows and an armed guard outside, and then drift lazily into a deep sleep that can only come when you feel safe and comfortable (with air conditioning going full blast!). Every day was exciting and provided its own stories to be told without having to resort to fantasy produced by some Hollywood Director who would probably "freak out" with fear or disgust over some of our daily experiences.

And since I'm in the mood to relate "freaky", isolated, but true experiences, let me write a little about some of the more "wild" aspects of primitive African cuisine. Speaking of Hollywood Directors, I would have enjoyed feeding one of them a full course meal with food so spicy hot that it could blister your lips; or place the head, tail and intestines of a large rodent called "Agouti" on their plate. Watching the reaction would have been maliciously delightful! But Agouti is a delicacy in that part of the world and anyone receiving such a meal is being honored (I know! I have been thusly honored!), as well as being served with the best the villagers have to offer (unless you want monkey or python or dog or fish with the head, or roasted termites!—and I've been privileged to eat all those things at one time or another). How do you eat a chicken head or fish eyeballs? Dip into the pot of common food, bring up the boiled chicken head, and place it in your mouth with the eye balls going in first into your mouth . . . . and suck! Yummy!

At this point, I would like to insert an article I wrote some years ago. It is written like a parable that Jesus would have told with pertinent application to our times. But it is a modern and very true-to-life parable, one that I have actually experienced (the part about eating rat) . . . .

The Agouti & Roasted Termites Parable

I will never forget the very first time that, as a missionary to Africa, I had the distinct "privilege" of eating rat! In the Ivory Coast, where our family spent two terms of service, this rat is called Agouti. There are different varieties of Agouti, as can be seen from the two pictures above. The one I first ate was the little guy that looks like a rat. It is a large rat, more the size of a muskrat, but very definitely, just a plain rat. The

Agouti leads a vegetarian life out in the bush and jungles of West Africa. They are not found in the cities or around garbage heaps. Chickens peck around sewers and garbage out in Africa, but not Agouti, they are vegetarians and grow up in the jungles on grains and plant life of various kinds. But nevertheless, eating rat, especially for a rookie missionary, is not a pleasant prospect. However, in the culture of that part of the world, a person is being honored, and shown the best of hospitality, when this local expression of gourmet dining is served. For my very first time of being thus honored, I was served the head, the tail, and everything in-between, including the intestines, nicely cleaned and laid on top of my bowl of rice. I can't believe I ate the whole thing!

Furthermore, acquaintances of mine from the Dogon Tribe in Mali taught me to eat and appreciate roasted termites. It was the way they cooked and prepared them that made the difference. I must admit that the taste is delicious; roasted termites make an excellent breakfast cereal—snap, crackle, and pop—the Kellogg Cereal company should be envious! Follow me one step further. Suppose with me, that, after having eaten my fill of rat, topped off with roasted termites for dessert, and that by some magic of modern technology I could be instantly transported to an American or European restaurant, and set down in front of my favorite meal,—a nice 12-16 ounce prime rib steak dinner. The question is, "Would I be able to eat it?" Obviously not, I am still too full of rat and roasted termites to be hungry for prime rib! And that is precisely our problem in the countries which are part of Western Civilization—and particularly on the North American Continent. We are <u>too full of the wrong things—too full of the cultural and spiritual equivalent of rat to be hungry for the Steak of Heaven</u>! We have also developed <u>priorities that express preference for these cultural, even religious rats</u>. Our rat-like priorities (what we watch on TV, what we think about, the songs we sing, the dreams, goals or desires of our hearts, how we spend our time, the kind of friends we enjoy) all too often lead us into the deception of a highly developed taste for Agouti! Our taste buds have gotten accustomed to the taste of rat!

Let me be clear by using additional illustrations what I am trying to say by the term, "religious rats" as compared to "the Steak of Heaven"!

Which would you prefer, wonderful music that satisfies your taste for particular genre of music, like contemporary music or the old hymns or choruses of a bygone day, or would you rather have the Manifest Presence of Jesus that transports your soul into His Presence without regard to the type of music? Some like one kind of music but others like something different. God is a God of variety, but He is not pleased with all the fighting over worship music that goes on in our day.

While pastoring a church I always instructed the worship team that they need to do two things: (1) themselves to be worshippers rather than connoisseurs of music. It isn't the music that is important but whether or not the music becomes a catalyst that transforms our emotions, thoughts and will into moments of high rapture as we make contact with His Manifest Presence; (2) I would instruct the Worship Leader to also take note of the reaction of the congregation to the particular song or type of music being presented. If what is being sung leaves the congregation just standing there with deadness and lack of emotional response, they may be mouthing the words, but, as the Worship Leader, you have the wrong song or the wrong genre of music! Change it immediately! Singing that song or music is like eating rat (Agouti)!

But if the song, the melody, the music helps the people to become emotionally enraptured, intellectually responsive and willfully involved, then stay with the song that is opening a door into Heaven! Consider singing the song again, and give people a chance to worship! Allow a chance for "all Heaven to break lose" so that people can be saved, healed, encouraged, strengthened and enraptured by His Presence. You may never move beyond the one song which serves like a doorway into the Manifest Presence of Christ! If you happened upon a song that meets people's needs, don't be in a hurry to change songs, going through a dead, dry Evangelical Liturgy just because you have a funny idea about time constraints or music preferences. It is NOT about Music! IT IS about following the Flow of the Holy Spirit Who is ministering to the needs of the people!!! And how and what the Holy Spirit blesses one Sunday may be quite different the next Sunday. Sensitivity to the Spirit, Spontaneity and Flexibility are keys that unlock people's hearts and open doors into God's Presence!

So what are some of the dynamics of True Worship? Let me try to answer that question. The overwhelming of the mind of the worshipper that allows he or she to forget all else and focus on how Wonderful Jesus is, the awe-inspiring Manifest Presence of Jesus that takes the emotions captive so as to more beautifully express uninhibited worship to our Glorious King & Savior, and the personal choice to surrender our Will to the control of the Lover of our Souls (as a wife might surrender herself to the attentions of her husband) all these and more constitute the dynamics of True Worship. Anything less is dead dry liturgy, (even Pentecostal, Charismatic liturgy), and the forfeiture of the Steak of Heaven for the perverted satisfaction of Agouti! How sad, how meaningless, how disappointing! No wonder some get bored silly with church and church people.

People who have learned to like Agouti cannot possibly imagine what all the fuss is about. As a missionary who spent much time in the "bush", I must confess that I did learn to enjoy Agouti,—but especially the roasted termites. It was, however, an acquired taste that came out of what I perceived to be the necessities of my lifestyle and ministry at that time. After a while, my wife, Ruth, and I were even ordering Agouti when we ate out at nice restaurants, bypassing the sirloin tip steaks also listed on the menu. Such was the transformation of our thinking and our taste buds!

To understand what I wish to say about the degeneration of our tastes and priorities regarding the usage of time, and/or our ability to make wise choices even in areas of methodology for doing the work of God, consider my confession about learning to like Agouti even to the point of ordering it in restaurants. Consider the possibility of being so full of "spiritual rat" that we have no hunger for God or even the ability to make choices that will cause us to develop that hunger. It is not natural to want to make one's self hungry. Instead, we have a deep desire to satisfy all our hunger pains. Jesus statement, "Blessed are they who hunger and thirst after righteousness" presupposes a willingness to go without all other "food" (things that satisfy inner longings) until we find that one particular kind of food—the righteousness of God, and the Manifest Presence of Jesus, that alone can ultimately help bring satisfaction to all desires, at every level of our being! Jesus promised satisfaction ONLY to those who are willing to go hungry until they find their spiritual prime rib. It should be noted that Jesus never pronounced a blessing on those who are full, satisfied, and content. His Blessing was reserved for those who were hungry to the point of starvation and thirsty to the point of dehydration (actual meaning of the Greek words, terms translated into English and found in Matt. 5).

The problem, for we members of Western Civilization, especially the species of "westerner" found on the North American Continent, is that we are surrounded with so much that is geared to bringing instant satisfaction to our every desire, our every hunger, our every thirst, that the self-discipline needed to starve ourselves long enough to be willing to eat only that food which comes to us out of the invisible, out of the realms of eternity, and more precisely the Throne Room of God,—that kind of self-discipline, most of the time, seems to be beyond the reach of our ability to choose. We really don't have time for God! We just deceive ourselves into thinking we do.

An illustration would be that of a man coming to his wife with the words, "Sweetheart, I have about an hour of free time for you in my schedule today. Would you like to be romantic? Let's hit the bed real quick and enjoy each other." Can you picture in your mind the wife's response? She probably would throw a shoe at him and tell him to come see her sometime when he isn't concerned about time limitations! The wife wants her husband's undivided attention. She isn't interested in being part of his hurried schedule.

In essence, we do that to God on a weekly basis! In reality, we are in too big of a hurry, too structured, too limited by the way we organize our time and priorities,—even in our "worship services"—to have time for intimacy and real fellowship with the Lover of our Souls! Shouting prayers and praise choruses AT God is not the same as "entering into His Presence", and staying there as long as He wants to love on us or encourage us to "love on Him"! We want God on our terms, and we want God to understand that our attitudes are for the highest good of His Kingdom;—so that we and our choices about music and/or time limitations for a church service (not the Holy Spirit's choices) can attract more people to Him. The truth is, that God does not need us to sing to Him! The choirs of Heaven far surpass any musical presentation we can come up with from our mortal abilities. The only thing we really have that God needs from us is our Love and Worship!

Our pride of intellect cries out, "God, don't you understand? If we take time to really wait on you, to wait for the Holy Spirit to begin getting His agenda accomplished in a particular service, if we wait for God's Will to be done, the people we have invited to church might not want to come back. God, don't you understand that we really know what is best for your Kingdom?" Thus, to a great degree, He is still standing on the outside of His Church asking to be admitted, to be loved, and to be granted the intimacy of true worship;—asking for the privilege of being the One who establishes the priorities of His own Kingdom!

It is the PROCESS of going hungry until we find the nourishment for our souls (mind, will power, and emotions) that comes ONLY from the pantries and tables of the Eternal Realms,—it is that process that constitutes much of what is known in Scripture as "seeking" or "searching" for God. A careful study of the four Hebrew words, and the one Greek word, connected with these two English words ("seek" & "search") is most instructive. The Prophet/Psalmist, David, describes his feelings during that process in terms of deep unsatisfied yearnings for the Presence and Knowledge of God and His ways, as did Isaiah and others.[38]

It was those very deep, unsatisfied, insatiable yearnings that allowed David to draw close to God. We need to understand, that, according to Scripture, the moment we feel satisfied and comfortable, the moment our heavenward priorities become mixed with earthbound priorities, (like wanting to be out of church at Twelve Noon) the process of seeking after God has been short circuited!!—And we lose our ability to draw close to God or enjoy intimate communion with Him.

Like a deep sea diver or snorkeler, the moment we start to think we can enjoy (by breathing in) the atmosphere we are swimming in, we are in danger of death by drowning! So, understanding the process—and the needed priorities for successful engagement in that Process—(the process of learning to prefer the Steak of Eternity over the Rat of a "North American style Christianity") becomes of paramount importance. Prime Rib priorities do not allow for Agouti preferences. And just as, according to Jesus, we cannot serve two Masters[39], neither can we long survive with two sets of taste buds!

---

[38]   Psalm 38:9; 42:1-2, 7-11; 63:1, 3-6; 73:25-26; 84:2; 143:6; Isaiah 26:9; Luke 6:21; I Peter 2:2

[39]   Matthew 6:19-24; Luke 16:10-13

Chapter Four

First Four-Year Term of Service in The Ivory Coast (Côte d'Ivoire) Part Two—Aspects of Ministry

1. The cultural setting of all Christian Ministry throughout Ivory Coast: the Sacred Dance.

Unlike Western Culture where there seems to be little or no connection between culture and religious beliefs, the culture and religious beliefs of primitive societies are intricately intertwined. Thus, for instance, to violate any kind of religious practice is to violate and thus pose a threat to, the wholeness or integrity of the culture or society of most primitive ethnic groups (i.e., tribes in Africa untouched by Western Civilization). Such threats to their religious superstitions are not tolerated and can bring severe injury, a demonic curse, or a quick violent death to the offender.

The culture protects the religious beliefs and the religious beliefs protect and reinforce the culture or society of each village or ethnic group. There are 64 tribes in Ivory Coast speaking 64 different languages with over 435 dialects out of those language groups. For instance, there are 35 very different dialects spoken by the Krou tribe with which Ruth and I lived and worked during our first four year term in Cote d'Ivoire, Afrique de l'Ouest (Ivory Coast, West Africa). I would often need to change translators when moving from village to village as I preached the Gospel. Most of the 35 dialects of the Krou language have no translation of Scripture in their dialect. And that is the challenge and opportunity presented to Wycliffe Bible Translators whose missionaries actually commit to spend their entire lives living among these segments of the Krou Tribe.

The villages and general population of Ivory Coast is animistic (worship of objects as a living god) and occultist. That would mean the inclusion of belief in and worship of evil spirits.

One of the prominent expressions of their animistic worship of evil spirits was something called, "The Sacred Dance". This event happened usually around the end of November and beginning of December. The women and children of each village that participate in the rituals of the Sacred Dance (and most villages in southwest Ivory Coast do participate in the dance) are required to leave their home village and go live in the jungle for two weeks while their husbands stay in the village to make Black Magic, Sorcery and all sorts of Jinxes or Evil Spells with body parts (animal and human) to be used against other humans or to protect the village from evil spirits. Most villages post signs outside the village stating that the Sacred Dance is happening in their village. I don't know what goes on or exactly what procedures are used in those séances but I do know that without the protection of the Blood of Jesus and God's Holy Spirit anyone can be subject to suffering as a result of curses pronounced by the local witch doctor, who, if he is legitimate is nothing more than a tool of Lucifer and demon spirits.

This is a very dangerous time of the year for everyone. Once when I was traveling alone and arrived after dark at the home of a missionary where there was a general meeting of the Missionary Field Fellowship members, I was roundly scolded by my concerned colleagues. The statement to me was, "Hey, Joseph, don't you know what time of the year this is?" Well I didn't and had never heard of the sacred dance or the danger it would pose to anyone out after dark. So this rookie missionary got an education about those facts. Another comment was by someone looking at my oversized head, "Boy they sure would like to have your head with which to make black magic!"

Can you imagine the danger to the African women and children who were required to sleep in the jungle forest during these events? Snakes abound in the jungle. What happens if, while a small child (or anyone) is sleeping on the ground and a cobra or mamba crawls up on you for body warmth? What happens when you turn over in your sleep or simply wake up to see the snake across your body? Well, one thing is for sure, if you have survived without being bitten up to that moment, you don't dare move until the snake decides to crawl away from you; far enough away so that it is not startled and turns to bite you when you move. The owner of the Mobile Gas Station in San Pedro was, reportedly, the biggest Head Hunter in the area with his own paid team of head collectors. I sometimes bought gas for my Peugeot at his place of business which was literally a cover for his real business; i.e., head hunting for sale of the product to those in the villages who carried out the Sacred Dance each year.

Two sources of Supernatural Power: Don't get them confused!

There are two sources to the supernatural. One is Satanic (from Lucifer and the Powers of Hell, and the other is from Jehovah God, Creator of all that exists both seen and unseen. For a better understanding of these matters the reader is encouraged to study the Scriptures listed in the footnote below.[40]

There are various demonstrations of demonic miracles that I could describe but the purpose of this book is not to glorify Lucifer or his demonic forces by describing their activities. One thing we did learn was that the power of God always defeats the power of Satan and demonic forces. Jesus made sure, by His death, burial, Resurrection from the dead and Ascension to the Right Hand of His Father in Heaven, that His Servants, the Apostles, Prophets, Pastors, Teachers and Evangelists of all ages and down through the centuries even to our own time in the Twenty-first Century, would always have all power needed to defeat the forces of evil.[41]

2. Ministry from within San Pedro and the local Assembly of God Church

Our first assignment after our arrival in Ivory Coast was to establish a working ministry with the local pastor, who was also the Presbyter with leadership responsibilities all over the southwestern region of Ivory Coast. Gnoué, Robert Samuel was a short, easy going pastor but beneath that easy going outward demeanor was a dynamic leader! Robert is pronounced according to French phonics, "Ro-bare). Robert's last name

---

[40] Ephesians 3:10 mentions "principalities and powers in heavenly places"; this is a reference to the spirit or unseen world of the Angels of God and the Demonic spirits of Lucifer's kingdom. Principalities is from a Greek word, "arché" A) RXH/ meaning "beginning, magistrate, authority, rank, power, dominion. So these spirits who need to understand the wisdom of God are Beings of authority. Jude 6 mentions them. Other references, Romans 8:38; Ephesians 1:3-6, 21; Colossians 1:16; I Peter 3:22; Revelation 16:13-14; II Thessalonians 2:9-11; I Timothy 4:1-3; II Timothy 3:1-7; I John 4:1-3

[41] Mark 6:13; 16:17-18; Luke 7:21; 8:2; 9:49-50; 10:17; 24:46-49; John 14:12; Acts 5:16; 8:7; 16:18; 19:12; Colossians 2:15; Hebrews 6:5; I Peter 3:22; Romans 8:38-39;

is pronounced with the "G" being silent (ny–owe–a [long "a"]). There were 35 known churches in the southwest area at the time of our arrival there. When we left, three years later, there were 150 Assembly of God churches. Many of these churches are deep in the jungle away from all influence of western civilization.

Robert's church, over which he was the Pastor, ran from 200 to 300 in attendance most Sundays. One of the things I remember about Robert's church was their all night prayer meetings every Friday. And I do mean, "all-night"! Prayer meeting started about 6 or 7 PM (African time) and lasted until 5 or 6 AM the next morning. And, Wow! Could those people pray! That, I'm sure, is part of the reason for the growth of churches in the southwest area.

The Sunday services (AM & PM) were animated and joyful even while monkeys swung from the rafters and large lizards (about six to eight inches, or even 12 inches long climbed the walls and rafters overhead, often urinating on the people below them). But in the middle of all the confusion, the Word of God went forth, usually translated into 4 or 5 different languages. Lives were changed, people were healed of diseases and marriages were strengthened. The Gifts of the Spirit were in full operation.

Church discipline was also part of their service to God. Everyone was required to attend the Friday night prayer meeting, and if you chose not to do so, the church Elders would pay you a visit to learn why you weren't in the weekly prayer meeting. If you were sick, they would anoint you with oil and YOU WOULD be healed! If it was a matter of having forgotten what day it was or if family had arrived from out of town and the demands of hospitality had been such that the person chose not to come to the prayer meeting that one week, if the person's heart attitude was still Biblical with no trace of rebellion or defiance then their absence was forgiven and the matter was dropped.

Discipline could also come with the matter of Tithing and the giving of offerings. When that part of the service was reached, folks were ushered forward one pew at a time. Two baskets had been placed on the altar (thank God, at least the African AOG have not done away with the "mourners bench—the altar"). One of the baskets was for tithe and the other for offerings. After giving their tithe, each person had their little booklet signed off on by the pastor indicating another Sunday of faithfulness to God with their finances. At the end of each month, every square had to be filled with the pastor's initials in order to prove the person had been faithful in tithing. They came dancing and singing bringing their tithes and offerings with them. Then danced and sang their way back to their seats. I was always thrilled with the beauty of this part of the church service. The musical voices of the people, particularly those of the ladies and their colorful outfits were an inspiring part of every service.

The discipline of people who claimed to be Born Again and looked to the San Pedro Assembly of God and Pastor Gnoué, Robert Samuel as their Pastor came in this form: anyone under discipline was required to sit in the last two rows of pews and were not allowed to sit any closer to the front of the Sanctuary than those two last rows; furthermore, they were not allowed to partake of the Holy Communion as long as they were "under Discipline"; they could not sing in the choir or participate in any other ministry within the church. They could, in fact, must, continue to pay their tithes with offerings unto the Lord. Failure to do so would result in the Discipline continuing until their lives demonstrated a submissive and cooperative attitude toward the church and its leadership.

How could the Discipline ban be lifted?

Any Discipline ban could be removed when a person repented by changing their attitudes and actions to comply with what the church and God expected of them, after which they could sit anywhere except the last two rows of pews. A visiting pastor or missionary was not allowed to sit down with the rest of the congregation but is required to sit on the platform. To do otherwise would indicate that the pastor or missionary was under discipline.

One last thing to mention: after we had been in San Pedro several months I was asked to preach in the Sunday AM service. As I recall, there were somewhere from three to five translators on the platform with me translating in that many different African languages but representative of the tribal or ethnic diversity making up that congregation. When I got up to preach I noticed that the entire front row of the church was filled with bare-breasted women, most of them nursing a baby. I thought to myself, "Okay, Joseph, you can do this! Just focus on your preaching and lift your eyes to the second row of pews and beyond." In African culture the female breast is not considered to be sexually provocative. However, to leave any part of her legs uncovered would be considered to be sexually provocative and not at all acceptable manner of attire for a Christian woman. Even pagan women do not show any part of their legs by the way they dress. Long dresses are required dress code.

A little side note: African churches often hold services in the midst of very difficult circumstances or distasteful, unhealthy environmental situations. Such was the situation with the "big church" in San Pedro. The San Pedro church where my friend, Gnoué, Robert Samuel, pastored was fronted by an open sewer that flowed through downtown San Pedro. It was necessary to walk a low bridge over the sewer in order to take advantage of the front entrance to the church. The church campus was made up of education annexes plus housing for the church staff and others attached to the congregation. When the annual rains came the sewer invariably overflowed its boundaries and covered the ground in between the various buildings (including the ground around the church). This kind of situation was often the case for city dwellers in Ivory Coast or other African countries and cities and always results in many health problems. Malaria carrying mosquitos as well as flies are attracted to these conditions and when the flies land on uncovered food disease, is even more easily transmitted. It was usually much more sanitary to live in the jungle than to live in a town. And, of course, the shanty-town on the outskirts of San Pedro suffered even more severe health destroying conditions.

3. Ministry in our Jungle Churches

Robert and I traveled many kilometers together as we ministered to the churches out in the jungle. It was also too frequently necessary for us to go into the jungle on missions of mercy to rescue our AOG church people from violent persecution.

Two examples come to my mind. The first is an account of young man and his Mother who lived out in a jungle village where a spiritual awakening was experienced and people were turning to Jesus Christ as their Savior. This young man and his Mother were being persecuted for their faith. Their mud hut, where they lived, was destroyed and they had been severely beaten by the villagers. A courier was sent in to San Pedro ask for help from Pastor Gnoué, Robert Samuel and myself. It was decided that the situation was dangerous enough for us to ask for help from the local Gendarmerie. Several of these Officers, in full battle dress and heavily armed with various weapons, were sent with us. We traveled in my 9-passenger French Peugeot station wagon. After a couple hours travel down badly maintained dirt roads and upon our arrival in the village, introductions were made to the village elders and the purpose of our visit described. The mood turned ugly and we realized that the situation was potentially explosive. For that reason, we stood with our backs to a large mud hut that served as a meeting place but that also provided protection so that no one could slip up behind us to do us bodily harm. The policemen, although heavily armed were obviously worried about what the outcome might be. The forest trees came right up to the edge of the village clearing and we knew that we could have been easily shot or killed with old muskets or spears or bows and arrows from the tree line. We could have also been beaten and clubbed or chopped to death by the angry villagers. Those kinds of things do happen and usually nothing is done about it.

I'm not sure how much time went by, but it must have been all of two or three hours. The entire village turned out for our meeting and discussion with the Village Elders. Our purpose, of course, was to get the young man (who had been cut with machete blows and beaten with clubs) and his Mother out of that village. They were now homeless because their mud hut had been destroyed and if we had left them in the village they surely would have been killed. The villagers were not happy with our interference or the fact that they might not be able to "finish off" these Christians. The entire confrontation was carried out in the Krou language which I did not understand. All I could do was to stand with Pastor Robert and the police. Finally, Pastor Robert said to me in French, "Pastor, get your car started, and as soon as all of us are in the car (including the young man and his Mother) get us out of here as fast as you can.

By God's Grace and Mercy we all arrived safely back in San Pedro.

Mahino-1 & Meeting the Tribal Chief for the Krou people

One other similar antidote will suffice. It happened in "Mahino-1". Again, word came to us by courier that Christians were suffering terrible beatings and abuse because of the refusal of the newly converted women to cooperate with the annual Sacred Dance, or as was expected, for the women and children to leave the village to go sleep in the forest (jungle) during the two weeks of the Sacred Dance.

Again, blood was already flowing and it would have been only a matter of time before someone got killed. I don't believe that my wife, Ruth, ever realized how dangerous were these forays into the jungle to rescue Christians from persecution, but I feel confident that she would have just prayed for me and trusted God along with me for His protection. But I never told her or the other Assembly of God missionaries on the Field the details of these trips.

So once again, we piled pastors (no police this time) into my nine-passenger Peugeot Station Wagon and headed out for another one of our jungle churches where God was moving powerfully to introduce His Son, Jesus, to this pagan village full of people who needed Salvation but didn't realize it.

I think it was on this trip that God provided a miracle of protection for us as we travelled. These roads were terribly rutted and one drove all over the road, from one side to the other, in an effort to be able to keep one's speed up fast enough to kind of glide across the tops of the worst ravines in the road. I believe I was driving about 45 to 55 miles per hour down this one lane dirt road when we met a logging truck barreling head on toward us at an equally fast pace. Without thinking about it, I took the Peugeot off the road and into the brush, then back onto the road behind the truck just as quickly as it passed by us.

I could hear the mumbling and fearful exclamations of the pastors in the car. Later, I would think about what had happened. We could have crashed into a tree stump after leaving the road or any other of many possible obstacles that would have caused flat tires or crushed front end of the car. We were deep into the jungle and there were no mechanics within many miles of us. We could have been hurt in the process with no medical help available. But God, our Heavenly Father was with us as the car crashed through the brush as if it were nothing, and then back onto the road without even a noticeable scratch or other damage to the car. Surely the Lord was with us that day!

Upon arrival in the village of Mahino-1 early that same morning we were granted a "tete a tete" with the Tribal Chief (not the village Chief, but Chief of the entire Krou Tribe of close to fifty thousand [42] people).

Our pastors were given first opportunity to address the Chief and shared with him for 2 or 3 hours stories about the greatness of the God of the Bible as well as the fact that He is not only God of the White Man but of all men! Many stories of miracles were shared. At stake, of course was the personal safety of the Christians who lived in Mahino, as well as our own safety once we entered the village.

Missing that day was the common African hospitality that made it culturally unacceptable to harm an invited guest. I know this because I have spent days and nights, as an invited guest, in villages, who still practiced head hunting. I was safe because I was their guest. But that day, as we sat in front of the Tribal Chief in an effort to work out a cessation of persecution for the members of the Assemblies of God church in that village, we were threatened by a semi-circle, located behind us, of the young men of the village all armed with machetes, spears and old muskets. We were being signaled that our lives were in danger and that all that was needed was a nod from the Chief and we would all be dead men!

At the end of several hours of testimony by our Pastors (African culture is event oriented, not time oriented, and thus never gets in a hurry) the Tribal Chief declared that he had not believed any of what

---

[42] Amount of population quoted from Wikipedia entry on the Krumen People. Also mentioned in that article is the possibility that the name of the tribe came from their activities in the 1700s to be "crewmen" on ships plying the slave trade during those years. This would be in line with comments to me by Pastor Robert Samuel Gnoué who claimed that his great, great Grandfather had participated in the slave trade and thus that his people were just as guilty as any White Man for having captured and sold slaves during that time. This came as part of a conversation in which I was apologetic for American guilt in participating in the slave trade. Robert's reply was that his people were as guilty as mine, so let's not even talk about those matters.

had been related to him about the God of the Christians. Furthermore, he challenged the Christian God by stipulating, "If your God is as powerful as you claim He is, let Him strike me dead! In fact, when that white man returns, you take your Christians out of here with you."

What happened next is all part of the same story. While we were all seated in front of the Krou Tribal Chief and testimonies in the Krou language (none of which I understood) were being offered by my pastor friends, a courier arrived from another village. The pastor of that village had been framed for murder by the village chief and had been arrested and jailed some distance south in the closest jail located at Tabou. Here is what probably happened. The local Witch Doctor, of the village where the Pastor lived, had been asked for help in the assassination of someone's enemy, and had probably agreed to a spiritual assassination to be followed by physical death and then for the death to be blamed on the local Assembly of God Pastor. This is not unusual. More Sorcery! More Black Magic done in the power of Satan and his demonic hordes!

It is claimed that a witch doctor can empower (when certain fees are paid) a person to project, after dark, their own spirit out their body, and find and "eat" the spirit of the person they want to assassinate. That person usually dies within 24 to 48 hours, without any marks being left on the body or any other medical evidence of violence, like poisoning. So what we have is spiritual assassination followed by physical death. Here are the facts as I know them: first, I have no proof that the spirit has actually left the assassins body (although I do not doubt it). What I do know is that some kind of curse had been pronounced and the object of the curse has died. It works! Only the covering of one's body, spirit and soul by surrender to Jesus, as an act of faith and surrender to His Sovereignty in one's life [43] can provide adequate protection from demonic curses. Even Christians can be impacted by these curses, becoming deathly ill, if they are not living in obedience and full surrender to the Lordship of Jesus Christ.

I had been asked to leave and go to the assistance of the pastor framed for murder. As I left the village compound of Mahino-1 that day, I had no idea about what I would encounter. All I knew was that this pastor needed a Brother in Christ to stand with him in his hour of need and to try to help him.

I drove alone for several hours down jungle dirt roads, deeply rutted with occasional wash-outs. This was wild untamed country full of pythons, mambas, apes, large lizards, white chimpanzees, and many other wild creatures of God's creation. In all of its savagery, it was gorgeous, beautiful country and I enjoyed the drive, just thanking God for the privilege of serving Him in West Africa.

I finally arrived in Tabou, a town with which I was familiar, having been there many times. I went straight to the jail and asked to see the pastor who had recently been incarcerated. After spending some time with him in prayer and visiting I asked to see the person in charge of the jail. What I said next was something of a bluff, but it worked! I identified the African Pastor they were holding as one of "our men", belonging to the American Assemblies of God that had come to their country to give ourselves in service to the Ivoirian people. I said, "Here we have come into your country not asking for payment or reward of any kind but simply the privilege to serve and be of benefit to the Ivoirian nation with all of its 64 tribes. And this is the way you reward our generosity

---

[43] The phrase, "surrender to His Sovereignty in one's life" is key to understanding the protection of God in moments of danger. If one is not living a life of surrender to God's Sovereignty that person is in mortal danger! Only the Grace of God can make the difference then! It is God's Sovereignty (over all His Creation, including Evil Spirits, that assures one's safety and destroys any vulnerability!

and selfless service to your people by arresting one of our pastors on only the word of a Village Chief who undoubtedly had ulterior motives in accusing the pastor?!". I played it up as best I could (all true of course) and then assured the Warden of the prison that the American Mission would contact the authorities in Abidjan to lodge a complaint if our pastor was not set free immediately. I went on to say that what would be preferable would be that the American Mission could work in harmony with the local police force. I think I remember telling him of some of the "rescue missions" I had already done, which, of course would take away from the potential work load of their own police force. I was told that it would take a day or two for the pastor to be released but that they would agree with me to do so. With that, I headed back to Mahino-1 and the crisis we were in the process of dealing with in that village. I had no idea whether the pastors I had left behind would be alive when I returned . . . or if, upon my return, I would survive. Like the Apostles of old, modern missionaries live daily, trusting in God's protection. However, I had peace in my heart about the matter, and knew for a certainty that God was in control. I fully expected to see the pastors again, alive and well.

As a side note, I do remember driving with Pastor Robert deep into the jungle on some mission when we came upon trees fallen across the road by some farmer trying to clear land for farming. Fortunately, I had brought my large, fancy machete (purchased in the USA). It was the only one we had with us and the only means by which we could chop through those trees and reopen the road. I was getting nowhere with that machete. Robert watched my efforts for a while but finally, could stand it no longer and asked if he could show me how to handle a machete. If he hadn't intervened, I might still be out in that jungle trying to chop my way through those trees. But Robert made short work of those trees and we began to drag pieces off to one side of the road, gradually opening up passage wide enough for us to drive the car through. What I wanted to tell about were the white chimpanzees that came out to scold and throw things at us while we worked. I had never seen white chimpanzees in the wild and so this was a treat with which I was fascinated. The chimpanzees were irritated and I was glad they didn't decide to attack us beyond throwing things at us. Fun! Better than TV!

Now, let's return to the scene in Mahino-1,—around 1982 or 1983. As I drove into the village compound I found all the pastors alive and in good health. In fact they were rejoicing at the miracle God had given them in resolving the issues for which we had come. After the Tribal Chief had issued his ultimatum and stated, "If your God is as powerful as you say He is, let him strike me dead!" our pastors went into a fasting and prayer mode the rest of the day. That night, in the middle of the night, the Chief came screaming out of the place where he was sleeping, almost berserk with fear. This, of course, was a great "loss of face" and embarrassment for a Chief to behave in that manner. When the villagers were finally able to get him calmed down so that he could speak coherently he told them that a man, dressed in a brilliant white garment and surrounded by a light that seemed to come from inside of Him had just stood over the Chief and spoken to him in his native Krou dialect. The Man declared, "If you drive these Christians out of the village, you are a dead man!" And then the brilliantly bright Man disappeared! Well it was the threat of death plus the appearing/disappearing act that completely unnerved the Tribal Chief. (I like to say, "It scared him so much that it almost made a "white man" out of him!") But of course that is only an effort to be humorous.

It is important to give Glory to God for this miraculous event! I did not see it happen, but the change of attitudes in the village was impossible to ignore. In addition, the Tribal Chief had ordered the Village Chief and his men to rebuild the place of Worship for the Christians that had been destroyed and told them he would return to make sure his orders were obeyed. We pastors were able to leave the village rejoicing in the victory God had given!

One final note is appropriate about the powers of darkness that we were up against that first term southwestern Ivory Coast. There was a village just half a mile from where we lived that did in fact practice ritual cannibalism. Once a year, and I believe this was about the same time of the annual Sacred Dance that occurred in so many parts of Ivory Coast, men from the village would engage in kidnapping infants from other villages. The babies were brought into the village where their hearts were cut out of their bodies for use in making Black Magic and Sorcery and the rest of the baby would be eaten at a ritual meal in the village. This was widely known in the area but never confronted. And it is the only village I ever became aware of where such awful practices were engaged in as part of their worship and effort to appease evil spirits. Robert and I never actively did anything about this, although I would often pray against.

Modern Example of winning the victory in the spirit world before experiencing it in the physical realm

I cannot help but jump forward briefly from the early 1980s to the year, 2013. Here is an example of "getting it done in the realm of the invisible spirit world" and reaping the benefits in the physical universe, actually here on earth. My Brother in-law, Tim Taylor, was diagnosed two years ago (2011) with Stage 4 cancer and given from two to six months to live. His response to the doctor, "Doc, I appreciate all you are trying to do for me, but when you tell me the same thing the Bible tells me, I'll take more seriously what you say." Tim knows what the Bible says about healing and its availability to all of God's children. Tim went on the internet to do a search for "Scriptures on Healing". What he found was a plethora of information. He downloaded several pages worth of Scriptures on Healing (both Old and New Testament) and began claim God's promises. Whenever fear, despair, discouragement or doubt would flood his mind because of all the negative medical reports he received on an ongoing basis. Tim was faithful to do the chemotherapy and keep all doctor appointments, but he was even more faithful to daily (or twice a day) read Scriptures that encouraged him to believe for the preservation of his life and for his healing from cancer. As time wore on, the reports became loaded with even more bad news. Early in 2013, he was told by three doctors that he now had three stage four cancers of various kinds and consequently should not expect to live much longer, in spite of the fact that he had not died as predicted earlier by the doctors. Again, Tim's response to the doctors was the same, "Well when you start telling me what the Bible tells me, I'll believe you." In late Spring of this year, all three doctors came to Tim to inform him that he is cancer free and all three stated that this is a medical miracle. As scientists they were scratching their heads in amazement. But they expressed their admiration for Tim and his steadfast faith and admitted that God had won!

In talking with Tim a couple weeks ago (September 2013) he stated to me that the key to faith is EXPECTATION! If you don't expect the outcome you have prayed for you really have not exercised any Faith! Tim is right! The Holy Spirit, in the book of Hebrews says that faith is the "substance" of things hoped for (i.e., faith brings what is unseen into this realm of reality and turns it into "substance" in the realm of the physical universe!); another translation would be, "the title deed"! That latter is amazing! How do you know you own your car? Because you have the legal Title which proves your ownership! So it is with faith for healing? If faith (expectation and assurance) has risen in your heart then you know that the demonstration of your healing in different outcomes to tests done by the doctors is just a matter of time! Faith is also the "evidence" of things not seen. This word, "evidence" is a word that comes out of the courtroom back in the days in which this verse was written; the word, "evidence" had the same meaning two thousand years ago as it has today. The word, in Greek, literally means, "Ground of Standing". "Standing" is something required in any courtroom and especially any Federal Court. So too, in the realm of the Spirit before the Throne of God! Faith gives one Standing before God, a right to be in His Presence and to claim certain outcomes as answers to prayer based on God's Word.

Here are two translations of the verse, The Amplified Bible and the New Living Translation, both of these versions of the Bible produced by committees of scholars that were expert grammarians of the Greek language.

The versions agree, they just state it differently.

Hebrews 11:1—AMP or Amplified Version

1 NOW FAITH is the assurance (the confirmation, othe title deed) of the things [we] hope for, being the proof of things [we] do not see *and* the conviction of their reality [faith perceiving as real fact what is not revealed to the senses].

Hebrews 11:1—NLT or New Living Translation

(NLT—New Living Translation) "Faith is the confidence that what we hope for will actually happen; it gives us assurance about things we cannot see.

So how is this expectation strengthened or established? One important way is the reading and meditation of God's promises about whatever you have need of. This is particularly true when one is praying about the salvation of a loved-one or the healing of your own body or someone else's body. When fear arises or doubt descends into your heart, refuse to consider any negative evidence remembering that the God Who created the Physical Universe has power over all the laws of nature (He created nature and so can overrule it at any time!). Bring the laws of the supernatural into the realm of the natural by using Scripture to destroy sickness & disease or the bondage of evil in the life of either a fellow Believer or an unsaved loved-one.

I learned an important lesson as I observed the ebb and flow of the spirit world out in West Africa. That lesson is that things are often accomplished in the spirit world before they are experienced in the physical or material realm of reality in which we live! If Witch Doctors empowered by demon spirits can accomplish miracles that originate in hell and thus get things done on earth by doing them first in the realm of the spirit world, it is logical (and Biblical) to understand that Christians, who have access to the Power of the Holy Spirit of God have a power far greater than any demonic power, and are also able to accomplish the miraculous for the Glory of God!

Do you have a loved one that is sick and or dying, accomplish their healing in the realm of the spirit world and watch it happen here on earth before your very eyes! For help with this concept please closely study the Scriptures referred to in this footnote = [44].

---

[44] Hebrews 1:14; 11:3; Romans 1:20; 4:17—"who gives life to the dead and speaks of the nonexistent things that he has foretold and promised as if they already existed.—(Amplified Version); Psalm 33:6; Jeremiah 10:11; Colossians 1:15; First Timothy 1:17; 6:16; John 1:18; Acts 17:24; Isaiah 40:25-26; Job 1:6-12, 20; 2:1-10; Isaiah 6:1-2; Luke 1:11-20, 26-38; 2:8-20

Chapter Five

Second Four-Year Term of Service in The Ivory Coast (Côte d'Ivoire)

Saying Good-bye to our Son

Our second term of missionary service in the Ivory Coast began with a "mixed bag" of both joyful expectations for a fruitful ministry, but also with deep sadness and foreboding regarding the future of our Son, Lance David. Lance had remained in the USA to begin his freshman year at Vanguard University in Costa Mesa, California. Vanguard University is an Assembly of God Higher Education institution that provides both Undergraduate and Graduate Degrees for Professional preparation in such fields as Education, Medicine, Law, Christian Ministry, Foreign Missions Service, Government, Social Services, Business and the Arts. Their stated purpose is to help each student fully integrate academic excellence with their Christian Faith and practical life experiences.

However, Lance had been struggling for a number of years with the seeming dichotomy between the values with which we had raised him and those of a large segment of the American culture that had become godless and hedonistic[45] in daily lifestyles. He obviously was torn between a desire to see and experience what "the world" had to offer and a reluctance to disappoint his parents by pulling away from the Christian Faith in which he was raised. I realized even then that Lance really had no hunger for spiritual things or the God to whom we, his parents, had been trying to introduce him. As his Father, I did not fully realize, until it was too late, the problem Lance was having even in the area sexual identity. However my concerns for the direction of my Son's interests and personal activities was so intense that when the moment came to say goodbye and leave our Son on the campus of the University my emotions overpowered me. With my body shaking from the force of choking sobs coming to the surface from way down inside of me, I suggested to my Son that maybe I needed to resign my missionary career to stay in the USA and be available as friend and Father to Lance. My offer was genuine and, at that moment, if Lance had hesitated or indicated in any way that he would appreciate me doing what I had just suggested, I would have made the decision to do just that! Instead, Lance assured me that he would be fine, that I had nothing to worry about as far as his welfare was concerned and, furthermore, that I was obligated to fulfill the Call of God on my life for service in Africa. I remember, as I drove away that day, leaving my Son standing behind the car (I watched him out of the rear view mirror) that hard sobs racked my body with such force that I could hardly control the car or keep it in my lane of traffic. Extreme emotions are no

---

[45] Meaning of Hedonism = the highest value or purpose in life is to enjoy life, have fun so that one comes to the end of life saying, "It has been a great life! I have enjoyed it and had a lot of fun! The focus of Hedonism is satisfaction of all one's physical, sexual and emotional desires. Laugh a lot, have fun, be entertained and happy with your life! But the Bible teaches that the highest purpose in life should be to fear God and keep His commandments because this life is only preparation for life in eternity. Read all of the Book of Ecclesiastes but especially the last chapter, chapter twelve which sums up wisdom.

viable substitute for a Father staying on top of matters that concern his children's psychological and spiritual wellbeing. In this I was a failure that only the mercy of God would eventually rectify. In the meantime, between my failure as a Father and God's merciful provision on my Son's deathbed, would come approximately eleven years of intercessory prayer and emotional suffering for us all. But an adequate treatment of that issue will necessitate another large segment of this book.

I watched my Son through the rear view mirror as I drove away. There he stood in colorful California style cutoffs, looking happy and relaxed, almost glad that we were leaving so he could begin this new adventure on his own. I don't suppose that is so unusual as children become young adults and look forward to spreading their wings and flying on their own. But I also remember the terrible sense of dread and foreboding that filled my heart. It was probably one of the worst days of my life up to that point and little did I realize the "hell" that would later confront us.

A few weeks later Ruth and I and our daughter, Lani Rochelle, arrived in Abidjan, the largest city in Côte d'Ivoire (Ivory Coast), West Africa. We had thoroughly enjoyed our nine passenger Peugeot station wagon of the previous term (1981-1983). I had often filled that vehicle with Ivoirian Pastors, and, at times, with Gendarmes when going on a particular dangerous mission into the jungle areas to deal with situations of persecution of our Christian people. However, this time we planned to buy a new Peugeot Sedan and were scheduled to pick it up right after our arrival in country. Faouzi David Arzouni and his wife, Linda, were part of the American Mission in Ivory Coast who met us at the airport when we arrived. Monsieur Montbuleau, from the French Mission accompanied the Arzounis.

I arrived with a Swiss typewriter (complete with the French version of the keyboard; accent marks on the keys) and our luggage from the USA. Faouzi and Montbeuleau immediately took me to a local bank with my thirty thousand dollar ($30,000) cashier's check where we purchased (seven million, five-hundred thousand Ivoirian (7,500,000) francs with which we filled a small suitcase and then proceeded to the local Peugeot dealership, where, after several hours of dickering we bought the Sedan.

Into a Hole full of rain water big enough to swallow the Mission Vehicle!

It had been raining hard the previous several days and many of the streets were flooded with water up to the top edge of the street curbs. On the way to the Peugeot Dealership we (myself, Faouzi and Montbeuleau) were forced to navigate these flooded streets in Faouzi's car. What we didn't know ahead of time was that a hole large enough to hold a car was in the middle of one of those streets. Water had filled that hole so that one could not discern that the hole existed because of the water that also covered the street up to the top of the street curbs. When Faouzi drove us into that hole, we suddenly found ourselves sinking to the bottom, and water rising outside halfway up the windows of the car. As water began slowly to seep inside the car eventually getting to the top of the car seats we found ourselves with wet bottoms and our feet and hands up in the air. We looked at ourselves and our predicament, saw our ridiculously funny we must be looking to the Africans who stood up topside on the edge of the hole looking down at the three white men in the vehicle. At that we saw the humor in the entire situation and started laughing hysterically. The African crowd that had now gathered around us outside the hole also began to laugh. I don't know exactly how it was done, except that I remember that enough large African men jumped down into the water that they were able to actually lift the car outside the hole and back onto the street above (with all three of us white guys still in the car)! I was elected, along with Montbeuleau, the French pastor, to physically push Faouzi's car down the street in an effort to get it started (which we did!). So I got my wet rear-end out of the car along with my new Florsheim shoes from the USA and began to push. We pushed long enough for Faouzi to coax the water logged engine into finally turning over, and long enough for me to ruin the leather soles of the brand new Florsheim shoes I was wearing. (Caution: never take Florsheim shoes to Africa!). Once the car engine came to life, we hopped back into the vehicle and drove off to the Peugeot Dealership. The miracle was that neither the typewriter with the French language keys I had bought in Switzerland nor the 7.5 million CFA (Ivoirian francs) which filled a brief case, both of which had been placed in the car trunk, were water damaged! It was those 7.5 million CFA ($30,000) that would be used to purchase our Speed the Light vehicle for this new term.

Over our Head & Swallowed up with Responsibilities

Ruth and I were returning to the Bible School in Daloa, Ivory Coast, West Africa. We began this new term of service with a sense of joy and keen anticipation of what the work of these next four years would allow us to accomplish for the Kingdom of God as we joined three other couples at the Institute of Pastoral and Theological Studies (in French, L'Institut Pastorale et Théologique) in Daloa. We had spent our first term on the coast, at San Pedro but were returning to this interior city to which the Bible School had been moved under the leadership of Rev. Willard Teague just before our first furlough of a couple years previous. It was sometime in the next year or so that I was given the opportunity to teach a short course of study at the West African Advanced School of Theology (WAAST). Since WAAST used a bi-lingual approach with its curriculum I faced the challenge of developing my classes in both French and English. The point being that anything we do in life will have its challenges and difficulties. But it was now that all the hard work of language studies in France and Switzerland would pay off.

Rev. Teague had moved to Lomé, Togo and the Presidency of the West Africa Advanced School of Theology. So he was no longer in Ivory Coast, and the Directorship of the school in Daloa had been given to our good friend, Faouzi Arzouni (and his lovely wife, Linda). I looked forward to working with Faouzi and the other two men on the Faculty. The plan was that I would assume the teaching of many of the Bible and Theology courses. This was a welcome challenge. I would now have opportunity to increase my fluency in French as I developed lesson plans and lectures for each subject. Ruth was asked to work in the campus Library and to teach Health and Christian Education classes to the wives of the pastors who were studying at the Bible School. She actually ended up being the Head Librarian and was charged with cataloging the entire French and English sections of the library using an American system: the Dewy Decimal System. She also eventually assumed the role of Bookstore Manager and Campus Nurse, charged with treating all sorts of tropical diseases.

Though she had no formal medical training in the USA prior to our departure for the Field, she daily consulted a manual which described symptoms and a second manual that gave suggested prescriptions matched to the symptoms. After coming to a conclusion on how best to treat a particular set of medical problems with a student, she would translate the suggested prescriptions into French and make her weekly trip to the pharmacy where her white skin was the only qualification she needed to purchase prescription medicine. In this role, Ruth was simply amazing! One is forced to the conclusion that she must have been helped with some supernatural wisdom. However, Ruth would often jokingly state that, "At least no ever died from my diagnosis and treatment for their sickness."

The "stormy" part of this tale has to do with what I am convinced was a demonic attack on the missionary family. Ruth and I had joined the team of three other couples and had no idea that we would eventually be the only couple left at the Bible College and would need to assume the work load that had been meant for four couples. We had specifically been asked to join the team there because the work load was too much for the three couples already in place. But there were problems, challenges, and the Enemy did his best to ruin relationships and destroy health. Eventually one couple would transfer back to the USA and their marriage would end in divorce. Another couple would be transferred to another Field of service and the third couple (Faouzi & Linda Arzouni) would take an early furlough so as to earn a higher academic degree. They would return years later and are now engaged in an awesome ministry in Mali, a country north of Ivory Coast and on the edge of the Sahara Desert. Faouzi David Arzouni, is fluent in Arabic, Bambara (aka, Djoula), and Woluf, [46] as well as French, and, of course, English. He's not too shabby in Greek and Hebrew either! Both he and Linda are fabulous Bible Teachers and it was a joy to work with them for the short time we had the privilege. Faouzi was a real "cut-up" with a sense of humor that frequently bubbled up to the surface even when the work load was extreme.

When Ruth and I arrived to take up our duties at the Bible Institute in Daloa, Faouzi was the Director and Academic Dean. Both duties would later fall upon me when Faouzi and Linda went to the States. After Faouzi and Linda went back to the USA for their study-furlough Ruth and I were left alone with one missionary intern to carry on the vision of the Bible Institute.

---

[46] Woluf is a language spoken by the tribal people of that name who constitute 40% of the population in Senegal, but also live in Gambia and Mauritania. Faouzi grew up in Senegal, and later in life became a naturalized citizen of the USA and a highly respected appointed missionary of the Assemblies of God. Faouzi, of Lebanese descent, married a beautiful blonde American girl whose Father was a Professor at Bethany Bible College (later, Bethany University) in Santa Cruz, California. Ruth and I enjoyed working with this delightful couple.

My work day began about 2 AM every morning and ended at 10 PM that night. As Interim Director, Academic Dean and Business Manager, plus Professor of Bible and Theology, all rolled into one person I was on a path toward a physical and emotional collapse. I was also the Field Fellowship Secretary-Treasurer and Christian Education Representative to the National Church. I arose at 2 AM to write my class lecture notes in English. For me it was easier to write in English and translate into French in my head as I lectured later in the day.

As Field Fellowship Secretary-Treasurer I not only recorded the Minutes and decisions of the Field Fellowship in business session, but also gave regular financial reports as part of my duties. Basically, I worked and kept financial records in three currencies (dollars, French Francs and Ivoirian Francs. The difference between Ivoirian and French Francs was a settled 50 to 1 but the differences, when dealing with dollars or French francs fluctuated from day to day. Thus each transaction (deposits and expenditures) has to be meticulously recorded with the proper exchange rate notes for each transaction. That also was part of my duties. To top it off, I had the same responsibilities for the Bible Institute finances and my own "work funds" as I did for the MFF (Missionary Field Fellowship). In regards to my position as the national Christian Education Representative I was responsible for making sure that all 200 Assembly of God churches in Ivory Coast were supplied with their "Sunday School" literature for their individual church and that on a monthly basis. I was further responsible for a report to the National Church at their annual business meeting. My duties as Academic Dean was to keep track of the academic grades and accomplishments of each student, keeping them on track toward graduation and making sure they were each taking the required courses. I passed out grades at the end of each semester and signed them each up for the appropriate classes for the following semester. As Interim Director I was responsible for the overall smooth operation of the entire college, including hiring the appropriate support workers, like cooks and grounds maintenance and making sure there was enough money to pay them once a month. I had a cash box for each area of financial responsibility (Bible Institute, Missionary Field Fellowship and personal work & ministry funds), each of which required careful attention to accounting details. And when we were short of cash, to pay the workers, for instance, I would put an I.O.U. in a different cash box and take out the money to pay the workers, etc. And so, of course, when balancing the books I had to pay back the I.O.U. from the cash box that had borrowed money to the original lending cash box. It got complicated when there was multiple I.O.U.s going back and forth in the various cash boxes." Running down to the bank to cash a check was not always possible. It will help the reader to understand that working in Third World Countries often precludes the use of checks or credit or debit cards as we are accustomed to do here in America. Cash is the only way to handle most financial transactions. And if the cash you have is in a foreign currency, that issue must be resolved before making local transactions, like paying workers, buying groceries or taking care of dozens of other daily needs requiring money for the College, Missionary Field Fellowship or other ministry involvements (taken from my personal work funds). If you feel confused with this explanation, trying working with it on a daily basis, week after week and & year after year.

The Ivoirian Assembly of God church of Ivory Coast was divided at that time between the French and American Assemblies of God from our individual countries. And so there was a lot of room for misunderstanding and/or "agreeing to disagree" but doing it agreeably. The top priority of the American Team was the unity of the Ivoirian Church, not tilted toward either the French or the American Missions.

Striving for Unity between the French and American trained pastors

And there was plenty of challenge as we sought to work in harmony with the French Assembly of God missionaries. Two issues with which we struggled to maintain harmony was our disagreement over the drinking of alcoholic beverages and what to do about polygamy throughout the Ivoirian National Church. As is common throughout all of Europe Christians, even Pentecostals, see nothing wrong with drinking alcoholic beverages. It is drunkenness upon which we could agree. But the American position was that of total abstinence. Believing as we did that the first glass of beer or wine or whiskey was just the first step toward becoming an alcoholic. We were able to share many examples to prove our point, but our French Brethren just did not agree with our conclusions. As a consequence, we did have some of our French Brethren that fell into alcoholism. I also remember Presbytery Meetings (a Board of Directors or Elders) in which the French missionaries and the National Church Leaders trained by them were drinking beer while the American missionaries and the National Church Leaders trained by us were drinking coca cola or water while we considered important matters concerning the work of God in Ivory Coast.

Another area of disagreement was concerning the question of polygamy. The French Missionaries took the position that all polygamy is sinful and that once a man comes to Christ he must dismiss all his wives but one. We heard of instances where a man would wait to declare his faith in Jesus Christ until he found a younger woman that he could marry so that he could have her after dismissing all his other wives. Of course those dismissed wives would then be without a home or means of support or love. One can easily see the grief caused by that position. But the French were adamant and so that was maintained in the section of Ivory Coast dominated by the French missionaries.

The American position was that once a man comes to Christ he must keep all the women to whom he is married (since marriage is a covenant relationship honored in Scripture). But that he must not take any more wives after becoming a Christian. Of course, for those who would be a pastor or elder in the church, they must be the husband of one wife and so if they are engaged in a polygamous relationship they are automatically disqualified to be a pastor or elder. Divorce was not an option since that too is forbidden in Scripture, especially for pastors and elders (husband of one wife; i.e., never married to another woman). Nowhere in Scripture is polygamy declared to be a sin. However, monogamy is obviously God's original plan (see example of Adam and Eve as well as other Scripture references. [47]).

How this was all resolved was as follows: In order to bring the French and American missions together into one National Church with one single governmental structure and with love and fellowship between all churches and pastors in Ivory Coast it became necessary to agree to

---

[47]   Genesis 2:24; Matthew 19:5; Mark 10:8; Ephesians 5:28-33

disagree on the above issues and leave it up to the conscience of each pastor and church as to what guidelines they would follow regarding these two issues.

Speed the Light & Boys & Girls Missionary Crusade Support Programs

Two American support programs continue to be crucial in helping us get the job done for the glory of God on the Mission Field. These two programs are called STL (Speed the Light) and BGMC (Boys & Girls Missionary Crusade). The youth (teenagers) in the state of Washington/ Northern Idaho raised enough money for me to purchase a French Peugeot station wagon and to use it for the four years our family was first in France and Switzerland for 18 months for language studies and then three years in the Ivory Coast, West Africa. My duties as Christian Education Representative for Ivory Coast took me all over that country plus from the border with Liberia to Accra, Ghana and publishing house there from which materials went out all over West Africa. I also served on the Board of Governors for the West African Advanced School of Theology in Lomé, Togo and used the Speed the Light Vehicle to get me to that locality. It was the vehicle I used to go to the rescue of persecuted Christians in some of the Assembly of God churches located deep in the forests of Ivory Coast.

The Boys and Girls Missionary Crusade was responsible for raising enough money to purchase Sunday School materials for children and adults in countries all over the world. Once a month boy and girls in the USA A/G churches would fill their "buddy barrel" banks with loose change and bring what they had saved to their church. The "buddy barrels" were emptied and taken back home to be filled over the course of the next four weeks. Two BGMC stories are worth relating.

The first has to do with a trip into the bush to preach in a Mossi village. I took as much literature with me as I thought I would need. Literature provided by BGMC. As the literature was distributed fights (pushing and grabbing to take away from someone else) broke out as people rushed to get their piece of literature. It is hard for an American mind to comprehend the hunger people in third world countries have for something to read. They want whatever they can get their hands on and their minds around. The opportunity to get the Gospel into the hearts and minds of West African people who live in the bush is a heartwarming but challenging open door for the presentation of the Gospel. This is the work of BGMC!

The second story is that of a young family (father, mother and two children) who were brought to the Mission House door where Ruth and I lived in Daloa. They were bruised, bloodied and beaten with clubs and machetes, and had been running for their lives all through the night. It all started when the young father of this family read a piece of Gospel Literature in which the plan of salvation was described. He gave his heart to Jesus and was transformed by the experience. Immediately he began to read that same one piece of literature to everyone that would listen. More people in the small village came to Christ. Soon the elders of the village became alarmed at the influence the young man seemed to have as he rose to be the pastor of the small church that sprang up. The reason he was brought to our home by other Christians in the town of Daloa was for us to pray with them that God would make them strong and also so that we could give them more literature. The young convert turned pastor needed more than one story from the Bible to read to the people of the village. And this is both the problem and the opportunity presented. We could not train African pastors fast enough to keep up with the demand as new churches sprang up faster than trained pastors could be sent to them. All of our pastors gave leadership to from three to five churches at the same time and did so before they even graduated from the Bible Institute. And, as fast as possible, they would train Elders within the church who would, themselves, start annex churches to the Mother church. And so it would go on down the line. And then there were repeated cases like the one I have just mentioned when someone got ahold of a tract (piece of religious literature) and would give their heart to Christ and immediately began reading the one piece of literature they had to others during the day or around the camp fire at night. More people would come to Christ and another church sprang up. I (and the other missionaries) were kept busy every weekend ministering to these "bush churches". No matter how hard we had worked at the Bible School during the week, on the weekends we were out driving down dirt roads filled with washboard or crevasses, on the way to some bush church where the people were hungry to hear more about Jesus.

Humorous Events

One humorous event worthy of mention had to do with the work of our "house-boy" who not only did all the sweeping, mopping, dusting in our home but also cooked our lunch and supper meals before the end of his day. His name was Abdoulye, a Mossi from the Mossi branch of the Assemblies of God in Ivory Coast. Abdoulye was a hard worker, reliable and trustworthy. He had dreams of one day becoming a pastor back in his home country of Berkina Faso (formerly, The Upper Volta). One day when Abdoulye was not at work for some reason, Ruth went to the freezer compartment of our refrigerator to get a chicken to thaw out for supper. [48] What Ruth found was a freezer bag full of chicken parts, including the head, feet and intestines. The next day when Abdoulye came back to work, Ruth asked him about the head, feet and intestines in the frozen package. His response, "Oh, Madame, ils sont des meilleurs parties de chaque poulet" (Madame, they, are the best parts of each chicken)!

Ruth's response (in French) was, "Abdoulye, des maintenant tu peut prendre des meilleurs parties de chacque poulet pour allez chez toi." (from now on you can have the best parts of each chicken to take home with you). One would have thought that Ruth had just given him a wonderful gift! He was most grateful!

---

[48] We raised our own chickens and Abdoulye also butchered them, placing them in the freezer for future use.

Another humorous memory comes to mind. It is the time a rich Jeweler, specializing in diamonds, offered to buy me a new Cadillac if I would give him my daughter in marriage. By this time, Lani Rochelle, was turning into a beautiful and mature young lady with gorgeous blonde hair and pretty face. Not a bad figure either. And so this older man of 40 to 50 years of age cast a hungry look at our daughter and offered me the Cadillac. When I did not respond positively to his offer, he must have thought I was trying to bargain for a higher price and so he offered me two Cadillac's. My response was, "You don't understand the American female. My daughter would never go to the bush or river to gather wood or water and then carry them back to your house on her head or cook over an open fire for you. Besides that, she would sass you and argue with you. You would not be happy with her". He agreed that such a wife would not please him, and that was the last I heard about buying my daughter for unholy matrimony.

A third humorous memory has to do with my Mossi Pastor friend, Zida Marcel (in African culture the last name is often written and spoken before the given name. Zida often visited me, riding his bicycle many kilometers over dirt roads, in from where he pastored thirteen churches out in the countryside. I bought more than one new tire for his bicycle and was delighted to do so. We became great friends and I still miss him to this day. Zida lived in a typical mud hut with his wife and two children. According to Mossi culture his wife normally would sleep on the floor with their daughter while Zida and his son were able to sleep in the only bed they possessed. I remember her as a very tall, lanky and shapely woman who cooked over an open fire out in the courtyard, bending from the waist to cook food and wash pots and dishes. Most African women work very hard, carrying wood and water on their heads (balanced on a cloth circled to form a cushion). Often, at the same time they would carry a baby on their back. In order to discourage the baby from wetting, or worse, down the mother's back, they are usually given an enema of water and very hot peppers early each morning. This is done by the mother filling her mouth with the water and peppers and, with their mouth, squirting the liquid up the baby's rectum. I have not yet been able to figure out how that works, but this was what was told my wife by the African women at the Bible School. That is the disgusting part; now for the humorous part!

One day Zida complained to me that his wife was pregnant again in spite of the fact that they had prayed she would not get pregnant. I asked him, "Zida, weren't you and Madame taught the rhythm method of birth control as part of the Bible School curriculum?" "So why didn't you stay away from your wife during that part of her monthly cycle?" His answer was typical African as he answered my question with a metaphor, "Oh, pastor, when one sleeps next to the Honey Bucket, it is hard to stay out of the Honey!" So much for birth control à l'Afrique! Is that why the birth rate among the white population in America is barely staying even with the death rate? Is it because white men do not "go for the Honey" in their own "Honey Bucket" often enough, and at the right time of the month?

My fourth humorous story (well, maybe not too humorous, when you read all of it): There are two ways to "use the restroom" when one is out in the bush. The first is obvious, find a bush! The draw-backs are twofold, snakes and children. If your "restroom" choice is a bush, it is always wise to take your machete with you and establish your "demilitarized zone" (snake free) in a wide enough area around the bush so that you have time to relax and let nature take its course. The second drawback to "using a bush" is, if you are a white person, the prying eyes of curious children who want to find out if a white person eliminates the same way an African does.

The second way to "use the restroom" out in the bush or jungle, and one a little more private, if provided by the local village, is a long path out into the jungle where, at the end of the path is located a very long and large fallen log. That is the community "outhouse". Try to find a clean spot on the log (and don't forget to take some toilet paper with you—none provided in any village)! climb up on the log and hang your bottom over the edge, letting nature take its course (if you can forget about the danger of snakes and manage to relax).

Once, using the "log method" of restroom visitation I complained to the African pastor I was traveling with about my fear of snakes while using the restroom facilities. His response? "Oh pastor, that is not what I worry about! "There are head hunters out in the forest just waiting to take advantage of some vulnerable person so as to take their head to be used for Black Magic at the next Sacred Dance!" He was serious! He definitely was not joking! Can you imagine how easy it was to relax the next time I had to visit the community log? I've tried both ways of "bathroom facilities". Neither is pleasant.

Okay! Enough of these stories! But I could relate many more on more tasteful subject matters. Just thought my reader would like me to open a little window onto the everyday life of people in general in that part of the world, including the missionaries who still take the Gospel into the Jungles and Deserts of many parts of the world. Next time you are prone to complain about traffic or some other aspect of American life, instead, just thank God for the good old USA! No rats or snakes or roasted termites or dog or monkey to eat, and somewhat better sanitation in our public restrooms! Toilet paper usually provided free of charge!

Challenge, Danger & Personal Crisis on the Mission Field

Houphouët-Boigny was the first President of Ivory Coast, a country which had gained full independence from France on July 11, 1960. Houphouët-Boigny was there George Washington and was celebrated as the wise old man of Africa. It was on Independence Day (I believe in 1984) while Ruth and I were in Daloa teaching and leading the Bible

School that President Houphouët-Boigny allowed all jail prisoners in the country (except for the most hardened murderers) to go free from jail as part of the national celebration of Independence.

But the result of that magnanimous gesture on the part of the President was rewarded by many of those who had been jailed who returned to their former lifestyles with violent acts of brutality, murder and robbery. When these criminals came to Daloa, where Ruth and I lived, they posted a notice on the bulletin board of a local grocery store bragging about which quarter of the city of Daloa they would attack that night.

I was so angered by the horrible murders and brutality that I had seen or knew about, and the fact that I was forced to take my 12-guage shotgun for several weeks, every night, to stand guard over the students in order to assure that they would not be brutalized or murdered in their sleep, that I posted a notice on the same bulletin board stating that I would be waiting for them with my 12-guage semi-automatic shotgun. That night, they did indeed come to our "quartier" (quarter of town) and appeared at the gate of the mission compound where Ruth and I lived. When our night guard, Moussa, pounded on the iron bars (anti-thief bars) over our bedroom window I grabbed my shotgun and ran outside in my pajamas. Moussa only had a single-shot African shotgun and was trembling with fear. And, yes, I was also probably out-gunned. But in my fury I charged the front gate with the shotgun raised and ready to fire and with every intention of sending some bandits to hell. Fortunately for me, and the Assemblies of God mission, the bandits ran!

In retrospect, all I can say is that God, in His Mercy, must have supernaturally intervened for all concerned, and granted a far different outcome than what could have been! I knew I could have been killed or injured, but in my fury over the brutality that was going on, I justified my reaction with the rationalization that I had to make a choice to let my neighbors be brutalized and killed (because they didn't have the means, as I did, to protect themselves); or, me possibly making the bandits pay a price, for a change, as I protected my wife and neighborhood (including other missionaries that lived just a block away!).

The police, as is usual in many third world countries, were useless, and many people had suffered death and horrible brutalization because of the inability or unwillingness of the local police to protect the citizens of Daloa. I had seen a fifteen year old boy hung by the neck in the courtyard of our immediate neighbor. It was enough! Maybe I would die, but so would some of the bandits!

I admit that my reactions were quite different than one would normally expect from a missionary who preaches the love of God and Salvation through the shed Blood of Jesus. However, my reactions were the result of anger at the atrocities that occurred nightly as well as my own determination to not just sit idly by while people suffered horrible injuries, and even death. The consequences for a lot of people, including Ruth, would have been horrible had I died that night, but so, possibly, would have been the consequences to the neighborhood if I hadn't put a little fear into the bandits. Is there any lesson to be learned? How about this one: do I stand by, when I have the power to intervene, and allow innocent men, women and children to be murdered? Or is it more Christ-like to fold my arms and just pray? Does God want me to protect the weak and helpless outside my home when I have the power to do so, or would He prefer that I just remain selfishly in the safety my own house, surrounded by my 8 foot walls topped off with jagged glass, and be content to protect myself and my wife? Where is the line of duty and compassion? What application might James 2:18-20, 26 have to this situation? Is it Godly and Christ-like to pass by on the other side, refusing to get involved because of the danger to myself and those I love if I do get involved? [49]

I was at the point of emotional and physical exhaustion due to my heavy work load, nightly guard duty on the campus, and doing my best to keep the Bible College open. Ruth and I had completely replaced three other A/G missionary couples who had left the College for various reasons and who had earlier complained that they were overworked, thus the need that Ruth and I be assigned to help at the College. So our position and work load was something like three times more untenable, more impossible and more difficult than had been that of the previous three couples we had replaced rather than just come along side of to help.

The only other time I used that shotgun was when the students sent word to the Mission House where Ruth and I lived and where my office was located. It was lunch time and a large snake of at least six feet in length was in the rafters of the lunch area covered with a thick interwoven thatched roof, and kept lunging at the students as they tried to eat their lunches. The students sent word for me to come quickly with my shotgun which I did. I saw the large head of that snake up in the rafters and raised my shotgun to blast off its head. As the headless snake recoiled and came out of the rafters falling to the ground in front of us I fired once more, being very careful to aim so that the students that surrounded me were not in my line of fire. I have a picture of Ruth posing with the body of that snake held up in one hand and what was

---

[49]   Luke 10:30-37; Dietrich Bonhoeffer is known for his book, The Cost of Discipleship. But he is equally well known for his involvement with the German Military Intelligence Office in a plot to assassinate Adolf Hitler. He was arrested by the German Gestapo not for his writings but for his participation in the plot to assassinate Hitler, and was himself executed by hanging in April 1945, just 53 days before the German surrender. He walked stark naked to his execution and after having ministered with no show of fear to the other pastors that would also be executed that day.

left of the head in the other hand. The students shuddered at that and remarked how brave Ruth was to hold up the snake for a picture.

Gradually, the bandits that had terrorized all of Ivory Coast were arrested or killed, and calm returned to the country. I returned to the 2 AM start up time for each work day and 10 PM bed-y-bye time when I was privileged to fall into bed and be instantly asleep from pure exhaustion. Not very good for the love life, but life was too hectic and dangerous for the "good stuff"! (tongue in cheek!)

Now comes the rest of this stormy weather scenario . . . .

Emergency Trip Back to the United States

Word came to us from my younger Brother, Harley Daniel and his wife, Debra, that our Son, Lance David, was homeless and living on the streets of San Diego. When we had left Lance to return to Ivory Coast I had bought him a nice car and left him enrolled in Vanguard University in Costa Mesa, California. We thought we at least had him headed in the right direction and had given him all the reasons to turn his life around and ultimately serve God. Vanguard University is an Assemblies of God liberal arts college with a Christian worldview through which all classes are presented: Nursing, Early Education, Business, Psychology, Religion and General Education degrees.

But Lance's heart was not focused on serving God, or even getting a good education that would qualify him for whatever field of endeavor in which he might be interested. Lance, so it seems, wanted to see what the rest of the world lived like outside the Christian worldview. He began visiting night clubs and eventually Gay bars. He began smoking and eventually got involved with drugs. Later, while he was dying, he would outline perfectly for me each step of the downward spiral that led to his death. He said, "Dad, if I hadn't started smoking I would not have started drinking, and if I hadn't started drinking alcoholic beverages I never would have got involved in drugs, and if I hadn't gotten involved with drugs I would never have gotten involved in homosexuality. I would add two additional steps at the very beginning, and that is "if he hadn't given in to a rebellious heart against God and his parents, he would not have turned his heart away from God nor been curious about the kind of lifestyle we had tried to train him to stay away from. And then all that he had stipulated never would have happened. In other words, his decline into deep sin that ruined his health and eventually killed him would never have happened if he had kept God central to his desires and if he had followed the Biblical injunction to honor and obey the teaching of his parents, the godly way in which he was raised. [50]

So when I heard that Lance was homeless and living on the streets of San Diego I got permission from the Area Director over all of Africa, the Rev. Don Corbin, to shut the school down for one trimester and come home to try to help my Son. Ruth and our daughter, Lani Rochelle, remained in Africa while I came home. Upon arrival in San Diego I went to live with my Brother Harley and his wife. They loaned me one of their cars so that I could find Lance somewhere out on the streets and then start spending as much time with him as possible. My plan was to get Lance into a Teen Challenge Facility or some similar Ministry to destitute men fighting against drugs and alcohol. I remained, mainly on the streets with my Son for the next six weeks. He would not allow me to help him and certainly wanted nothing to do with Teen Challenge or any other religious organization. So Lance had made his choice! Like the Prodigal Son [51] he wanted to see city life, drinking and making merry in a way never experienced with his father, who expected a disciplined lifestyle, with respect for each other, obedience to his parents and good times in the home, with an occasional family outing and party-celebration without all the excesses of those who neither have nor want godly values. I returned to Africa a broken hearted Father.

---

[50] There are no age limits to the command for children to obey their parents that are mentioned in Scripture. I interpret that to mean that even adult children are expected to honor their parents by maintaining Biblical standards of holiness no lower than those required by their parents. In fact the next generation should always honor their parents by requiring that their own children obey and honor their grandparents and by teaching their children a system of values that would not shame what was already valued in the family. Notice I did not say man-made rules, but Biblical standards.

[51] Prodigal or prodigality meaning, "extravagantly wasteful"; synonymous to "lascivious lifestyle, dissipated"; in some places it is translated as "riot" or participation in a riot. See Luke 15:11-24

Lance would find shelter and food from a man who ran an antique (junk) shop. The man's name was Peter and once Lance moved in with him, Peter began to verbally abuse him, as well as to beat him and rape him almost on a daily basis. This continued for two years and was how Lance became infected with AIDS, for Peter was a prolific homosexual who carried on several different relationships with other homosexuals.

It was during this time that Ruth and I were completing our last two years of a four year cycle in Africa before coming home for furlough and to raise money for our next four years in Africa. It was during the time that I had closed down the Bible School in Ivory Coast to come home to be with Lance that I found myself driving around Peter's place trying to decide whether I would go into that house to beat Peter to a bloody, senseless pulp or maybe just kill him with a knife or baseball bat. Lance had already told me about Peter's physical and emotional abuse. Peter would verbally belittle him before he raped him and Lance was losing all self-respect and certainly, since he was dependent on Peter for shelter and food felt no ability to resist him. I am ashamed now to admit it, but my reaction was similar to the one I had experienced a year or so earlier when bandits in Ivory Coast were beating, mutilating and killing innocent men, women and children. My rage knew no bounds! Murder was in my heart like a southern California brush-fire out of control. And I know this, I never want to feel like that again! But Lance had rejected my efforts to help him and chosen to move in with Peter. For Ruth and Lani's sake, so they wouldn't lose a husband and father because of me going to prison, I decided not to give in to my desires to take vengeance on Peter and rationalized my decision on the basis of Lance's refusal to let me find a place at Teen Challenge or similar Christian organization.

I know this, too, that it is only because of the Grace and Mercy of my Heavenly Father, and my life-long habits of listening to the Holy Spirit, that I was able to retrieve some sanity to my thinking and pull back from an awful reaction to the death sentence Peter had passed on my son when he beat him and raped him for those two years. Peter lived long enough to return to London, England and die there. Also, by God's Grace, I was able to forgive Peter and pray for his healing and salvation before he died.

I benefited the most from what God had done in my heart. To Him I owe my life, ministry and freedom from some horrible consequences that would have come, not only to myself but to my precious wife and daughter had I not repented of what was in my heart.

There is a very graphic lesson to be learned here! And I still can't bring myself to say that I have it all figured out as to when violence is justified and when it is not. I am convinced of these ideas: that there defiantly are times when violence is justified, but also that, in most cases, it is NOT justified. One time violence is never justified is for the purposes of revenge. God said that only He is qualified to take vengeance for His people. [52] When we take matters into our own hands then God will not act on our behalf. But patience, love and self-sacrifice are almost always better tools for winning the day! Each of us, in humility before God and His Word must sort through all that for ourselves.

The Bait Stick and The Bait of Satan

John Bevere has written a book entitled, The Bait of Satan. (And I highly recommend that every Christian read that book, as well as all the rest of John Bevere's books. Certainly God has used that Brother as a modern day prophet.

---

[52] Deuteronomy 32:35-36, 43; Romans 12:19-21 says: Dear friends, never take revenge. Leave that to the righteous anger of God. For the Scriptures say, "I will take revenge; I will pay them back,"*. . . Also, in the Deuteronomy passage we are assured that "their foot shall slip in due time". So, as far as vengeance is concerned we need to leave that and its' timing in God's hands.

One of two Greek words in the New Testament for "offend" or "offense" is the word, ska/ndalon (skandalon) [53] which refers to a bait stick or bent sapling in a trap. When the bait is taken the trap is sprung and the animal is entrapped. This imagery is used to refer to what happens when a person is offended. That person is entrapped by Satan who now controls his thoughts, emotions and choices or decisions. Scriptures that use this word are: Matthew 13:41; 16:23; 18:7; Romans 9:33; 11:9 where it is translated, "stumbling block" and 14:13 where it is translated, "occasion to fall"; Galatians 5:11 mentions the "offense of the cross"; I Peter 2:8 speaks of a rock of offense, even to them which stumble (offended) at the Word, being disobedient". The "Stone of stumbling (offense)" is Christ over which many of the Jews who were unwilling to recognize Jesus as the Messiah stumbled and fell into condemnation & perdition. First John 2:10 describes one who loves his fellow Brother in Christ and shows his love by not allowing any occasion of stumbling (offense) in his own life. Revelation 2:14 speaks of the doctrine of the Prophet Balaam who taught Israel to sin Numbers 31:16 and cast a stumbling block before them causing them to be involved in "religious immorality" (similar to temple prostitutes). Part of the doctrine of Balaam was to follow the money, wherever his position as a Man of God would cause him to be paid the highest fee.

What needs to be remembered here is that when our emotions are high and we are scandalized or offended for some reason we have sold our souls (emotions, will and thought life) to be under the control of Satan.

I do not believe that when I rose up to protect our neighborhood from murderous bandits that Satan was controlling my emotions any more than he was when David killed Goliath or Elijah beheaded by his own

---

[53] Strong's Greek/Hebrew Definitions—NT4625

sword the prophets of Baal, or when Dietrich Bonhoeffer participated in the plot to assassinate Adolf Hitler.

But certainly my high emotions and desire to take the life of the man who beat and raped my Son and gave him AIDS was wrong (because of the motive of revenge[54]), and much evil would have come out of such an action. I had a lot of repenting to do for those emotions and ungodly desires (revenge) and am ashamed that I ever gave myself over to those passions, but also thankful that the Lord delivered me out of the trap and caused me to turn loose of the "bait stick" before I yanked on it by the act of performing what was in my heart.

---

[54] Leviticus 9:18; Psalm 94:1; Hebrews 10:30; Rom 12:19-20 (Amplified Bible) 19 Beloved, never avenge yourselves, but leave the way open for [God's] wrath; for it is written, Vengeance is Mine, I will repay (requite), says the Lord. [Deuteronomy 32:35.] 20 But if your enemy is hungry, feed him; if he is thirsty, give him drink; for by so doing you will heap burning coals upon his head. [Prov 25:21,22.]

Chapter Six

Perseverance through Storms Experienced, Victories Won And Lessons Learned during Intense Spiritual Warfare

The Struggle for our Son's Life and Eternal Destiny

Lance's Story:
(and ours)
"For Such A Time As This!"[55]

> This document began to be written on Tuesday, June 8, 1999 from notes previously taken.

THE MIDNIGHT CALL

There was a chilly breeze (25 degrees below zero) the evening of October 4th 1993 in Fairbanks, Alaska. Although we had traveled many places around the world we had looked forward to this first trip to Alaska. We never dreamed that before the evening was over a chill would sweep through our bodies that would freeze our very souls. Our travel as Itinerating Seminar Speakers brought us to the North Alaska Sectional Minister's Conference of the Assemblies of God. We would

---

[55] Esther 4:14

145

be speaking to this section's pastors and their wives for three days. The Conference began that evening with a banquet for all the ministers and their spouses at a Restaurant in Fairbanks. After the meal I challenged and encouraged them through the teaching of the Word. The evening was concluded with a time of praying for one another and getting acquainted. As the couples dispersed, we gathered our luggage from the guesthouse of the Grail Assembly in Fairbanks where we had just taught a weekend Seminar. The remainder of the Ministers conference was to be held at the Assembly church at North Pole, Alaska. Therefore, Pastor Gordon Welk and his wife Shirley were busy transferring our things to their vehicle to drive us to their home. We would be staying with them an additional week because we were also scheduled to minister to their congregation the week following after the conclusion of the ministers conference. We arrived at their log home at midnight exhausted but looking forward to the following week with great anticipation. We were very surprised when our hosts informed us that there were three emergency phone messages for us.

We had learned just before flying to Alaska on September 30th that our Son, Lance, had collapsed at work and his wife had rushed him to the South Bay Hospital near Manhattan Beach in Southern California. They had determined that Lance was very sick with pneumonia. We had called and talked with Lance by phone from Fairbanks just the day before the conference started. At that time we were told that the Doctor suspected there were other problems and was taking further tests. Therefore, on learning of the emergency calls we immediately suspected that the calls had to do with Lance's test results. The first call was a message from my Brother, Harley Daniel, in San Diego. The second was from Lance's new bride of five months. The third message was from our daughter, Lani, whom we were surprised to learn had flown down to be with her Brother. The messages all said to call immediately no matter how late the hour.

Lance had been calling us frequently the past three months, since their return home from their honeymoon cruise. He had become sick on the cruise and was having difficulty keeping his food down. He was very concerned and had repeatedly asked us to pray for him. He had complained that he was growing very weak. We had encouraged Lance to get a complete physical as soon as possible. After several doctor appointments and many tests Lance had reported to us that the only thing definite the Doctors had learned was that he was very anemic.

I placed my first call, from the private guest bedroom to my Brother, Daniel. Harley informed me that Lance was now in serious condition with Cryptococcus Meningitis and Encephalitis, in addition to the pneumonia. His next words resounded like a bomb going off in my head; "additional tests indicate that Lance tested positive for the Human Immune Virus."(HIV). He suggested that we get down to Los Angeles as soon as possible. We immediately called the hospital and talked to Lance's wife Rose as well as to our daughter Lani Rochelle. We were told that a second test had been taken to determine whether or not Lance's condition had progressed yet to the Auto Immune Deficiency Syndrome."(Full blown AIDS) The final results of that test would not be known for 24 Hours. The Doctor had said that any one of these viruses by itself could be fatal to an HIV patient, because the HIV patient's immune systems becomes very compromised and therefore, is unable to fight off the viruses. The chance of Lance surviving all four of these viruses at the same time made his recovery very doubtful!

Words cannot describe the heavy, foreboding that overwhelmed us like a blanket trying to suffocate us. On completion of the calls we threw ourselves into each other's arms and wept. Lance David was our first child and only Son. How could this be happening? It seemed as if a knife had been plunged into our hearts ripping them open and leaving them to bleed. Our hearts ached for our Son. We prayed that this would turn out to be just a horrible nightmare that would disappear when we awoke. However, that was not to be.

As soon as we were able to recover our composure sufficiently we rejoined our hosts in their living room and shared with them our devastating news. We were deeply touched and comforted by the sensitivity and loving support Gordon & Shirley gave us at that critical moment. What a blessing they were to us! God knew exactly what we needed and was one step ahead of us. Here we were just seven hours before we were to teach the morning sessions, and wham-o! Gordon and Shirley helped us talk through the reality of the news and encouraged us in the Lord. We wept and shared together for a couple hours. After praying together we decided to go ahead and teach the first morning session while working on the arrangements for changing our return flight. With that decision made, we fell into bed and tried to sleep.

After only a few hours of fitful sleep we made another quick call to the hospital to check on Lance's condition. We were able to speak with Lance briefly and were shocked by the frailty in his voice. We assured him that we were making plans to come to him as soon as we could make the necessary adjustments to our tickets. Lance assured us that it was not necessary for us to leave in the middle of the conference. We reassured him that he and his welfare took priority over any other obligations. It would have been impossible for us to concentrate on teaching knowing our Son's life could be at stake. Although we were obligated, after the Minister's conference, for another week of meetings at North Pole Assembly we simply committed the matter into God's Hands. We were sure Pastor Welk and his congregation would understand.

Before the morning session the leaders of the Conference had special prayer with us in the Pastor's Office. They had special prayer for our Son and that God would help and strengthen us for what lay ahead. Providentially, the subject I was to teach in that morning session was Intercessory Prayer. Pastor Roger Davis who was in charge of the conference shared with the pastors and their wives that our Son was very seriously ill and in a hospital in the Los Angeles area. The Holy Spirit empowered me in a special way that morning as I spoke on the Biblical principles of Intercessory Prayer. I encouraged the pastors to apply those principles to their individual lives and ministry and to realize that we are in spiritual warfare against the enemy of our souls. The teaching that morning was followed by a powerful time of individual and corporate intercessory prayer. Everyone present was greatly impacted by the teaching of the Word, and came to a new understanding of the relevance and importance of intercession; not just intercessory prayer but actually getting involved in another person's life to rescue them from whatever it is that has brought their life under bondage to financial situations, sickness, evil of any kind like drugs, physical abuse or molestation. Whatever is tearing someone else's life apart and another person has the power or influence to bring that to an end is a form of intercession.

Pastor Davis from Fairbanks was diligently working for us behind the scenes in an effort to expedite matters and hasten our departure. Ruth and I were anxious to get to our Son in California. At noon there was a quick lunch in the church fellowship hall. Joseph taught Ruth's afternoon session so that she could go to the pastor's home to get our things repacked. Ruth then brought the luggage to the church. At the end of that session Pastor Davis met us with our new tickets. We learned that it had been necessary for him to make a special trip all the way to the Fairbanks airport in order to exchange our tickets. We said a quick goodbye to everyone and loaded our things into Pastor Davis' vehicle. Pastor Welk quietly handed us a check of $600 dollars as an honorarium for the services we were to have with him the following week. They also gave us remuneration for being guest speakers at the Conference, even though we only fulfilled half of our obligation. The thoughtfulness, prayers and support of everyone there was overwhelming and ministered to us in a special way. On arriving at the airport we rushed to the gate just in time to board our plane, which was being held to accommodate us. We flew out of Anchorage at about 4 PM.

Our return flight took us to the Sea-Tac airport just south of Seattle. Ruth's Niece, Tammy, had made arrangements for the first available flight to the L. A. International Airport. Ruth's Brother Dan Taylor and his wife, Barb, met us at the airport at 9 PM, Tuesday night, October 5th and drove us to our apartment in Tacoma, Washington. We quickly did our laundry and repacked our suitcases in preparation for our early morning flight to Los Angeles. The telephone rang at 1 A.M. just as we were ready to tumble into bed. It was the early hours of Wednesday the 6th. Our daughter Lani was calling from the hospital in L.A. She was sobbing so hard we could hardly understand what she was saying. She begged us to get there as soon as possible. She was alone with Lance who was now in the Intensive Care Unit. Lance's wife, Rose, with her Sister and Mother had gone home for a few hours' sleep. They had asked Lani to stay with Lance while they tried to get some rest. Lance was running a raging fever and was delirious. Lani was frightened and having a very difficult time emotionally seeing her Brother in that condition. She was very scared and told us that, "Lance is out of his mind." We informed her that our flight would be leaving in a matter of hours and that we would meet her at the hospital by early afternoon.

We fell into bed for a few hours of exhausted sleep. On awaking, we drove to Dan and Barb Taylor's home at Lake Tapps and they took us on to the airport. We arrived at the L.A. International Airport at 2:30 PM, rented a car and drove straight to the hospital where our daughter met us.

On arriving at the South Bay Hospital Lani took us to the Intensive Care Unit to see Lance. Lance's wife, Rose (pseudonym), as well as her Mother and Sister were all in the hall just outside the IC Unit. Ruth and Rose melted into each other's arms and wept together. Rose had been with Lance almost continually since he had been admitted to the hospital. Rose is a very beautiful young woman, however, at that moment the heartache and grief etched on her face had aged her. We received permission to go into the Intensive Care Unit to see Lance alone. Because we were his parents the nurses allowed both of us to go in together rather than insisting we go in separately.

Entering Lance's room we were shocked and horrified at his condition. He had lost a lot of weight and looked like a skeleton. The left side of his face sagged because of paralysis due to the encephalitis which caused swelling of the membrane around his brain. This swelling was putting pressure on his brain that resulted in the partial paralysis. We immediately noticed that his wrists and ankles were tied to the bed with long cloth cords. This was to keep him in bed since he was continuously trying to get out of bed. Lance was delirious and kept reaching up into the air to pet little pink kittens he thought he was seeing. We quickly went to the head of his bed and said, "Hello, Son. He turned his face toward us and we looked into his eyes that seemed like empty pools. His response was, "Who are you?" Because there seemed to be no indication of recognition we identified ourselves as his Mother and Father. He looked at us with a blank stare and said, "I don't know you. Get out of here, I'm not feeling well." He then raised his voice to call for a nurse to have us removed from the room.

Ruth leaned over the bed and said, "Lance, this is Pepper." This had been her nickname when she was in college and Lance also would often playfully call her "Pepper". On hearing the name "Pepper", Lance's eyes brightened and he said, "Oh, my Mother is called Pepper too." Ruth responded by saying, "I know, Son, I am your Mother." We watched as he struggled to assimilate what she had just said. Slowly, he came to realize who we were. The nurses would not allow us to stay with him very long due to their desire not to tire Lance out. So after a short time we returned to the waiting room where Rose (pseudonym) and her Mom (Lance's Mother in-law), and Sister were waiting. We took turns spending short periods with Lance throughout the day. Someone from the family was at the hospital at all times.

One time Ruth went in to see Lance and he seemed to think he was back in his store (at Godiva's Chocolatier) taking inventory of the stock. Another time, Lance expressed his concern about getting back to work because he was afraid of losing his job. Another time he thought he was driving his car. He was trying to put his foot on the brake and to steer the car so as to avoid an accident. We stayed at the hospital until late that evening and then got a motel room for the night. Rose was to stay with him that night as we had not had much sleep the previous two nights.

Rose was having a particularly hard time. They had just been married five months and the news of Lance having AIDS was a devastating blow to her. All her hopes and dreams for the future were being dashed to pieces before her very eyes. She was slowly realizing that she was in the process of losing her new husband, as well as her dream for a family.

Rose's Sister, Mary, and a friend were working with hospital administrators in an effort to get Lance transferred to Cedar Sinai Hospital and under the care of Dr. Pasolski who is one of the foremost AIDS specialists on the West Coast. The Cedar Sinai Hospital is known for its AIDS Ward which covers the sixth floor of one wing of the hospital. After several days of phone calls and personal appeals with both hospitals and doctors, permission was granted to have Lance transferred. We were not aware that June's Friend had claimed to be Lance's Sister in an effort to add validity and authority to her negotiations. However, we did appreciate all their efforts on Lance's behalf

After spending several hours with Lance on Thursday morning we went to the I-Hop Restaurant for lunch. We went back to the hospital about 2:20 PM. On Thursday evening, about 7:30 PM, October 7th, Lance was transferred by ambulance from the IC unit at South Bay Hospital to the AIDS ward at Cedar Sinai Hospital in Beverly Hills, California. The transfer was probably at least partially responsible for

Lance's life being saved at that point. The move between the hospitals was unsettling to Lance and seemed to cause him great anxiety. He was continuously inquiring about where he was and what was going on, and we could hear the doctors and nurses trying to calm him and reassure him. It was necessary for the nurses to give him something to calm him down. Soon after his arrival at Cedar Sinai, the doctor immediately examined Lance. We were informed that the doctor was going to make adjustments in the strengths and combinations of medicines to bring Lance's condition under control. After the doctor checked him he called Rose and our families into a room to have a serious talk. He said that the paralysis on the left side of Lance's body and the delirium could be permanent. He said that we would just have to wait and see, but that we wouldn't know anything for sure for about a week. He said that there was a possibility that the virus could have gotten into Lance's brain. He emphasized that if that were true and Lance did live, that in all probability he would be a vegetable the rest of his life. We went back to the motel at Manhattan Beach at 1 AM Friday morning emotionally and physically drained.

On Friday the 8th I called my Sister, Norma Jean Boggs, and she asked if we needed her to come down to be with us. This morning Ruth was having a very difficult time emotionally, handling everything. Lance had a very restless day. Debbie, Harley Daniel's wife, came up on Friday and spent several hours with Lance. She spent the night with us at our motel. We lived at the hospital during the day and took turns with Rose spending the night at the hospital with Lance. On Saturday, the 9th, Joseph's Brother and his wife[56] came up from San Diego to see Lance. Many of Lance and Rose's friends and family members were also coming in and out for visits during this time.

---

[56] Harley Daniel and Debra Meyers

On Saturday morning we went to the hospital after breakfast and spent the day with Lance. Debbie's husband, Harley Daniel, arrived about 9 PM and we all visited with Lance until 11 PM. Danny asked me to have prayer with Lance before we left that night. We then got our things from the motel and spent the night at Lance & Rose's house in Manhattan Beach, since Rose was staying at the hospital with Lance that night.

On Sunday, October 10, 1993, we met at a restaurant and had breakfast with Dan and Deb before going to the hospital. We then went shopping to get streamers, a card, candles and a gift for Lance for a celebration of Lance's 27th birthday. On the way to the hospital the traffic got backed up and Dan's car was hit from behind by another driver. There were actually four cars involved and we were the fourth car. So we were delayed by the police and the need to fill out forms. Except for a temporary sore neck for Ruth, no one else in our car was hurt. We finally arrived at the hospital to find Lance sitting up in bed and laughing and joking with those around him. Rose and her family had provided a birthday cake and some soft drinks. They helped Lance blow out his candles. Then he opened the gifts that everyone had brought for him, and had a nice party. The nurses and staff came in to help us sing Happy Birthday to Lance. Lance was very happy and talkative, and he talked to about 7 or 8 different people who had telephoned to wish him Happy Birthday. Dan and Debbie left after the party to drive back to San Diego. They both had to be at work the next morning. It was a wonderful day and everyone was rejoicing that Lance was so much better, which meant that the immediate crisis was over. We immediately began talking about when he could return home. Ruth and I spent the night at the hospital with Lance.

On Monday, Lance was exhausted after all the talking and excitement of the day before. Rose became very pensive and was doing a lot of thinking and questioning. Rose called us aside to talk to us privately and ask us if we aware when Lance knew he had been exposed to the HIV virus. She also questioned us about Lance's relationship with Peter. We told her that Lance had cut off his relationship with us during that time so we were only aware of what rumors we heard but did not have any facts. We informed her that we had received a letter while we were still in Africa from a relative who said they had heard that Lance had been tested for HIV virus and it had turned out positive. But that when we arrived home from Africa and questioned Lance about it that he had denied it. Months later on questioning him again he acknowledged that he had tested HIV positive but that since the HIV positive results at that time were sometimes false, he was told to have a second test taken. He had told us that the second test had turned out negative. We told Rose that we understood her concerns but if she wanted the answer to these questions she needed to speak to Lance openly and honestly about her concerns; that he was the only one who knew the truth about these matters.

Tuesday, the 12th,—Ruth asked Lance about his relationship with God. Lance acknowledged that he had lived his life only to please himself, without any thought of anyone else. He realized that he had made a lot of mistakes and wasted many years. Lance told Ruth that if he lived through this crisis that he was going to make some changes. One thing he mentioned that he would like to do was to become a hospital volunteer to help others that are going through similar things to what he had experienced. Another desire of his was to write a book for children who found it necessary to go into the hospital. The purpose of such a book would be to help relieve their fears. Ruth talked to Lance and told him that he needed to share the details of his past with Rose (pseudonym) in an open and honest fashion. Ruth made the observation that he (Lance) owed that to his wife. Lance later told Ruth that he and Rose had talked. But he did not share with Ruth the contents of that conversation. We again spent the night at the hospital with our Son.

Wednesday—October 13th—Lance was very emotional this morning and had obviously been doing some thinking. He asked Ruth's forgiveness for what he was putting her through. He said he was sorry for not having listened to her and her advice in the past. He said that Ruth and been right and he had been wrong. At that time he said that it wasn't worth it. We left the hospital and drove down to Dan and Debbie's home in San Diego and spent the night with them. There was something we needed to get from Dan and Debbie but don't remember what it was. We returned to Cedar Sinai on Thursday morning, the 14th. Lance was very weak and was not able to hold food on his stomach. He had a slight seizure when his nurse, Greg, tried to get him up. Lance was talkative during the afternoon. He wasn't able to keep his dinner down and watched some TV for several hours that evening. However he got a terrific headache. Ruth and I spent the night at the hospital with him and he had two more small seizures during the night.

Friday—October the 15th—Lance was not able to keep his breakfast down again this morning and later had two more seizures. Ruth reported this to the nurse and Lance was immediately rushed to the Intensive Care Unit (about noon). Lance had a terrible headache most of the day. It was on Friday, the 15th that the doctor talked to us and told us that the next 48 hours were critical and would determine whether Lance would survive or not. We got on the phone and called Family and Pastors around the country so that they and their congregations could pray. We went to Rose's (pseudonym) place about 6 PM to take a much needed shower and short nap and then went back to the hospital at 9 PM. The drive between Lance and Rose's place in Manhattan Beach and the hospital in Beverly Hills was about a 1 to 1 & ½ hour drive, depending on traffic. Lance had a severe headache about 11 PM.

Saturday, October 16th—Lance was very anxious, agitated and depressed. He was unable to keep down his food. In the afternoon he had several visitors. He seemed a little better and able to visit okay.

Rose, Dolly (pseudonym), Debbie, Ruth and I all spent the night at the hospital. Lance had another very severe headache. At times he would take his fist and beat his head as if he were trying to make the headaches stop. Later the doctor ordered that Lance be taken down for a CAT scan in an effort to find the reason for the headaches. It was a very restless and anxious night. Different ones were going into the IC unit to spend time with him, so he would know he wasn't alone. Much of the time, whoever was with Lance just sat quietly, without talking (unless he wanted to talk). But he seemed to be comforted by the knowledge that someone was there.

Sunday morning, October 17th—Ruth stayed with Lance in the Intensive Care room from 4 AM, on. Debbie came in later and spent some time with him, because she had to leave at 1 PM to go back to San Diego. Ruth and I spent the afternoon with Lance, who was very restless and wanting to leave. During this time there were several "code blue" calls and each time we were afraid it might be for Lance. That night we had dinner with Rose (pseudonym) and Dolly (pseudonym) in the hospital cafeteria. We then went to Lance and Rose's house to get a shower and good night sleep.

Monday—October 18th—Lance had improved enough that he was moved out of the IC unit and back to his room on the sixth floor. I visited with him for a while and said goodbye to fly back to Tacoma and my speaking engagements in the Northwest. I had been there 12 days but needed to continue our meetings in the churches. It was decided that Ruth would stay with Lance until we could be sure that he was through this second crisis and on the road to recovery. Lance was able to be placed in a wheelchair and go for a brief ride outside on the hospital plaza. Ruth visited with Rose (pseudonym), which was nice because she had been a little cool and distant since the conversation in which we had discussed her concerns about when Lance first knew about being HIV positive. Lance seemed unusually quiet. Lorenzo (another

Godiva manager that Lance knew) and a girlfriend of Rose's came to visit Lance. Lance was able to keep all of his food down for the first time that evening. Ruth spent the night alone with him. Ruth took the opportunity to speak with Lance about how seriously ill he was. She shared with him what the doctor had told us about their uncertainty that Lance would live. And also, that if he did live that there was a possibility that the virus had gotten into his brain, which would have left him a vegetable if he did live. Lance shared with Ruth that when he was in the Intensive Care Unit he thought he was dying. He also shared how his headaches were so severe that if it had been possible for him to get out of bed and get to a window he would have jumped out and taken his own life. Lance was able to sleep most of the night.

Tuesday—October 19th—Lance was able to keep his breakfast down and sat in the shower, which was his first shower in three weeks, and then was able to eat lunch. Marcie, a hospital volunteer and Ruth and Rose (pseudonym) took Lance in a wheelchair for a ride on the plaza to get some fresh air. The nurse's also removed Lance's catheter. Lance started to have severe headaches and chills again later that day. But the pain medicine seemed to stop it. He started to have another seizure but Ruth told him to take slow, deep breaths and he was able to stop the seizure. Ruth spent the night at Dolly's house that night.

Wednesday, October 20th—Ruth had breakfast at Dolly's and she showed Ruth the house. They then went to see Lance at the hospital. Lance had eaten three bowls of cereal for lunch and was keeping his food down. They took him out for another wheelchair ride, but later he became very short and snappy. Rose, Dolly (pseudonym), Mary (pseudonym) and her friend, Sally, left about 7 PM because of Lance's attitudes. After they left, Ruth confronted Lance about his bad language, attitudes and shortness with people who had been there for him for a couple weeks now. Lance became angry, so Ruth left the room and went out to the waiting room for an hour. Lance thought Ruth had left for the night so when she came back an hour later he was grateful to see her, and had adjusted his attitude. They watched 101 Dalmatians together. Ruth spent the night with Lance in his room. Lance woke up about 3 AM and Ruth got up from the couch to see how he was doing. They ended up having a very nice talk from 3 to 6 AM.

Thursday, October 21ˢᵗ—Lance was able to sit up and feed himself breakfast. The nurse came in and talked to him about home care and learning to do his own IV and also spoke of the need for physical therapy. Lance and Ruth visited alone for a while until Rose (pseudonym), Mary (pseudonym), Sally and Dolly (pseudonym) came with donuts they had brought for him. Lance was doing well enough that Ruth felt she could safely leave and go home to Tacoma, Washington. The last half-hour with Lance was very difficult. She told him that we would keep in touch by phone and that we would be praying for him. He cried and thanked Ruth for coming. Said that he didn't know how he was going to get along without his Mother. Rose's Mother, Dolly (pseudonym), and her friend, Lynn took Ruth to the LA airport and I picked her up at Sea-Tac and then drove to Dan and Barb's home at Lake Tapps (near Tacoma, Washington) where we ate dinner with them. We called Lance that evening. He said that the doctor had told him he could go home on Friday. Ruth went home and got unpacked and fell into bed. She slept from 10 PM until 11 AM the next morning.

Friday—October 22ⁿᵈ—we called the hospital at 1:30 PM and talked to the doctor. Lance was doing much better and was getting ready to be released. We left home at 3 PM in the afternoon and drove to Richland, Washington where we spent the night with Gary and Julie. We visited with them until 1 AM Saturday morning.

Saturday—October 23ʳᵈ—we had breakfast with Julie and the children and left about 10:30 AM to drive to Caldwell, Idaho. Julie had packed a lunch for us for the trip. When we arrived in Caldwell there was a prayer meeting at the church from 8 to 9 PM. After the prayer meeting we stayed and ran off the study guides for the Sunday School class the next morning before going to the motel. We called Rose from the motel and she said that Lance was enjoying being home.

Monday—October 25th—we called to see how Lance was doing but there was no answer.

Tuesday—October 26th—We called Lance; he was in the tub. Rose (pseudonym) said that he was gaining his strength and walking on his own now.

Thursday—October 28th—we drove to Boise, Idaho and stopped at the church to see Lyle Dodson, and then went on to Lyle and Claire's apartment where we shared with them about Lance. We called Rose and learned that Lance had come down with pneumonia again and was on oxygen.

Friday—October 29th—we left Boise at 8:30 AM and arrived in Tacoma at 6:30 PM where we called Rose (pseudonym). Rose was feeling a little overwhelmed with her responsibilities of caring for Lance with his IVs, etc. Ruth offered to return to Manhattan Beach to help her. But she said that nurses were coming to the house every day to help her with Lance and that she was feeling more relaxed about taking care of his IVs.

Sunday—October 31st—Rose called to tell us that Lance was taken back to the hospital because of difficulty breathing. The doctor wanted to keep him there for several days to stabilize him and make some changes in his medication. We called the hospital and talked to Lance later that evening.

Monday—November 1st—Lance and Rose's six month wedding anniversary.

Saturday—November 13th—Ruth left to fly down to be with Lance who was in the hospital. Debbie Meyers picked Ruth up at the airport and they went together to see Lance. That was the day that Debbie told Ruth that she was going to divorce Joseph's Brother, Danny.

Ruth spent the night at the hospital with Lance who had a bad case of diarrhea.

Sunday, November 14th—Ruth spent the entire day with Lance who was continuing to have a bad problem with diarrhea. Rick and Michelle from AIDS Research Ministries came to see Lance that afternoon. Lance was in the middle of being cleaned up and at first he didn't want to see them. He asked them to wait in the hall for a few minutes and then he would see them. They visited with Lance for a while and had prayer with him and then Ruth spent the night at the hospital with Lance.

Monday, November 15th—Lance was released from the hospital about 4 PM and Rose picked them up and took them to the house in Manhattan Beach. A nurse came to the house that evening and hooked Lance up to his antibiotics and his nutritional feeding which he had to take intravenously because he was having trouble keeping food down again.

Tuesday, November 16th—Rose (pseudonym) left for San Francisco to spend five days with her Sister, Mary (pseudonym), and to get some rest and a break, R&R from the stress and anxiety. A nurse came to the house to show Ruth how to do Lance's IVs and medications. Because Lance could not keep enough food on his stomach, he had lost a lot of weight. To build him back up again he was being fed intravenously (pick line). They had inserted the pick line in his arm while he was still in the hospital. And this relieved the necessity of the continuous insertion of needles every time they needed to give him medication or to draw blood. So part of Ruth's responsibility every day before he could use them was to flush the lines.

Wednesday, November 17th—one of the negative side results of the intravenous feeding is that it often causes diarrhea. Lance had a bad case of this today. He was laying on the floor and Ruth had received a phone call from the insurance company asking about how Lance was doing. Suddenly, he had to go to the bathroom and tried to get up. Ruth couldn't help him because she was on the phone. Suddenly Lance had the diarrhea all over himself, the rug and everything around him. So then Ruth had to get him in the tub and bathed. Ruth had to get the gloves on and clean up the rug, linen, etc. Lance and Rose (pseudonym) had no washer and dryer in the home. So they were running out of clothes and towels because they were all dirty. Ruth called Pam (Rose's Aunt) to ask her if she could go to the store and buy some disposable undergarments for Lance. Pam wanted to know what the problem was and Ruth told her. She offered to go to the store for Ruth to get supplies she needed. Pam also offered to stop by and pick up the dirty clothes and towels and do a wash, which she did. Took them home, washed, dried and folded them and brought them back. Every night Ruth would hook Lance up to his nutritional IV. When it was time for Lance to go to bed, she hooked him up for his feeding. The process took several hours (about 4 to 6 hours—although Ruth's memory is not clear on this). There was a pharmaceutical company that delivered the large bags of nutritional feeding, and Ruth kept them in the refrigerator. But she had to take it out of the refrigerator a couple hours before the feeding so that it would not be a shock to his system. On top of his intravenous feedings, Ruth was still preparing three meals a day for him of simple things she felt he could keep on his stomach. This was done to help him gain weight more quickly and get his body used to eating and keeping food on the stomach again. Also she gave him liquids.

Thursday, November 18th—Lance was doing better today and Ruth talked him into going outside on their enclosed patio to sit in the sunshine for about an hour.

Friday and Saturday—the 19th and 20th—no special notes were made because it was about the same. Bouts with vomiting and diarrhea, also with depression. Although he was determined, at first (until later on when Rose (pseudonym) decided to divorce him) to beat the disease.

Sunday, November 21st—Ruth and Lance watched the Crystal Cathedral together. Rose arrived back from San Francisco that afternoon. She and Ruth went to the store to do some shopping. They bought groceries and then went to Target to buy Lance some flannel pajamas and shorts because he was complaining on being cold. Ruth noticed a definite change in Rose's attitude. She seemed withdrawn from both Ruth and Lance. She did what she needed to do but there was not the warmth of husband/wife love.

Monday, November 22nd—Rose (pseudonym) cleaned up all the dirty clothes and took them over to Pam's place to do a washing. That evening Ruth and Lance watched the movie, Joni, together. Rose was either in the bedroom or kitchen and never joined Ruth and Lance to watch the movie.

Tuesday, November 23rd—that morning Ruth packed her things, got Lance bathed and dressed and ready for his doctor appointment, and then they took Ruth to the airport and dropped her off at the airport about 1 PM. I was in Revival Meetings in Canada and so Barb picked Ruth up at Sea-Tac and took her home. When Ruth got home she called Lance and Rose to find out the outcome from his appointment with Dr. Palkowski. They said that Lance had gained 8 pounds and now weighed 123 pounds. The doctor was trying to find out what medicine was causing the vomiting.

Thursday, November 25—Thanksgiving. Ruth called me where I was staying in Canada and told me that she would be spending Thanksgiving with Esther. I agreed to pick her up at Esther's place as soon as I drove in from Canada.

Friday, November 26th—Wes and Marcia took us to the airport and kept our car while we flew to Ketchikan, Alaska and our meetings there. Lee and Karla met us at the airport and we stayed in a room in the downstairs of their home. We did a Marriage Seminar on Friday and Saturday. And I began a teaching on Sunday on the Healing of Broken Relationships.

The next week, December 5-8, we were in meetings at the North Pole Assembly of God church and on Thursday, December 9th, in celebration of Ruth's birthday, I took Ruth to a special restaurant just 15 miles north of Fairbanks.

Lance was out of work for six months. His recovery was very gradual. He finally got where he could hold down his food but was still quite weak. Several times when he tried to venture out with friends he lost his balance and would fall due to the residual effects of the paralysis on his left side. Thankfully, the only evidence of paralysis on the left side of his face was that when he slept his left eye did not go all the way closed. And it seemed that he was peeping out at you, even when he was fast asleep. Due to a clause in his company's medical insurance Lance was forced to make the choice to either go back to work or lose his medical coverage. So in March of 1994, in spite of the fact that he had not regained his strength he went back to work as Manager of the Godiva Chocolatier Store in Sherman Oaks Fashion Square in Sherman Oaks, California.

Earlier in the year there had been a severe earthquake with the epicenter at Sherman Oaks. As a consequence, the Mall where the GODIVA store was located was severely damaged. The parking lot had completely collapsed and all the glass from the windows and the display cases was broken and scattered all over the floor. The whole Mall had been completely shut down since the earthquake. By March 1994 several of the stores had been able to reopen. Lance's first responsibility, in going back to work, was to get his store cleaned up and ready to reopen. Lance worked hard to bring the sales back up and to increase his volume of product. He was very creative in finding ways to introduce the store and its product to potential customers. Within a short while he had his store up and selling at previous levels. Lance was a warm and friendly manager and took a personal interest in all his customers.

In was the second week of March, 1994 that we were in meetings in Prince George, British Columbia that we received almost nightly phone calls from our Son, who was in tears, telling us that his wife had informed him that she was planning on leaving him. This was partially due to the fact that she felt that he had not been completely open and honest with her regarding the condition of his health and his past lifestyle. She was also having trouble handling Lance's sickness and the loss of a future for them together. However, she continued to live with him for several months after that. Lance was understandably devastated. He felt that with her gone there would be no reason for him to continue to live.

Rose's forthcoming departure created another serious problem for Lance. Their car was a wedding gift to Rose from her Grandmother, and thus Rose's departure would leave Lance without transportation or the ability to get back and forth to work. That situation caused Lance a lot of anxiety because he couldn't afford to lose his job. Lance did not have the means or the credit to buy a car. Therefore, we stepped in as his parents to help him. We were able to get a loan, which we used to buy a small, economical vehicle for him so that he would have transportation to work. He promised that if we would do that, that he would send us the monthly payments. Ruth's Brother, Dan Taylor, drove the little 1991 Geo-Metro down to Lance in Manhattan Beach. Dan said that he averaged 50 miles per gallon on the trip. Lance was thankful, and very relieved to have a vehicle of his own.

The rest of the Spring and Summer of 1994 we were back on the east coast doing seminar and revival meeting work in the churches. While in New Jersey during the month of August we spoke to our Son several times by phone. By this time his wife had left and he was alone. Lance was having a difficult time adjusting to her absence in his home and life and was experiencing deep depression. We called Lance several times that month. Several times when we called he burst into tears and talked to us about suicide and about having lost his will to live. We tried to encourage him as much as possible. We reminded him that he could still accomplish things with his life and tried to get him to focus on that possibility. Because of his mental and emotional state we felt it was important for him to have someone with him for support. So we discussed the possibility of Ruth flying out to be with Lance in Manhattan Beach for as long as she felt she was needed. We called Lance concerning what we felt we wanted to do to help him. Lance let us know that he did not want Ruth to come. However, considering his emotional state we felt we needed to do what was best for his physical welfare. We notified Lance of Ruth's flight schedule and I took Ruth to the JFK International Airport and sent her off to Los Angeles. Because of Lance's work schedule he contacted Rose and arranged for her to pick Ruth up at the L.A. International when she arrived. Rose took Ruth to Lance's house.

From the beginning, Lance was suspicious of Ruth's motives for coming. When Ruth informed Lance that she was there because she loved him and was concerned about his welfare, and that she just wanted to be there for him, he did not believe her. We have learned through the years from study and research that often the human tendency is to assign to other people's motives what are actually our own motives or thought patterns. In fact, Lance said to Ruth that there had to be some other reason for her coming, besides just wanting to be there for him because she loved him.

Ruth tried to explain to him that that is what love is all about; namely, relationships and being there for each other. It seems like the focus on so many relationships has become what someone can get for themselves rather than what they can give to the other. This causes people to become skeptical and suspicious of other people's motives or of the "real thing" when people really do care for them. Ruth learned later that Lance thought she had come to control his life and to tell him what he could and couldn't do, as if he were a little boy again and living at home. Ruth assured him that such an attitude was not even in her mind, nor did she have any desire to do such a thing. Ruth pointed out to him many examples as proof. For instance, Ruth had not said anything to him about smoking in the house even though he knew that Ruth was allergic to the cigarette smoke and it caused her to cough uncontrollably. Ruth endured his blaring rock music without a word, in spite of the fact that he was aware that it was physically painful to her ears. When he came in late, Ruth never questioned where he had been or what he had been doing. Ruth was preparing meals for Lance every night but soon stopped doing that because Lance refused to eat what was fixed (things Ruth thought he liked) and would prepare something different for himself—even after Ruth had gone to a lot of work to prepare food for him.

Since Lance was working during the day Ruth mainly concentrated on getting his house cleaned up. Lance remarked that his house hadn't been that clean for a long time. The longer Ruth stayed the more hostile and fearful he became. Until one night he didn't even come home from work. At that point, Ruth decided that there was no reason for her to stay any longer. So Ruth contacted me and asked me to get her a plane ticket. She then flew out and rejoined me in Chicago.

1996

On the 26th of February, 1996 Lance came to work to find his District Manager in the store. He was surprised to find them there so early in the morning and without prior notice. Lance was informed that this would be his final day of work. He was shocked and asked them what they meant. He had just received a large bonus check for having surpassing his previous month's production goals. He was told that they were closing the store. Lance asked them why the store was being closed since he had brought it out of the red and it was doing better now than it had been under the previous manager. Lance had been working with the GODIVA Chocolatier, Inc. company for over 5 years and had at one time received national recognition as the nation's top manager in the area of customer relationships. He had received a personal letter of commendation from the President of the company. During his years at GODIVA he had never heard of the company closing down a store without previous notification to the manager and employees. His District Manager, who had also been accompanied by the Regional Manager, told him that the store was being closed because the lease had run out. They also informed the employees that this would be their last day of work, as well. Lance was devastated. He now had no means of being able to support himself. Physically, Lance's health had deteriorated. However, what upset him the most was the way the company let him go with no recognition of all the hard work he had done for the company, and no consideration for the emotional or financial impact of the abrupt termination of his employment.

Lance was under a tremendous amount of stress during this time, due to the fact that he had hundreds of dollars of medication to buy every month. As a result of all the anxiety and stress Lance had a Grand Mall seizure and several additional seizures on Sunday, April 21st. Lance ended up in the hospital where they struggled for some time to get the seizures under control. Once again Lance came very near death. The doctor told us that Lance needed to have someone with him 24 hours a day because of the possibility of additional seizures. When Lance was stabilized, and we had an opportunity to speak with him by phone, he was very weak. The doctor informed us that in all probability Lance only had weeks or, at the most, months left to live. We told Lance that we would be more than willing to take help him and take care of him however long he needed us. Lance was anxious to come up to Tacoma, Washington to visit his Aunts, Uncles and Cousins whom he had not seen for ten years. He seemed to know that he did not have a lot of time left. And this would be his way of seeing everyone a last time. In spite of the fact that there was no one in California available to be with Lance 24 hours a day as he needed, Lance insisted that he wanted to return to California to be near his friends. We agreed to purchase him a round-trip ticket as soon as he was strong enough to travel. However, we let him know that because of Ruth's need for continued physical therapy due to recent injuries received in an auto accident we could only care for him in our home in Tacoma.

We were both very disappointed that Lance was not willing to stay in our home so that we could help care for him. Being there for him was important for several reasons. First of all, we simply wanted to spend with Lance whatever amount of time was left for him to live. Secondly, we feel that our children are our first and highest priority, after our relationship with each other and the Lord. Thirdly, God spoke to our hearts and let us know that caring for our Son was also His Will for us at that time. Since Lance was an adult we simply had to commit him into God's hands and leave it to God to change Lance's mind. So although it was not voiced to Lance, we knew in our hearts that we would be caring for him. How Ruth's Mother's heart ached to hold her Son close once more and for them to share their hearts with each other once again as they did when he was young! We have learned through many situations that God has many ways of bringing about His Will in our lives.

The Taylor family scheduled a family reunion in honor of Ruth's Father's Sister, Bea, who was turning 80 years old. At the same time everyone would be there to see and spend time with Lance. The reunion was to take place at Ruth's Brother's lakeside home at Lake Tapps. Lance was thrilled when he learned about the family reunion and began counting the weeks. We immediately made reservations and purchased an airline ticket for Lance to fly to Tacoma on June 29th. He was scheduled to return to L.A. on July 10th. Once Ruth knew for sure that Lance had improved enough to be released from the hospital and was regaining his strength, she flew to the Midwest to rejoin me in my Ohio Meetings. Ruth had not been able to travel with me for a year now because of some health problems and the necessary recuperation and therapy after her car accident. Since she had basically been cooped up in our apartment by herself, for a year, I felt that she needed to get away for a couple weeks break before Lance's arrival at our home. From Ohio, we drove to West Virginia and ministered in a church there, plus visited a few of Ruth's relatives in the South. We arrived back home in Tacoma, Washington on June 27th, just two days before Lance's arrival.

On Saturday the 29th of June, 1996 we went to the Sea-Tac airport to meet Lance. We knew that Lance was very sick and had lost quite a bit of weight again, but we were not prepared for what we were about to experience as the passengers began to disembark. We stood there anxiously waiting to greet our Son. However, most of the passengers had disembarked from the plane and we still did not see him. At first we were fearful that he may have missed the flight. Then suddenly, we saw one of the flight attendants supporting a tall, skeleton like individual as he slowly walked toward us. He was dressed in a bright mustard yellow suit and was carrying in his hands a bouquet of flowers. After our initial shock we realized that this was our Son. We both embraced him and told him how thrilled we were to have him home with us for a while. Lance handed the bouquet of flowers to Ruth and began to apologize for the condition of the flowers. He explained that he had to literally run through the L.A. airport to avoid missing his plane. He was still so weak from that expenditure of energy that he asked if he could sit down and rest for a few minutes. I asked Lance if he would like a wheelchair to ride in and Lance was quick to say, "Yes" so I quickly went to a service desk and ordered a wheelchair to be brought to our location. Lance kept up a cheerful chatter as we waited for the wheelchair to arrive, and then began to wheel him out of the airport and to the car. I tried to hide my face and the fact that I had to keep brushing tears from my cheeks. I didn't want to create a scene or to make Lance unhappy by my reaction. This was indeed a bitter/sweet moment. Although we had talked to Lance by phone many times I had not seen my Son since those awful days in October 1993, and Ruth had not seen him since a year and a half earlier when she flew to be with him when he was going through such emotional upheaval after Rose's (pseudonym) departure.

As the people kept getting off the plane, I was looking for my Son. Even as Lance and the Flight Attendant were first approaching us, I was looking past them, wondering where Lance was. I kept thinking to myself, "Where is my Son?" And then there was this voice that said, "Hi Mom and Dad!" And I knew that this tall skinny person walking slowly toward me, that I had not yet recognized, was my Son. Tears streamed down my cheeks and were hastily brushed aside as I moved to embrace my Son. Lance was trying to explain to us why he had almost missed his plane. They had actually called for a special electric transporter to convey Lance to the terminal gate, but it was taking so long for it to arrive and out of fear of missing the plane they decided not to wait and had run through the entire terminal to Lance's departure gate. Lance also explained to us that he was suffering from numbness in his feet and legs caused from a lack of blood circulation.

The day before Lance's arrival we had removed some furniture from the back bedroom that Ruth was using for her office, to make room for a twin bed for Lance to sleep on. Ruth helped Lance unpack his small suitcase. Even Lance was surprised by what he had brought, and what he had failed to pack in his suitcase. Lance was very excited, but by this time, also beginning to show signs of fatigue. Later as he went to bed, he snuggled down under the covers and said, "Oh, I love this bed. It is so comfortable." At that Ruth explained to him that this was the bed she had slept in as a young girl until she left home. Lance was very pleased to be sleeping in the bed that his Mother had used when she was a girl. Ruth sat on the edge of the bed and visited with her Son for a while. On seeing that he was very tired she had a word of prayer with him, kissed him goodnight and told him that they could talk more tomorrow.

July 1996

The first few days were a time of reminiscing. Lance was still quite weak, and therefore spent quite a bit of time in bed. Ruth would sit beside his bed as they recalled the many happy memories from his childhood. One evening, as they were talking, Lance asked her if she would lay down beside him and just hold him. Ruth laid down on top of the covers, with her arm around her Son. At that moment, Lance said, "Oh, Mama, this is just what I have needed." He went on to say, "It seems like it has been so long since someone has just loved me." She shared with him stories about his Grandma and Grandpa Taylor's background and conversion to Jesus Christ. Lance had never heard those stories before. Lance had been very close to his Grandma Taylor. In fact, we had lived with her for two years, in-between pastorates. However, Lance's Grandpa Taylor had died when Lance was only 10 months old. Lance enjoyed the stories Ruth shared with him of her own childhood and being raised with her seven brothers and two sisters. When she finished one story his automatic response was for her to tell him another. He seemed to be soaking up the good times and memories of three generations.

One of Ruth's and Lance's favorite memories was in September 1971 on Lance's first day of school. It was a difficult day on Mama to let her son go. On their parting and saying goodbye, Lance turned around and waved and said, "Keep happy harmony in your heart, Mama." At that Mama lost it and burst into tears. Those words became a frequent expression in our home, and even into his adulthood.

A lot of time was also spent with Lance sharing his memories of our times together as a family, as well as our many sightseeing trips throughout Europe and our adventures in West Africa. Lance enjoyed talking and could chatter away for hours as long as someone would listen to him. Lance had an extraordinary, even superior, memory, especially for all kinds of detail. One example was the Sunday that his Father presented his ministry as a prospective Senior Pastor for the First Assembly of God in Ellensburg, Washington. During the following weeks Lance recalled to us what specific people were wearing, the color co-ordinations, and if the persons and shoes of the women matched or not and whether the men's ties went with their suits or not. He never missed or forgot a detail. Years later, as a student at the Ivory Coast Academy in Bouake, Ivory Coast, West Africa Lance's eye for fashion and color proved to be a useful asset. Many of the teen boys came to Lance not only for haircuts but also for advice on their wardrobes for special occasions.

Another memory was the embarrassing time that Lance's Father was serving communion as Interim Pastor at Spanaway Assembly. The Presence of the Lord was very powerful and as I was sharing a few preliminary words I began to weep before the Lord. Ruth had failed to provide me with a fresh handkerchief that morning. When my nose, as well as the tears, began to flow, I found himself in desperate need for something with which I could blow my nose. On not seeing anything immediately available, I proceeded to remove the linen napkin that covered the communion emblems and used it to blow my nose. Ruth remembered that at the time, Lance, upon seeing what his Father was doing, was so embarrassed that he had scooted down in the pew so no one could see him. As Lance and Ruth shared that memory they both burst out laughing uncontrollably until their sides ached. They ended up having to wipe the tears out of their eyes. Lance made the comment, "I still can't believe he did that." Ruth's response to Lance was, "Well, that was better than him using his suit sleeve."

At the Taylor Family Reunion, on the 4th of July, Lance had the opportunity to visit with his Aunts and Uncles and most of his cousins whom he hadn't seen for so long. It was a very happy occasion and memory for him. At first, his emaciated condition was a shock to some. But throughout the day many expressions of love and support were given to Lance. This meant a lot to him and he knew by the end of the day that he had a loving and supportive group of friends and family around him. The day ended with the Family gathering together to sing favorite hymns and choruses. There was also a time of special prayer both for Aunt Bea and Lance. Dan and Barb's home at Lake Tapps held many special memories for Lance. Throughout the years there had been many Family gatherings there, with times of swimming, boating, waterskiing, roasting wieners and marshmallows over an open fire by the water, laughter and good times with the Family. All of these memories came flooding back to Lance that day. As well as the memory of the Taylor Family's "bon voyage party" that was given for us before we left in 1979 for Europe to learn French.

Lance was having a great deal of difficulty eating, and could only eat small portions at a time. Ruth was kept busy trying to come up with appetizing meals in order to encourage Lance to eat and to build up his strength and body weight. When Lance arrived we discovered that he was completely out of some of his medications, and others were almost all gone. In order for us to find out what all his medications were and the schedule for taking them it was necessary for Joseph to talk to his doctor in California. We received a list of Lance's medications from the doctor and were told that we could contact the pharmacy down there and that they could call in an order to our pharmacy in Tacoma.

As soon as we received all the medications Ruth set up a schedule for Lance and brought his medications to him at the proper times throughout the day. Lance had been taking his morning and evening doses all at one time, in the mornings so that he would not have to bother with them at night. The doctor was very concerned because some of these were very toxic medications and he was actually overdosing on them by the way he was taking them.

We also soon came to realize that simple things like handling his own medications, paying bills and taking care of insurance matters, was too mentally and emotionally stressful for him to handle. When his bills were brought to him he didn't even want to see them because he knew he didn't have the money to pay them and it was too upsetting for him to deal with them.

Another immediate problem was the CMV virus (a form of cancer)[57] that he had contracted and which was attacking the retina of his eyes. His eyesight was deteriorating and he had lost most of his peripheral vision. As a consequence, any personal mail and letters he received he was unable to read for himself. So when his mail was brought to him he would ask us to either read it to him or to lay it aside for later. Before

---

[57] Copied from the CDC (Centers for Disease Control & Prevention) WEB site: CMV may cause severe and occasionally life-threatening disease in immunocompromised persons (meaning people with weakened immune systems), such as organ and bone marrow transplant recipients, cancer patients, patients receiving immunosuppressive drugs, and HIV-infected patients (see You Can Prevent CMV, A Guide for People with HIV Infection) A primary (first) CMV infection can cause serious disease in immunocompromised persons. Once a person has had a CMV infection, the virus stays in their body for life. The virus stays dormant (inactive) most of the time, but it can reactivate (become active again) and cause illness. Reactivation of a previous CMV infection is a more common problem for persons with weakened immune systems than primary infection since the majority of people are infected with CMV by the time they are 40 years old. Immunocompromised patients who are concerned about CMV should consult their physicians about the best ways to avoid problems from CMV infection.

Lance had left California he had been included in an experimental program for a new intravenous medication for the CMV virus. His trip to Washington had temporarily interrupted his schedule. He had been told that he could get his infusion (treatment) up here. However, on our investigating the availability of that medicine in Washington State we learned that it was only available in California during this trial period.

To complicate things further Lance began having consistently high fevers, especially at night. Nightly it became necessary to try to cool his body with cool cloths and alcohol rubdowns in an endeavor to bring his temperature under control. There were several nights that his temperature reached 105 degrees. Since Lance belonged to an HMO and was planning to return to California he did not have a doctor here in Washington State. We finally discovered that the fevers were the result of a bad tooth. Since Lance did not have any dental insurance we were scrambling to try to find a dentist that would take him. After contacting the AIDS Foundation here in town we were informed of a clinic that specialized in servicing the welfare and low income people of this area. We soon learned that their schedule was so full already that they only had room for two new appointments per day. And those slots were created in order to take care of any emergencies. However, in making numerous efforts to reach them by phone Joseph realized that he would need to go down at 7 AM and stand in line outside the door until they opened, so that when they opened he would be the first one in line. This assured Joseph of the opportunity to get an appointment for Lance, and was necessary because they would not accept new appointments over the telephone. Even when Joseph did get the appointment there were no openings for two weeks. When Lance was finally able to see the dentist his tooth was terribly abscessed, and the dentist gave him an antibiotic to try to bring the infection under control. It was not until his next appointment, two weeks after the first one that the tooth was pulled and the infection came pouring out of the hole.

Lance had been a very heavy smoker. However, since his seizure he had cut way back to smoking only 5 or 6 cigarettes a day. Because Lance had only expected to be up here for 10 days he had only brought $20 with him. Thus he quickly ran out of funds. Although the doctor had warned Lance that both smoking and drinking were detrimental to his immune system in its present weakened state Lance's attitude was that he was dying anyway so a few cigarettes a day wouldn't make that much difference. We agreed with him and so I offered to purchase his cigarettes for him. Lance was very shocked at my offer offer, knowing that I did not approve of smoking and was aware that the people at the Albertson's Supermarket where we shopped knew that I was a minister. Thereafter, I kept Lance supplied with cigarettes and often paid for them with my own money. As Lance's eyesight deteriorated it even became necessary for me to light his cigarettes for him, since Lance could not see well enough to find or light the end of the cigarette. The only condition we set was that, because of our throat problems and not being able to handle cigarette smoke that Lance would do all his smoking outside on the patio. Lance quickly agreed to that.

On July 10th, in the middle of Lance's dental problems he was scheduled to return to California. However, because of his severe weakness and high fevers Lance was really too sick to travel. We explained to Lance that he needed to make a decision as to whether he would stay on up here in order to have the necessary around the clock care he needed or whether he would return to California. He understood that he was still too weak to return. We explained to him that it would be a simple matter to get his airline ticket changed due to the fact that it was good for a year. Lance said that before he made a decision that he wanted to discuss the matter with Rose (pseudonym). Rose questioned us concerning Lance's condition and our willingness to continue caring for him. We assured her that we would be more than happy to care for him as long as he needed our help. Rose then expressed to Lance that she thought it would be best for him to stay with his parents so that he could get full time care. Lance agreed to remain in Tacoma and we had his flight cancelled.

Now that we knew that Lance would be staying with us in Tacoma, we were overwhelmed with the work involved in getting all of his medicines and care providers transferred to Washington State. We soon came to realize that caring for Lance, plus making all the telephone contacts to get all of Lance's benefits transferred to Washington, in the beginning, was more than one person could handle alone. Thus we agreed that I would concentrate on the business end of things while Ruth would focus on Lance's personal care—and getting him to and from his doctor appointments. However, in practice there was a lot of overlap. There were many times when I helped Ruth with Lance's personal care. I spent many hours daily on the phone, working with doctors, hospitals, health care givers, insurance people, social security people, social service workers, AIDS foundation workers, and the list goes on and on.

In my inquiry with Lance's medical insurance company we learned that his insurance with them had been terminated as of May 31st of 1996 due to the termination of his employment with GODIVA. Lance said that he thought he had applied to COBRA for future benefits. However, in contacting COBRA they informed us that they had not received the application or the first premium. We made a quick call to Rose (pseudonym) who was staying in Lance's house at the time and asked her to see if she could find the necessary paperwork. Rose agreed to find the paperwork and get it filled out and sent it to the company with the first premium payment. However, the monthly premiums were $144 per month and Lance was concerned because he desperately needed the coverage but, being on Social Security, could not afford the premiums. It took weeks of being transferred from one person to another, filling out forms and applications, plus getting special permission from Lance (including sometimes written permission) for every detail that needed to be taken care of before we were able to get Lance medically situated in Washington State.

We contacted the AIDS Foundation in Tacoma and explained to them our concern regarding the payment of Lance's medical insurance premiums. We were informed that the foundation had a program (called The Evergreen Program) which helped people with AIDS pay their insurance premiums. On July 19th someone from the AIDS Foundation came to our home to help us fill out the necessary paperwork so that Lance could be involved in the program. The Evergreen Program[58] was a great blessing for Lance and paid his monthly insurance premiums up through his death. I was checking weekly with the AETNA Insurance (insurer for the COBRA Program) to make sure that Lance was actually covered. There was some confusion over whether the paperwork and premium payments were to be sent to COBRA or to AETNA. This caused many weeks of additional delay in Lance receiving the benefits of this program. The first check was returned to Evergreen because, not only was the address wrong, but the premium amount were not correct. After weeks of my continuous telephone follow-up with AETNA, COBRA and The Evergreen Foundation we finally got the problem resolved.

On July 20th, Lance was sitting in the living room with us and said that he wasn't feeling well. Suddenly, he began to perspire profusely. Perspiration was dripping off of his face, running down his arms, and soaking his T-shirt. As soon as we dried him off he would be soaked again. At this point we called a family member who was a Doctor of Internal Medicine. He suspected that Lance needed a transfusion and suggested that we take Lance to the Emergency unit of a hospital, since he did not as yet have a doctor up here. On mentioning this to Lance,

---

[58]   Named Evergreen because Washington is the "Evergreen State"

he let us know that he did not want to go into the hospital. He still had bad memories of his experience in the Fall of 1993 when he almost died. He was afraid that if he went to the hospital that they would want to keep him there, and that he would not be able to come back home. We assured him that we would not let that happen. On that basis he agreed to go. This was sometime during the second or third week of July. It was necessary for Lance to receive several pints of blood. They did insist on him staying overnight for observation, but he was released the next day.

July was passing quickly and Lance had still not received his CIDOSOVIR infusion because the medical insurance refused to pay for it unless a doctor gave it that was especially trained in the protocol necessary to the administration of that medicine. Finally, on July 23rd his local doctor, Dr. Demaio, contacted APRIA Health Care providers to come to our apartment weekly to give Lance his infusion. Lance had to take a pre-medication, Probenecid, at 9:30 AM and then the nurse would start the hydration process about 11:30 AM, followed by the infusion at 12:30. This process was continued weekly through August.

It wasn't until after several weeks of filling out much paper work, making many phone calls, required referrals, and going through much red-tape before we were able to get Lance's first primary care giver appointment in Tacoma. The paper work was necessary to get his medical records transferred from California to Washington. Our greatest obstacle in finding a primary care giver was the limited number of doctors in this locality who were certified physicians with Lance's HMO. Of the eleven who were certified all but two had full patient loads and were not taking any new cases. It was not until I called the last doctor on the list that he found a primary care giver for Lance. It was only after seeing this primary care giver, Dr. William Lee, that Lance was able to obtain a referral to a local AIDS specialist. Lance found a Doctor Demaio, who was an AIDS specialist, and who agreed to accept him as a new patient. However, he was not certified by Lance's HMO. However, because of the seriousness of Lance's condition he agreed to go ahead while he was working on his certification, and to delay the billing until the completion of the certification process. We were very thankful and appreciative to Dr. Demaio, for his sensitivity and efforts on our Son's behalf. So much time had already been lost and Lance was losing ground fast. One of the first things Dr. Demaio did was to put Lance on the new Pro-Tease Inhibiters. This new combination of medicines is not a cure for AIDS but has had success in slowing down the process of AIDS in some patients. Dr. Demaio started Lance on these medications one at a time so that Lance's body could adjust to them more easily, and also so we would be able to better determine how Lance's body was responding to them individually. The doctor warned us that these medications were very toxic so that it was very important for him to take them at exactly the times prescribed and not on an empty stomach. Since Dr. Demaio was starting Lance on the new medications so late in the progression of the disease he could not guarantee that these would help Lance. Most of the AIDS patients who are helped with this combination are those in the early stages of HIV infection. Lance was now in the very last stages of AIDS and his T-Cell count was down to 8 or 9. This meant that Lance's body and immune system no longer had the ability to fight against bacteria, viruses or diseases.

Because Ruth was having such difficulty with getting Lance to eat, the social service sent out a nutritionist to see how we could increase Lance's intake. She began by asking Lance questions and filling out a personal profile on Lance. It was during this time that Lance revealed to her that the two weeks before his arrival up here he had completely stopped eating and taking his medications. In fact, he acknowledged that he had spent most of his days and nights laying on his bed crying and asking God to take his life. On hearing that, Ruth was overwhelmed with emotion to realize that our Son had been at such a desperate point and we were totally unaware of his emotional state. We were so thankful for the opportunity that God was now giving us to be with and care for our Son. Many times during those first few weeks Lance would apologize for all the extra work he was causing us. Ruth quickly told him that it was not necessary to apologize and that that was what love and family was all about. She added that she counted it a privilege to be able to be there for him and care for him.

Later, as the nutritionist was taking measurements of Lance's arms and legs Lance shared some insights on himself. He told her that he had been an extra in a Hollywood movie. The nutritionist was very interested and inquired about what movie he was in. He told her that he was an Extra in the film, Schindler's List. She responded very excitedly and said that that was one of her favorite movies. Then she asked him what part he had played. Lance responded with a straight face and said that he had played the part of one of the men behind the barbed wire fence of the concentration camp. The nutritionist remarked about how lucky he was to have had an opportunity like that. Even Ruth spoke up and said, "Lance, you never told me that." Lance's response was made with a continued straight face, as he said, "Oh, Mother!" with a tone of unbelief at our gullibility. At that, the nutritionist and Ruth both burst into laughter. This was another example of Lance's ability to bring humor into negative and even life-threatening situations. In spite of Lance's physical ups and downs he never lost his ability to make people laugh. The nutritionist provided Ruth with recipes for enriched drinks that would make it easier for Lance to take in sufficient calories and possibly keep up his weight.

Several weeks after his arrival in our home Lance began to complain of severe itching. It was then he informed us that he contracted scabies several months before. He had gotten medication from his doctor in California and thought he had gotten rid of the problem. However, on examining Lance, it was evident that the scabies were back. He evidently either had not taken the medication long enough or had not adequately washed all his bedding, towels, and clothes. We were able to get the necessary medication from his Doctor. Ruth rubbed the crème all over his body, from head to foot. It was also necessary to wash all his bedding, towels, clothes, etc. to make sure that not one knit or egg was left alive. The process was then repeated a week later, just to be sure. It was about this time that Ruth realized that she was now itching and scratching. Guess what? She had contracted the scabies from Lance. More medicine was gotten and the process was repeated with Ruth. This required that all of our bedding, towels and clothes also had to be washed in hot water. The surprise with this particular episode was that I did not contract scabies also since Ruth and I sleep in the same bed. We were all relieved when that ordeal was over. Scabies is sometimes referred to as "the seven year itch".

Some additional insight on the care of a person who is dying of aids might be helpful to the younger generation considering questions about lifestyle.

Because of Lance's increasing problem with diarrhea we placed plastic runners down the hallway of our small apartment. I frequently helped my Son from his bed, down the hallway to the bathroom. Frequently Lance would be defecating as he walked toward the bathroom. By this time he was no longer able to care for himself and so I would need to wipe his bottom for him and clean him up then get him back down the hallway and back to bed. We would need to avoid the feces he had left behind him when we first came down the hallway toward the bathroom. After getting him back to bed, I would need to get a bucket of hot water mixed with a strong disinfectant and clean up the mess. This was a process of cleaning and disinfecting several times for each event. It was important to get the plastic runners and also any carpet area affected totally disinfected for the benefit of all three of us (Ruth and I and our Son).

Once, while bathing him, I was leaning over the tub when Lance became sick. The vomit came out of his mouth like a gusher and covered my face (eyes and mouth). Lance's immediate response was to say, "Oh Dad, I'm so sorry!"

So there I was, gagging and wiping my Son's vomit out of my eyes and off my mouth while I tried hard not to regurgitate back on top of him. Finally, I was able to respond, "Son, it is too late to be sorry but I love you and your Mother and I will continue to care for you and help through this process." Lance had a fear, a dread, of being stuck back in a hospital there to lay until he died. Ruth and I promised that we would not allow that to happen, but would do all we could to keep him in our home and care for him until the end.

So we had to let the dirty water out of the tub and clean us both up before putting fresh warm water back in the tub and continuing Lance's bath. By that time, I also needed a shower, but that would have to wait. Such is life as one cares for a Loved One dying of AIDS.

August, 1996

Sometime during the first part of August we were informed by Suzanne, Lance's AIDS Foundation Case Worker, that Ruth was eligible for benefits as Lance's Primary Home caregiver. Suzanne came to the house and filled out the necessary paperwork for Ruth's official appointment. Even though these benefits would not amount to a significant income, every little bit helped since we had ceased teaching their seminars in order to give Lance the 24 hour, around the clock care he needed,—and thus had no income. Suzanne also told Lance that it was important that he consider filling out the necessary paperwork for: (1) a living will; and, (2) for his parents to have a power of attorney which would give us the legal right to make emergency medical decisions for him. Lance decided to do as Suzanne had suggested and she helped him fill out the necessary paperwork. Lance stated in his living will that he did not want to be put on a life support system or to be revived when he died.

On August the 7th, Dr. Demaio called us informing us that Lance's blood count was down to 19 and that he was in need of another blood transfusion. Arrangements were made through an APRIA Health Care nurse for the blood transfusion to be given Lance here at the house the next day.

We learned that on Lance's termination from his employment that Lance had filed a suit through the California Department for Fair Employment and Housing Agency against GODIVA. Lance felt that the main reason he was terminated was because he had AIDS, not because the lease was up on the building, as had been stated to him. Lance had previously managed a GODIVA store in San Francisco and it was when the lease on that building expired that Lance was transferred to the store in Sherwood Oaks. On August 13th, 1996 Lance received a communication from the California Department of Fair Employment concerning a response to the suit. At this point the evidence was inconclusive and they wanted to do some further investigation into the matter. Lance let her know that he wanted the case to be pursued because he felt that after all the years of hard work that he had put into the company that he was not treated fairly in the manner of his termination or the terms of his severance pay. In Lance's physical condition the sudden termination without proper notification caused him a great deal of stress and emotional trauma.

It was about this time that a friend of Ruth's that she had known from childhood, Mrs. Margie Craighead, came to Tacoma for a visit. Ruth's Sister in-law, Barbara Taylor, called and suggested that Ruth take advantage of Margie's visit to get away for a couple days of R&R. This would also give Ruth some time to visit with Margie. I offered to care for Lance and encouraged Ruth to accept the invitation. Lance and

I took Ruth to Lake Tapps and then stayed for dinner before returning to Tacoma. It was a much needed and welcome break for Ruth from all the stress and responsibility. Margie and Ruth spent hours talking and sharing together. Lance and I drove up to the Lake on Sunday afternoon to pick Ruth up.

Toward the end of August a Social Worker came to see how Lance was doing. During the visit Lance made a comment to a Social Worker to the affect that he is his Mother's favorite child. Several days later the subject came up again between Ruth and Lance. Ruth explained to Lance that she loved both of her children. She emphasized that each of them were special to her in their own unique way. Her exact words of reassurance to Lance were, "Son, you have always held a very special place in my heart as my first child and only Son. And you always will. No one could every take your place." Ruth also explained that due to their similar personalities, temperament and interests, that they had much more in common with each other and thus found it easier to communicate with and understand each other. However, Lance was greatly offended and refused to be comforted or reassured by this. The earlier comment hurt him deeply and he refused to turn loose of the hurt, no matter what explanations and reassurances of love that Ruth gave him. This became a catalyst for him turning against his Mother with great bitterness. In retrospect what needs to be realized is that, in retrospect, it is obvious that Lance wanted to return to his childhood and to be a little boy again. He just wanted his Mommy to hold him and let him be a little boy again. He was dying and knew it. But, for a while he wanted to pretend that he was his Mother's favorite and to emotionally hold on to the security of being his Mommy's little boy again. Those were the feelings he was already having that first night as Ruth tucked him lovingly into bed, talked with him as she had so often done during his boyhood, and then kissed him goodnight.

Toward the end of the conversation the Social Worker inquired if we had had any discussion concerning Lance's funeral arrangements. Ruth was very appreciative that the subject had come up because Lance became very upset if she brought up any negative subject. Ruth quickly spoke up and acknowledged that we had not yet discussed the topic. The Social Worker told us that we needed to talk about it so that we, Lance's parents, would know his desires. Lance spoke up and said that he really preferred to be cremated. The thought of cremation was horrifying to Ruth and I and she expressed that she would have a hard time with that. Ruth expressed to all of us that it was hard enough losing her Son at such a young age without having to deal with his cremation on top of everything else. The Social Worker told us that we needed to discuss this further and come to some agreement.

Lance's Cousin, Tammy Taylor Krob, offered to purchase tickets for Lance and his Sister so that they could attend the Jesus of Nazareth play in Puyallup. Lance was very excited and was looking forward to seeing the Play. However, when the time arrived for getting ready to go, Lance was not feeling well and just the thought of getting ready seemed too much to him. So we ended up not going and called the Play Office to free up those seats.

Lance's bedroom was right across the hall from Ruth's and my bedroom. Since Lance was having so much difficulty getting around because of his loss of eyesight we kept the hall light on in case he had to get up during the night to use the restroom. His bedroom door was always left open at night so that he could go toward the light to get to the bathroom and also so we could hear him in case he needed us. Ruth had a habit of trying to sleep with one ear open in case Lance called.

One night, about 1 AM, Ruth woke up very suddenly. In spite of the fact that she had not heard any sound she intuitively knew that Lance needed her. She jumped out of bed and rushed into Lance's room where she found him on his hands and knees in the middle of his bed. Lance appeared to be digging with his hands. Ruth asked him what he was doing. He said that he was trying to get rid of the snakes in his bed. Ruth reassured him that there were no snakes. After several minutes of reassuring and calming him she was able to get him sufficiently awake so that he could tell her what was happening. Lance said that he had dreamt that he was in a pit with snakes in it. He said that he hated snakes and that he was trying to kill them, but that they would not die. He said that as soon as he seemed to get one snake killed it just came back to life again. Ruth asked him what he thought the dream meant. Lance said that he didn't know. Ruth then asked him if he remembered what snakes represented in the Bible. Lance seemed still to be a little groggy and did not answer her question. Ruth then reminded him of the story of Adam and Eve in the Garden of Eden and asked him who it was that came to tempt them. He said it was the devil. Ruth told him that throughout the Bible snakes were representative of Satan and evil spirits.

Ruth then applied the dream to his own life and shared with him how Satan had gotten many footholds in his life over the past ten or twelve years. Ruth explained how Satan had ensnared Lance with many bad habits and sins, and that Satan did not want to let go of his hold on Lance's life. Ruth shared with Lance that he, Lance, was the only one that could decide who it was he was going to allow to control his life— God or Satan. She shared with him the Scripture that says that we are to choose "this day who we will serve". Ruth warned him that he was running out of time and that he needed to make his decision soon. Lance responded by telling his Mother that he did love God. Ruth replied and told him that it isn't enough to say that we love or believe in God but that our lives, actions, and words should demonstrate our love and belief in God. Lance was very open and receptive to Ruth's sharing with him about spiritual things. Ruth then asked Lance if he wanted her to have a word of prayer with him, and he said that he did. So Ruth prayed with him before going back to her bed.

Several weeks later Ruth was again awakened out of a sound sleep with strong impression that Lance needed her. She rushed into his room to find him sitting up in the middle of his bed and just staring into space. Ruth asked him if there was something wrong. Lance told her that he had just had a terrible experience. Ruth asked him if he would like to share it with her and sat down on the edge of his bed. Lance told his Mother that the Devil had just come into his room. He went on to explain that he had seen a figure standing just inside the entrance of his bedroom doorway, dressed in a black, hooded garment. Lance said that the figure had looked at him and pointed his finger at him and laughed at him. Lance demonstrated for his Mother what the laugh sounded like; and what that was could best be described as a "hideous or mocking laugh". Ruth then asked Lance about how he had responded. Lance told her that he had said something like either, "Devil, I plead the Blood of Jesus against you" or "I rebuke you in the Name of Jesus".[59] Ruth told him that he had responded correctly, and then asked Lance what had happened next. Lance said that the figure had simply disappeared, and that then Ruth had come in. Ruth took the opportunity to share with Lance that the Devil was letting him know that he had no intention of loosening his hold on him. Ruth reminded him that John 10:10 warns us that the Thief (Satan) comes to steal, kill, and destroy. Ruth explained to Lance that the devil was not just out to destroy Lance's physical body but that he also was out to destroy Lance's soul and send him to hell. Ruth also shared that the Bible tells us that Christ came to bring us life, not only life on earth, but eternal life where we would reign (rule) with Him forever. Ruth asked Lance which Master he was going to serve. Lance responded by saying that he hated the devil because he had influenced him to make wrong choices and ruined his life. Ruth reminded Lance that he could turn that around by resisting the Devil and

---

[59]   We can't quite remember which it was

189

choosing to serve God. Lance again told his Mother that he believed in God, and she responded by reminding him that the Scripture says that even the demons believe and tremble. She went on to say that "to truly believe in God" means that one will choose to live according to God's Word. Ruth emphasized with Lance the importance of surrendering our Will to the Will of God and of allowing Him to guide and direct our lives. Lance was very receptive to all that his Mother had said to him. Lance was deeply touched by what Ruth was sharing. Ruth reminded Lance that there was a battle going on for his soul and that he was the only one that could determine who would win, the Devil or God. Ruth asked Lance if she could have prayer with him and he quickly agreed. After a word of prayer Ruth tucked him under the covers, kissed him goodnight, and went back to bed. This experience had really sobered Lance and caused him to do some serious thinking.

One night, about this time, I had a dream that greatly disturbed m but that was to later prove to be a helpful guide to us for understanding the dynamics of what was going on behind the scenes, in the spirit world. I dreamed that I was standing beneath a row of large blackbirds and was trying to scare them away. At first, in the dream, I tried shouting at them and waving my arms in an effort to frighten them away. Next, I tried throwing things at them (rocks and sticks), but the birds only looked at me and did not move. Then I came over and stood directly beneath them and began to jump up towards them. The longer I jumped the higher and closer to them I got, until I was jumping up and looking directly into their eyes. But the birds just stared at me with a piercing gaze, unblinking and undisturbed. I was frustrated that I couldn't drive the birds away and continued to jump up and look into their large, yellow glowing eyes. The birds continued to look at me, but did not move.

Ruth had learned to tell when I was dreaming because of the noises I made. This time, my feet were moving in response to the dream and Ruth shook me awake and asked me if I were dreaming. I then told her the content of the dream. Ruth wanted to know if I thought the dream had any meaning. At first, I responded by saying he wasn't sure, but I knew I was disturbed by the dream. The dream continued to haunt my mind until, several nights later as we lay in bed, Ruth said, "I know what the birds represent!" She continued, "They represent demonic or evil spirits." In later discussions about the dream the meaning would gradually unfold. The birds represented evil spirits waiting to attack Lance. They were hindered from attacking him because Lance was in our home, which was protected by the Blood of Jesus. This was so because of Ruth and I being, ourselves, redeemed by the Blood of Jesus and thus under His Covenant Protection. It was for this reason that Ruth and I would be so disturbed by later events, and people's actions. Events and people who would be used of Satan to try to get Lance out of our home and out from under the protection of the Blood of Jesus which protects our home. During the last few days of Lance's life, I became very protective of Lance and would not allow people to come visit him who might carry with them evil, or demonic influence. This was not understood by some, but in the end, Lance would experience great spiritual victory, unhindered by demonic pressure through other people.

Thursday—August 29th—Lance was having occasional pains in the area of his intestines so Dr. Demaio ordered that an ultrasound be given on August 29th to try to determine the cause of the pain.[60] The results of the ultra-gram came back negative with no answers about why he was experiencing these pains.

September, 1996

Labor Day was coming up and we decided that we would have a Bar-B-Que. Lance was all excited and wanted to help because he

---

[60] How long was Lance in the hospital or was this an outpatient thing?

enjoyed cooking. However, because of his lack of stamina it was his Mother that ended up making most of the preparations. I got the Bar-B-Que ready on the back patio and cooked the shish kabobs for us. Ruth fixed a macaroni salad and a Jell-O salad, plus a fresh vegetable plate with lots of dip. On the completion of the meal we all sat down to enjoy the food. We were all disappointed when, after three or four bites, Lance said he was full and could not eat any more. However, no one was more disappointed than Lance. The effects of the wasting syndrome plus all the different medications that made him sick every day were really having a negative effect on Lance's physical condition. The medications were extremely toxic and very hard on his already weakened condition. In spite of the fact that Lance wasn't able to enjoy the meal it turned out to be a wonderful family experience.

One of the problems that Lance was having concerned the need for blood samples to be taken regularly. His arms soon became like pincushions. One day, on Lance's exiting from the Laboratory; Ruth noticed that he had about eight cotton balls taped up and down both arms. When Ruth inquired concerning the reason for the cotton balls Lance said that each one represented a place where they had tried to draw blood. Ruth's heart ached for him because of the unnecessary suffering those cotton balls represented. So, on Lance's next visit to the doctor we inquired about the possibility of something being done to alleviate the problem. The doctor informed us the possibility of inserting a life port in Lance's chest. A Life Port is small plastic or metal disk with a slightly raised rubber injection site that is inserted just below the skin. The rubber injection site is called the Port Septum. The Septum is made of a silicone material which reseals itself after each use. This allows the Septum to be punctured many hundreds of times with a special needle. Attached to the base of the Port is a narrow flexible tube or catheter. The catheter is inserted into a large blood vessel and delivers the infusion through the Port directly into one's blood stream. It can also be used to draw blood samples so that it becomes unnecessary to insert needles into the person's body when drawing blood. At first Lance did not want to have something inserted into his chest. However, after some time of contemplation and remembering all the painful encounters with needles he chose to have the Life Port inserted into his chest. This was done at the hospital in day surgery. However, when the time came for him to be discharged he had not been able to keep anything on his stomach. Therefore it was insisted that he stay in the hospital overnight. He was discharged the following day.

On Monday—September 9th, Lance was back in the hospital suffering from severe pain in his intestine area. The doctor had tests run and x-rays taken to try to determine the cause of the pain. The Doctor suspected that the CMV virus may have spread from Lance's eyes to his intestines. The Doctor told us that if that were the case that Lance would probably only have several weeks to live. Even before the results of the tests were known Dr. Demaio decided to go ahead and begin treatment in an effort to counteract the possible presence of the CMV virus in the intestines because time was of the essence. The pain became so severe that none of the pain relievers they tried even touched the pain. It was decided to put Lance on a morphine drip so that he would not suffer.

After being at the hospital all day with Lance, the reality of the doctor's prognosis suddenly overwhelmed Ruth and she went home physically and emotionally exhausted. We called our daughter, Lani Rochelle, to let her know of her Brother's worsening condition. Lani decided to come to Tacoma after the 10th so she could spend some time with her Brother on the 11th. We had tried to contact Lance's X-wife, Rose (pseudonym), earlier in the day to let her know of Lance's worsening condition. However, we were unable to reach her and left a message on her recorder. After tumbling into bed, we held each other and cried and prayed together before falling into a fitful and disturbed sleep. Suddenly the ringing of the phone beside our bed awakened us. Our first thought was that it was the hospital but we were greatly relieved that it was Rose returning our call. We informed her concerning the doctor's prognosis and that if she wanted to see Lance again she needed to come as soon as possible.

Rose let us know that she definitely wanted to see Lance again and that she would get back to us concerning the time of her arrival. We let her know that she was more than welcome to stay with us at our apartment and that we could provide transportation for her. Rose (pseudonym) called us on Wednesday, September 11th to let us know that she would arrive late that night in Seattle, with her Sister, Mary (pseudonym), plus two of Lance's friends.

Lance's doctor in California had warned us at the time of Lance's Grand Mal seizure in April concerning the deterioration of the mental condition of many AIDS patients. He explained that many patients experience dementia, a progressive loss of memory, confusion, a lack of concentration and sometimes paranoia. We were beginning to see some of these symptoms displayed from time to time. At this time these manifestations became even more pronounced due to the effect of Lance's morphine drip. For example, Lance was having a problem with his lips becoming chapped. He could not find his chap-stick in the drawer of his nightstand beside his hospital bed. He asked if Ruth would check his coat pocket to see if he had left it in there. When Ruth reached into his coat pocket he became very agitated and angrily asked Ruth why she was getting into his things. Ruth responded that she was simply doing what he had requested. Lance's reaction was just a blank, puzzled look, as if he didn't understand what she was talking about. These experiences of forgetfulness and confusion were happening more and more frequently. Lance was beginning to see us as a potential threat to his independence or privacy.

On receiving the results of Lance's tests, the doctor learned that the CMV virus had indeed spread from Lance's eyes to his intestines.

Because the doctor had quickly begun the treatments Lance's condition was beginning to improve. The doctor was already beginning to talk to us about preparations for Lance to go back home. Since Lance had lost a lot of weight due to his inability to keep food on his stomach, the doctor suggested that if Lance continued to improve we might be able to give him some intravenous feedings to bring his weight back up. Lance wanted to have the intravenous feeding and was looking forward to leaving the hospital and coming back home.

It was about 1 PM on Thursday, September 12th when Rose (pseudonym), Mary (pseudonym), and Lance's friends (Fortino and Tom) arrived at the hospital to see Lance. Ruth had been there that morning but had gone home for lunch. I was at the hospital when they arrived and stayed in the room with them for a short time, then left in order to give them some time alone with Lance. I returned to Lance's room about an hour later and was in the room only a few minutes when my Sister, Norma, and her husband Tom Boggs arrived from California. Norma and Tom and not seen Lance since his wedding day and were anxious to see him. Norma and Tom visited with Lance for about an hour before joining me in the waiting room. It was at this time that Ruth returned to the hospital and visited with myself, Norma and Tom Boggs in the waiting room. Shortly thereafter, Tom and Fortino came out and told us that Lance was hungry and that they were going to get him something to eat. While they were gone we decided to go back in and visit with Lance for a while since Ruth had not yet seen Rose (pseudonym) and Mary (pseudonym).

When Fortino and Tom came back with some food for Lance, Rose and Mary decided that they would go down to the cafeteria to get something to eat. Ruth and Norma decided to go with them. While sitting in the cafeteria visiting with Mary and Rose, Ruth brought up the subject of the need to begin thinking about Lance's funeral, and the necessary arrangements. At that point Rose inquired if Lance had talked to us about his desire to be cremated. Ruth responded that the subject had come up once while talking with a Social Worker. She explained to Rose that Lance's wishes had been discussed at that time only briefly, and that Lance had stated that he preferred to be cremated. Ruth then said that the subject had never been discussed again, but had been left hanging and never resolved. Ruth let Rose know that she was having a hard enough time dealing with the impending loss of her Son without having to also deal with the idea of him being cremated.

Ruth also informed Rose that we had contacted a personal friend who works at a mortuary and had asked him for estimates on funeral costs. This friend had offered to help us in any way he could and had given us some preliminary cost estimates. Ruth didn't remember exactly how the subject came up but she thought that Rose indicated that she felt that Lance's wishes should be respected. This brought up the subject of how Lance's funeral expenses were to be paid. Ruth informed Rose that Lance had said that he had lost his life insurance policy at the termination of his employment with GODIVA. Therefore, as far as Ruth was aware, Lance had no money available to cover those expenses. Ruth then inquired of Rose if she was planning on paying the necessary expenses. Ruth told her that it looked like we were going to end up having to cover the funeral expenses, and that since we are basically unemployed that will require us to borrow the money to do so. Rose then stated that there was some money that would be available to help with the funeral expenses. Ruth asked her what the source of the money would be and she said that she would rather not divulge that. Ruth told her that if we were going to be left having to pay all of the expenses we felt we should have something to say in the final decision.

After returning from the cafeteria we all went in to see Lance again. After visiting for a while it was decided that Norma and Tom Boggs and Ruth and myself would return to our apartment and give Lance an opportunity to visit with his friends from California. So we went home and had dinner with Norma and Tom and took the night off for some R&R.

The next day, Friday—September 13th, we were not in a hurry to return to the hospital because we knew Lance's friends would be there, saying "goodbye" to him. Shortly after breakfast the telephone rang. It was Rose who was calling from the hospital and was very upset. She evidently had shared with Lance our conversation from the previous day. Rose talked as if we had already made all the arrangements and said that we were being very selfish, and only thinking about what we wanted. She made several other accusations concerning our motives and Lance's money.

Ruth arrived at the hospital after Lance's friends had left to go back to California. However, when Ruth arrived at Lance's room, a Hospital Social Worker by the name of Lynn was in talking to Lance. Ruth later learned that at the time Lance's friends left Lance had begun sobbing very loudly. Lynn had gone in to find out what was wrong with him. Ruth waited outside his room until Lynn was through talking with him and then went in to see her Son. That afternoon I came to the hospital and talked with Lance about my concerns regarding the disrespectful way that he often spoke to his Mother. I emphasized with Lance that we wanted to continue to care for him, but that his way of talking to his Mother was not acceptable behavior. I told Lance that if he refused to change that we would have to make other arrangements for his care. Lance became very angry at that point and made the statement that he was going to get the last laugh. After that statement, we told Lance goodbye and went home for the night.

Saturday—September 14th—Arrangements had been made through Dr. Demaio for nurses to come to the home and train Ruth for the task of giving Lance his infusion to counteract the CMV virus and also on how to hook up his daily nutritional feedings. Lance was originally scheduled to come home on Saturday, September 14th. However, all of the arrangements had not yet been completed. Ruth called Lance that morning before going to the hospital. Ruth reminded Lance of his two experiences with the Forces of Darkness several weeks previously and of the dream his Father had concerning demonic forces. Ruth also reminded him that there was a battle going on for his soul. Ruth told him that she believed that Satan wanted him out of our home because our home was covered by the Blood of Christ and that Lance was protected by God's Grace in our home. Ruth told him that the choice was up to him whether he wanted to come back to our apartment or not but that if he chose to go elsewhere he was removing himself from God's protection, and making himself vulnerable to Satan's attacks. Ruth then asked him if he had made up his mind for sure whether he was coming home or going elsewhere. Lance told Ruth that he guessed he could try once more. It was at that moment that Lance informed her that Dolly had just arrived in his room. Ruth then told him that she would be coming to pick him up to bring him home.

Ruth then left for the hospital. The reason I didn't go with Ruth was because both she and Lance were pretty upset with each other at that moment. After discussing the matter, Ruth and I agreed that there would be a more calm transition and less chance for unpleasant words if Ruth went alone. Lance was also very upset with me because of the ultimatum I had given him the night before concerning his verbal abuse of his Mother. And I was feeling pretty fed up with Lance's attitudes.

On arriving in Lance's hospital room Ruth encountered Dolly and Karen. Dolly said that she was going to the cafeteria to get some lunch. Ruth reached out to touch Karen and said to her, "We need your prayers, Karen. We are under satanic attack." Karen said, "I know, Auntie Ruth." And with that she also left the room. Ruth and barely begun her visit with Lance when the hospital social worker, Lynn, came in. She asked Ruth if she was aware of the fact that Lance wanted to go back to California as soon as he was strong enough. Ruth informed her that we were very much aware of that. The social worker then informed Ruth that Lance had decided that he did not want to come back to our home, but that he wanted to go someplace else. Ruth told her that she was very surprised to hear that because she had talked to Lance by phone just that morning before she left for the hospital and that he had said that he had changed his mind and wanted to come home. At that, Lynn turned to Lance and asked him what he wanted to do. Lance agreed with Lynn that he did not want to go back home and that he thought it best if he went somewhere else. Lynn said that they had set up a plan for him for regaining his weight and strength so that he could return to California to be near his friends. Ruth was in shock because she knew that there was no one in California that was willing to care for Lance or be there for him.

Ruth learned that because Lance had changed his mind about coming home the social worker had cancelled the orders for the home nursing training for Ruth and other preparations such as the installation of a hospital bed in our apartment. A short while later, Dan and Barbara Taylor came to visit. After they had visited with Lance for a while Ruth asked for Barb to go out to the waiting room with her where Ruth shared with Barb what had transpired. She shared that the change in Lance's decision not to come home had come about immediately after the departure of Rose and Lance's friends. She also shared with Barb that they had not only had an influence on Lance but had actually encouraged him not to come back home. Barb asked Ruth why they would do that. And Ruth told her she didn't know, but for some reason they seemed to feel that they needed to protect Lance from us. Ruth shared with Barb about Rose's upset over the cremation issue and indicated she felt that could have played a part. Ruth told Barb that another person had come up in a conversation between Lance and the Social Worker. Lance had requested that the Social Worker deliver an envelope to this other person. Ruth explained that she had no idea of what the envelope was all about. It seemed that suddenly there was a group of people who were committed to support Lance and his wishes no matter what the cost was to his parents who had expended so unconditional love and practical caring for him. Ruth was feeling betrayed and was uncertain who she could trust. Ruth was so upset that she was weeping uncontrollably. Ruth said that she did not understand how it could be that, since she was Lance's caretaker, that she had not been informed ahead of time about the change in plans. Ruth had not even been consulted or given an opportunity to give her side of the story about what was going on with Lance.

Looking back on it later, Ruth realized that even someone on the medical staff had been involved in this because he had been trying to persuade Ruth that she was not able to care for Lance. We thought that strange at the time because Ruth had been involved in that very process down in California. Ruth inquired of the doctor where they were going to send Lance. And he informed her that two friends of Lance's were out looking for a place for Lance at that very moment. In talking with Lance later Ruth learned that it was a cousin and his x-mother in-law, Dolly (pseudonym), who were trying to find a place for Lance to go to from the hospital.

Ruth was so distraught that she sat out in the waiting room by herself crying and staring into space. It was difficult to believe that after all of our prayers for God to make it possible for us to care for our Son at the end of his life, that Lance was being stolen away from us at this critical moment. There seemed to be nothing we could do about it. Ruth's heart was broken because her greatest desire at this time was to spend whatever time was left with her Son.

On arriving home that evening Ruth poured out her soul to me and our mutual friend, Judy Shelton. Judy had come over to bring some food to us. She had been a tremendous blessing to us by making arrangements with the women from her church, Abundant Life Fellowship, to bring evening meals to us every other day, in order to free up Ruth's time. Judy had brought the food and then tried to leave, but was not able to get her car started. Thus, she was still at our apartment when Ruth arrived, and was there for Ruth at a critical moment when Ruth really needed her. Ruth shared with Judy and I the unexpected happenings of the day. Judy joined us for supper and we talked for an hour or more. That night, I held Ruth in my arms and let her cry herself to sleep.

The next morning, Sunday, September the 15th, Ruth returned to the hospital to see Lance. When Ruth entered Lance's room, Dolly (pseudonym) was sitting at the head of Lance's bed holding his hand and Lance was telling her how glad he was that she had come and how much he had missed her. Ruth was struck with the incongruity of the scene because Lance had often spoken to us about how much of a problem he had with getting along with Dolly and had often spoken of her with words of disdain and criticism. After a while Ruth left the room. Lance was visiting in a very animated way with Dolly and almost completely ignored his Mother. Obviously, they were carrying on for the impact that it would have on Ruth. When Ruth returned to the floor she sat for a long time out in the waiting room because she was having a hard time emotionally dealing with what was happening. What she didn't realize was that actually Dolly had left to go check out some health care facilities that the social worker had told them about. There were a lot of things Ruth would like to have expressed to Lance at that time, but didn't because emotions were running too high, and Ruth also knew that anything she would say Lance would put a negative twist to and would repeat it to Dolly and others.

Ruth continued to sit there alone, trying to contain her emotions, when all of a sudden she saw this young woman walking through the room on the way to the elevator. Suddenly, she turned around and looked toward Ruth and mentioned that she had seen her there quite a bit over the last several days. She came over to talk to Ruth, and Ruth informed her that our Son was there as a Patient. She said that she had noticed Ruth earlier and that Ruth looked familiar to her. The two women began to recount different places where they could have met. Ruth mentioned that her husband was an Assembly of God minister. At that, she stated that her Father was an Assembly of God minister. Then Ruth inquired about her Father's name, and learned that her Father was Leland Gross who had been our Presbyter when we pastored our first church in Yakima, Washington and was now on the Board of Directors of our ministry organization, Church Renewal Ministries. Crystal (the young woman Ruth was talking to) had recognized Ruth from years earlier. When Ruth learned about Crystal's identity, the feeling arose in her that Crystal had indeed been sent to her by God to minister to her at this moment. Ruth began to pour out her heart to Crystal, explaining the turn of events and how everyone seemed to have a word of influence in our Son's decision except for her. Ruth let her know that she didn't understand how they could justify making decisions concerning us and our Son, without our knowledge and without first consulting us.

It was at this moment that Dolly (pseudonym) came back and rushed over to Ruth with the report that she had found a room in a wonderful health care facility for Lance. They had talked to the person in charge at the Bel-Air Health Care Facility and had been assured that Lance would be able to have a room by himself that was clean and bright. On the completion of her bubbly report to Ruth, Ruth turned and introduced her to Crystal. Crystal in turn introduced herself to Dolly as the Administrative Director of the Fifth Floor where Lance was located. Shortly thereafter Dolly left to share her exciting findings with Lance. On learning Crystal's position there, Ruth suddenly realized how timely the conversation was she was having with Crystal. Ruth immediately apologized for taking so much of her time and so freely expressing her concerns. Crystal responded by saying that she felt God had ordained the conversation. The two women had a quick word of prayer together and then she had to leave for an important meeting. Ruth had at last found a sympathetic ear and someone to whom she could express her concerns and pain.

While Ruth was talking to Crystal, Suzanne from the Aids Foundation came over to talk with them. She had just visited with Lance. Lance had told her that his friends had come up from California to visit him. Then she remarked about how wonderful it was for Lance to have someone to visit him who really loved him. The emphasis she had expressed made Ruth feel that we (Lance's parents) were not included in "the ones who loved him". Ruth went in to Lance's room to spend some time with him. After another extremely difficult and emotional day Ruth returned home.

The following day, Monday, September the 16th, arrangements were being made for Lance to be transferred to Bel Air. Ruth again went to the hospital to spend time with Lance. During one of her breaks from her visit with Lance, Ruth went to the Waiting Room and was joined there by Dolly (pseudonym). Dolly began making comments concerning certain things she had heard about our relationship with Lance. One comment was that she was aware of the fact that we did not approve of Lance smoking. Ruth felt that what she was inferring was that with Lance going to a health care facility so that we would not need to be bothered any more. It was at that point that Ruth informed her that his Father had actually been buying Lance's cigarettes for him and had even lit them for him. Ruth told her that since Lance only had months left to live, at the most, that his smoking or non-smoking was not an issue to us. Dolly had no reply to this. Ruth explained to her that our only request was that he not smoke in the house, but that, because of our own health problems, he should do his smoking out on the patio. And this he had gladly agreed to do.

Another comment Dolly made was that she understood how busy we were when we were on the mission field and that we had for that reason sent the kids to Boarding School. Ruth was again surprised by her comment and informed her that she had personally taught Lance and Lani at home our first year in Africa. Ruth let her know that we believed very strongly that the children were our responsibility and we had no desire or intention of sending our children to Boarding School. However, after a year of interaction with other missionary's children and hearing all of their exciting stories about their lives together at the Boarding School Lance and Lani suddenly felt left out and alone. Lance and Lani begged and pleaded with us to allow them to go to Boarding School with the other missionary kids for the coming school year. At first we told them, "no", however, after their continued pleading with us we recognized their need and the importance of social contact with children their own age. We therefore, told them we would consider it on a trial basis for one quarter, but that if they wanted to change their mind all they had to do was let us know. Each additional quarter they were given the same option and each time Lance and Lani both chose to go back to the Boarding School. Ruth explained to Dolly (pseudonym) that Lance had only attended the Boarding School for two school years, for a total of 18 months.

Another topic of discussion was Lance's behavior and the disrespectful way he talked to and treated other people. Ruth made the comment that he was not raised that way; but that he had been taught to be polite and respectful to others. Dolly began to excuse his behavior by saying, "Oh that's just Lance. He talks to everyone that way, but doesn't mean anything by it." Ruth told her that she was not aware of many parents who would tolerate disrespectful and vulgar talk from even their younger children, let alone one of their adult children old enough to know better. Ruth told Dolly that impoliteness and disrespect was unacceptable behavior coming from anyone. Ruth then asked Dolly why it was that everyone makes excuses for Lance. She finally acknowledged that Lance had many times been disrespectful and talked in an inappropriate manner to his own wife, as well as many other people.

Ruth had overheard Lance talking to Lynn, the hospital social worker concerning an envelope that he wanted to give to another person. Ruth was surprised that Lance was asking the social worker to do that, rather than asking his Mother to deliver the envelope. It appeared that Lance was obviously doing something he didn't want his Mother to know about. Ruth expressed her concerns to both Barb and Joseph. She remarked that the other person must someway be involved in Lance's plans. We were obviously being left out, but of what we had no idea. Neither Lance nor the Social Worker made any explanations to Ruth. We were sure that this other relative was not yet aware of what had transpired that weekend during the visit of Lance's friends from California. Therefore, we felt that she was, in all probability, completely unaware of all that she would be getting involved in.

Tuesday—September 17th—On this day, the hospital had made arrangements for Lance to be transferred to Bel Air Health Care Center. When Ruth said something about taking Lance over to Bel Air in our car, she was informed that they had already made arrangements for him to be taken by ambulance. This was another instance in which Ruth, who was his legal executor and official caregiver was ignored and left out of the loop by the hospital social worker. Ruth gathered up all of Lance's belongings, and followed the ambulance over to the health care facility. Dolly (pseudonym), Lance's X-Mother in-law also went by car to Bel Air.

On arriving at Bel Air Lance was not taken to the private room that had been promised for him. Instead, he was taken to a room with another Patient. As soon as he was transferred from the gurney to his bed the first words out of his mouth were, "Oh my God, what have I done?!"

Then he turned to Ruth and said, "Mom, if I apologize to Dad do you think he will forgive me and let me come back home?" Dolly was in the room when Lance made these statements. Ruth turned to Lance and said, "Son, you know it is not a question of forgiveness. We have always and will always forgive you no matter what." Ruth then explained, "It is a question of your attitude and whether you are willing to work together with us to make this time we have together as pleasant and stress free as possible." Within a few minutes the Administrator came with the necessary admittance forms which required Lance's signature. Lance immediately informed her that he was not going to be staying. Dolly was standing in one corner of the room with a sheepish look on her face because getting Lance into a health care facility had been her personal project, the reason she had come to Tacoma. At this point Dolly spoke up and questioned the Administrator concerning the private room that had been promised to Lance. The Administrator responded by apologizing, and explaining that that had been a mistake because those rooms are reserved for people with certain needs because none of the other rooms had the necessary electrical plug-ins. And that Lance's needs did not require that. The Administrator went on and explained to Lance that it was already 5 PM and impossible for them to make any change in plans at this late hour of the evening. He said that if he had to he would just walk out. She begged him not to do that and asked for his cooperation to give them time to work out the details. She said that it normally takes a couple days to make those arrangements. So Lance responded by asking if he could just go home with his Mother. The Administrator explained to him that all the home care nurses and medications and infusions had been cancelled because of his decision not to go back home and that it would take several days to get all that in place again. She promised Lance that this was not a prison and that if he insisted on going elsewhere that he was free to do it. However, it was necessary for him to stay there until the necessary arrangements could be made.

She assured him that it was necessary to fill out the paperwork because he would be staying there until other arrangements could be made. Lance finally agreed to sign the paperwork. However, he once again emphasized that he would not be staying. Ruth assured Lance that she would talk to his Father for him concerning his coming back home, but that the decision really depended on Lance's willingness to cooperate with us and treat us with respect. Ruth stayed long enough to get Lance calmed down and reassured him that she would return in the morning.

Wednesday, September 18th—Ruth purposefully waited until later in the morning to go see Lance in order to give Dolly an opportunity to have some private time alone with him before she returned to California. It was later that day that Lance met and made a new friend in the person of Hal Heine. Hal had been an AIDS patient for 16 years, and, at that time, was the longest surviving AIDS Patient in Washington State. Lance and Hal met when they went both were out in the inner courtyard for a smoke. There was an immediate rapport and friendship established. Lance told Hal that he was very unhappy there and did not plan to stay. Hal suggested looking into the possibility of getting Lance transferred to his room. Lance responded positively to the idea and said that at least he would have someone to talk with. Ruth spent most of the day with Lance.

Thursday, September 19th—The arrangements for Lance's transfer to Hal's room were completed. Lance was to move in with Hal that morning. While the staff and personnel were moving Lance's bed and personal affects, Ruth inquired if there was a private room where she could spend some time talking to her Son. They took Ruth and Lance to an empty room and there Ruth expressed to Lance our concern and hurt over the methods that were used concerning his decision to come to the Bel Air Health Facility rather than coming back home. Ruth let Lance know how hurt and devastated she was to be completely excluded from the decision, as well as the decision making process. Ruth also shared with him our hurt on learning that he had led people to believe that we were not treating him properly. Ruth told him that we loved him and were making every effort to care for him and help him in all his areas of need. Ruth explained that it was painful to have one's hand bitten by the person you are trying to help. Ruth further explained to him that such behavior on his part is not an expression of love from him. Ruth went on to say that true love meant looking out for the welfare of the one you loved, and that was what we had been trying to do. Ruth shared with Lance again that we were more than happy to have Lance come back home and for the privilege of caring for him, but only if he stopped fighting against us. She went on to say that we didn't know how much time he had left to live and that we wanted to take advantage of this time to build happy memories. Ruth also confessed to him that at that moment the memories in her mind were not happy ones. Lance's only response was that he did love us; however, he denied that he had criticized us or made arrangements of any kind without our knowledge. In fact, he said, "Mom, there has not been a conspiracy against you and Dad, even though it might appear that way." In light of the fact that we had never mentioned the word (or concept) of conspiracy to Lance in connection with his activities it was very enlightening to Ruth and I that Lance would make that assertion. Lance did go on to make some vague statement about being sorry (although he never identified what he was sorry for) and then said that he still wanted to come home if we would let him.

Friday—September 20th—The doctor had started Lance on his nutritional feeding (known as, TPN) but had to discontinue the treatments. He said that Lance was having a problem with his liver and thus was unable to continue the feedings until his liver healed. He was also giving Lance white blood cell shots. Lance was extremely upset when he learned that the doctor would not be able to continue the feedings due to the condition of Lance's liver. Lance was anxious to gain 20 pounds so that he could go back to California.

Fortino, one of Lance's friends from California, called again to check on Lance's condition. We informed him that Lance was in a health care facility and that we were planning on getting away for the weekend because of the emotional trauma we had been through with Lance the previous week. I informed Fortino that Ruth had been very distraught over how we had been treated and all the whole transfer came about without our knowledge. It was at this point that Fortino shared with Joseph his surprise and unbelief at the conversations between Lance and the friends from California who had come to visit him that last morning. He made the statement that he had seen a side of Lance that he had never seen before. He also expressed to us his appreciation for our efforts to keep him informed on Lance's condition. He also shared with us that he was aware of our love for Lance and the sacrifices we were making to care for him. He let us know that he respected us very much for what we were doing.

Friday—September 20st—We informed Lance that since he was being well cared for that we were going to take several days off for a much needed period of rest and recuperation. We informed him that we would come in to see him when we got back on Monday. I had originally planned to take this opportunity for us to stay in the home of some friends in the Longview, Washington area so that he could discuss a possible business venture with the friend. Due to Ruth's emotional exhaustion she could not handle the thought of even being around people. I realized that it was important for Ruth and I to spend some time alone for some emotional healing, so I called the friend and backed out of the arrangement.

Saturday—September 21st & 22nd—Ruth and I went to the Holiday Inn Express of Longview, Washington (3 miles off the freeway) and spent Saturday and Sunday alone in the room. We took all our meals in the room and would not even allow the girls to come in to clean the room. We spent much of those two days watching TBN (a Christian network) and crying and talking and sleeping. We arrived back in Tacoma on Monday the 23rd about 1 PM and went directly to Bel Air to see Lance.

Lance inquired on a daily basis if the arrangements had been made for him to come back home. We told him that he was going to have to be patient because the arrangements would take time for completion. However, since he was the one that had made the decision to go to the health care center we felt he needed to suffer the consequences of his choice for a short period of time. Later, after the daily nutritional feedings had begun he again inquired how soon he could come home. We told him that he needed to complete the nutritional feedings first since the feeding arrangements had already been set up for the health care center and also because Ruth had not yet received the necessary training for that activity.

We were both making daily visits with Lance during this time. Ruth would visit Lance in the morning and I would visit Lance in the afternoon and evening. In fact I would often go out and buy special lunches or dinners at fast food places for him and Hal. We would take Lance out into the courtyard for his smokes and would visit with Hal Heine as well. Since Lance would be staying long enough to complete his feeding program he decided he wanted a phone and television in his room. So we made provision for a phone to be installed and he asked us to use $200 of his Social Security check to purchase a portable color TV for him.

Tuesday—September 24th—I talked to Dr. Demaio who said that Lance was back on his TPN and should be able to come home next Monday, the 30th. He said that Lance should be through with his TPN by then and that he would give him steroid pills to help him gain more weight.

Thursday—September 26th—I had made an appointment to meet with Crystal and Lynn, the hospital social worker, concerning the lack of communication with us about where Lance would be going when he was dismissed from the hospital. Crystal had volunteered to mediate the meeting between myself and Lynn. The hospital social worker had taken it on herself to cancel the arrangements for the home care that the doctor had special ordered for Lance, and had done so without informing Ruth, whom Social Services had approved as Lance's Care Giver. A hospital bed had been ordered for our apartment and a portable commode and walker for Lance. The doctor had arranged for nurses to come in and train Ruth in administrating Lance's TPN (his intravenous nutritional feeding). This was all cancelled with not so much as the courtesy of a phone call from the Tacoma General hospital social worker.

My desire was to confront the Social Worker with the fact that she had overstepped her bounds by ignoring Ruth who was Lance's appointed caregiver. I also confronted her with the fact that there was enough pressure on families these days without a government worker interfering in private family matters, especially when they neglected to get the whole story or consider the feelings of everyone concerned before taking action. The feeling was that there had been a conspiracy behind our back and that the Social Worker's job should have been to help bring peace and understanding to the situation instead of aiding and abetting the confusion. Lynn responded by saying that Lance was a 30-year-old man, and that since he was an adult her only obligation was to Lance. After an hour of discussion the meeting came to an end with nothing really resolved.

I hurried home after that meeting to get ready for his annual Board of Directors meeting for Church Renewal Ministries which was held that evening in Kirkland.

Hal, the AIDS Patient that Lance shared a room with took Lance under his wing and was a real friend and helper. By this time Lance's eyesight had further deteriorated and Hal was always there to help him find the bathroom at night when he needed and to help him out into the courtyard so he could have a smoke. Lance was excited about having a buddy that he could talk to. Their relationship had its ups and downs. Their friendship got strained for a while when Hal got on to Lance concerning the disrespectful way he talked to his Mother. Lance did not appreciate Hal's giving him advice in what he considered was a family matter. Hal said that he could not handle being there and hearing Lance's rudeness to his parents, so Hal got where he would leave whenever Ruth came to visit Lance. On learning about the problem Ruth and I had a talk with Hal. We explained to him that Lance had a lot of hurt and anger inside and that since we are the ones that are there he took it out on us. We begged Hal not to allow Lance's problem with us to interfere with his relationship and friendship with Lance. We told him that we were going to continue to work with Lance concerning the problem.

At one point Hal had experienced some small seizures, which had temporarily affected his ability to walk. As a result he was confined to a wheelchair. Lance and Hal decided that they wanted to go out in the courtyard for a smoke. And since none of the family was there at the time to help them, Lance began pushing Hal in the wheel chair down the hallways to the courtyard. Because of Lance's deteriorated eyesight Hal was giving Lance verbal directions about when to turn to the right or left or to go straight ahead. By the two of them working together they managed to arrive safely at their destination.

When Lance got his private phone and TV in the room he shared them freely with Hal. Even when Lance finally left Bel Air he allowed Hal to keep and use his phone and TV the remainder of the month. That way Lance was able to call Hal from home and keep in touch with him. Lance had invited Hal to his 30th birthday party on October 12th.

However, Hal was not physically strong enough to come because of the result of a seizure due to having received a flu shot. Hal and Lance were both very disappointed. They kept a close and warm friendship up until the time Lance died. Hal even came to visit Lance during his last hospital stay. We tried to contact Hal at the time of Lance's death to let him know about the memorial service. However, he was no longer at Bel Air, but stayed at an assisted living apartment here in Tacoma. We were unable to reach Hal but left a message with the caregiver there. About six months after Lance's death we had an occasion to visit Hal at his apartment in downtown Tacoma. He was extremely happy to see us again and cried as we went over memories of he and Lance. He told us how much he missed Lance and expressed his appreciation for our friendship and personal interest in him. Hal later got transferred to the Bailey Boushet hospice in Seattle. We were able to talk to him by phone two or three times but were never able to see him again. The last time we called we talked to a nurse who informed us that dementia has set in and that Hal was no longer able to always discern reality from fantasy.

Saturday—September 28th—During Ruth's visit with Lance today they went out and sat in the courtyard at Bel Air so that Lance could smoke a cigarette. Ruth took advantage of their time alone together to discuss a problem area with Lance that she was concerned about. She talked to him about the importance of forgiving those in his past who had hurt him. Lance indicated that he thought he had forgiven most of the people in his past who had hurt him, except maybe Peter. Ruth expressed that he seemed to have a lot of anger and resentment in him that had built up over the years. Lance seemed surprised by that statement and said he didn't feel angry. Ruth then shared with him how that often he reacts in anger and resentment when something happens he doesn't like or when confronted or disagreed with. Ruth told him that she felt that he had never really dealt with those issues that had built up inside of him. She then talked to him about the importance of working to bring healing and forgiveness to any that he is holding grudges against. Once again she reminded him that we were looking forward to him coming back home so that we could care for him. However, he needed to make some adjustments in his attitudes and reactions. One does not treat someone they profess to love with disrespect and resentment. Ruth shared with Lance that this was a very stressful and difficult time for all of us and that we needed to work extra hard at being sensitive and kind with each other.

Monday—September 30th—Lance had finished his TPN program and the doctor had told him he could come back home now. The administrative staff, with social services, had arranged a meeting with myself and Ruth to make arrangements for Lance's home care. They told us that in spite of the fact that Lance had complained and wanted to come home the whole time that he had developed some close friendships and enjoyed himself, in spite of himself. We were in the middle of discussing Lance's home care when Lance suddenly entered the room. He expressed his desire to continue the TPN feedings until he got his weight back up to 120 pounds. Everyone was in shock, including Lance, who said, "I can't believe I'm doing this." They said they would talk to the doctor and see if that could be arranged. The nurses mentioned the importance of Ruth being trained to give Lance the intravenous Ganciclovir. Since Lance decided that he wanted to stay longer the training was postponed until just before Lance would go home. The Bel Air staff contacted Dr. Demaio concerning Lance's desire to continue the intravenous feedings for several more days and Dr. Demaio consented for that to happen.

Tuesday—October 1st—Dr. Demaio said it was necessary for Lance to have a blood transfusion. For some reason, they were unable to do that at Bel Air. For that reason, Lance was transported by ambulance to the Tacoma General Hospital for a blood transfusion. He was then kept overnight for observation to make sure that he was stabilized. We then picked him up in the car and transported him back to Bel Air. It was at this time that Paul Dodson, who was in charge of the MK Program (MK=missionary kids) for the Assemblies of God Division of Foreign Missions out of the international headquarters in Springfield, Missouri, happened to be in town. Paul was a close friend to Lani and offered to bring Lani to Tacoma to see her Brother. Thus, Paul Dodson and Lani Rochelle were able to visit Lance while he was still in the hospital.

Wednesday—October 2nd—Lance was to be discharged from the hospital today. Ruth went and picked him up in the car and drove him back to Bel Air. During Lance's stay at Bel Air I would often go and spend several hours in the afternoons and evenings with Lance. Lance would often call me and ask me to bring him some "real food" (like, ham & cheese hot pockets, or a hamburger and French Fries or a taco from Taco Bell). He would also ask me for a Milk Shake which I was delighted to get for him. We tried to get as much food down him as possible because he was very anxious to get back up to 120 pounds. Several times I got special permission to take Lance on short outings in order to get him out of the health care facility. I would take him for a drive and sometimes we would stop and get something to eat. Lance made it clear that he enjoyed our times together, and, of course, the feeling was mutual. It was during one of these drives that I took him to Wells Fargo so that he could open his own Bank Account and have his social security checks wired directly to his account.

The decision was made for Lance to be discharged on Saturday, October 5th. Therefore, arrangements were made for Ruth to come in early in the morning of the 3rd and 4th to be trained in giving Lance his

Ganciclovir. [61] Since Ruth was already going in each morning it just meant that she would go in a little earlier. The possibility of having a nurse come to the home to help bathe Lance was discussed, but we said that wouldn't be necessary at this point in time. The nurse also mentioned that we could contact the Olsten Kimberly Home Health Care. These people are skilled nurses and able to give us a lot of help. We did obtain their services. One of the things the nurse did for us was to regularly change the bandages around Lance's life port which was embedded in his chest.

Lance was thrilled and excited when he finally attained the 120 pounds that he had been working toward. So on Saturday, October 5th, Ruth and I went to Bel Air to get our Son and bring him home. We gathered all his clothes and belongings together which necessitated several trips to the car. The nurses and other patients were coming in to tell Lance good-bye. He had a particularly hard time in saying good-bye to Hal Heine, who had become a very good friend. Lance assured him that he would keep in touch with him and left his phone there for Hal to use for the remainder of the month. This made it possible for Hal to call Lance whenever he wanted to talk, and Lance could call him. Lance also left his television there for Hal's use, since we had a television at our home that he could watch. The one disappointment for Lance, in coming back home, was the fact that his bed had been taken out and a hospital bed installed in its' place. The hospital bed was not as comfortable.

---

[61] Ganciclovir is used to treat cytomegalovirus (CMV) retinitis (eye infection that can cause blindness) in people whose immune system is not working normally. Ganciclovir capsules are used to treat CMV retinitis after the condition has been controlled by intravenous (injected into a vein) ganciclovir. Ganciclovir is also used to prevent cytomegalovirus (CMV) disease in people who have acquired immunodeficiency syndrome (AIDS) or who have received an organ transplant and are at risk of CMV disease. Ganciclovir is in a class of medications called antivirals. It works by preventing the spread of CMV disease or slowing the growth of CMV.

However, it was much easier on Ruth's back, and allowed her to raise and adjust the bed when needed. It also made it easier for Lance to get in and out of bed. I purchased plastic runners which we installed from his bed to the door, and then down the hallway to the bathroom, and beyond to the Living Room. Because Lance was so skinny the diarrhea would often leak from around his underwear and down his legs. Often it was necessary for Ruth to mop the bathroom floor several times a day. Ruth and I were delighted to have Lance back home again, even though we knew we were in for a lot of hard work in caring for him.

It was during the next couple days (Sunday and Monday mornings) that a nurse came to our apartment and instructed Ruth on the techniques necessary for hooking up Lance's Ganciclovir and flushing the lines to his Life Port. Lance's Ganciclovir was hooked up to a different machine than what was at Bel Air, and this necessitated Ruth being re-trained for the new machine. The nurse emphasized with Ruth the importance always putting on gloves before she started connecting Lance to the lines. In fact, Ruth had to put on a second pair of gloves over the first pair as added protection because it was warned that the Ganciclovir is chemotherapy, and very toxic. The nurse warned Ruth that if she should accidently get any of the Ganciclovir on her skin that she was to stop what she was doing immediately and to go and wash her skin thoroughly with soap and water. The Ganciclovir is so toxic that it can actually burn and damage the skin. On hearing that, Ruth understood a little better Lance's complaints about pumping the poison into his veins. It was this toxic medication that caused Lance so much nausea and vomiting. However, the Ganciclovir was necessary to control and slow down the growth and spread of the CMV virus that had already gone from his eyes down into his intestines. If the CMV virus continued to spread in his intestines and other organs the pain would become unbearable. As it was, it was necessary for Lance to be on pain medication continuously.

Tuesday—October 8th—On this day I received a phone call from my Sister, Norma, who explained that her husband, Tom, was in the Redding, California hospital for an angioplasty, necessary for unclogging an artery. The doctor had said that he was on the verge of a heart attack because of the severe blockage. I later received another phone call saying that the procedure had been postponed until the next day. I then called Tom and at his room in the hospital and had a word of prayer with him.

Wednesday—October 9th—This was the day before Lance's 30th birthday and I went to pick up Lani from the bus stop. Lani had come from Seattle to see her Brother and spend his birthday with him. Lance gave me $10 to get him a key so that he could use the apartment complex tanning bed any time he wanted. Dan and Barb were going to be leaving on a trip the next day so they came by this evening to see Lance and to bring him a birthday cake and wished him a happy birthday. So we all had cake and something to drink and sang Happy Birthday to Lance.

Thursday—October 10th—Lance's 30th Birthday! Ruth and I had been so busy with preparations for Lance's homecoming and care that we did not have much time to make special plans for his birthday. Ruth talked to Lance about a party, but he said he didn't want one. So we just planned a cozy family celebration for him! Lance wanted to go on a trip to Seattle with his Dad for his birthday. However, one of his cousins said she had a gift and card that she was going to bring by. So it was necessary to wait and not leave until after her visit. Ruth even called the Cousin to check to make sure she was planning on coming. The Cousin assured Ruth that she would be coming but a little later than she originally stated. She never did show up that evening and Lance was very disappointed and upset. Because he had waited all day to make the trip to Seattle but now it was too late and he was too tired. I assured him that he would take him another day. Ruth overheard Lance talking with a friend in California and mentioning that this had not been much of a birthday. Ruth determined right then that she would go ahead and give him a special birthday party. She felt that the fact that Lance had reached his 30th birthday was something to celebrate, so she began to make plans for a belated party.

I took Lance for an outing several days later. Once again, the Cousin had called and said that she wanted to bring Lance his birthday card. Lance and I waited until after the time she said she would be here but when she had not arrived at the pre-arranged time, Lance said that he did not want to miss a second outing. Later on, this Cousin called to let us know she was going to be late, but Ruth informed her that they had left on a pre-planned trip to Seattle. Lance was really upset by this second time that this family member had "stood him up". They started to go to Seattle but, because Lance was having a problem with diarrhea, they decided it was best not to go that far. So they went to Point Defiance Park instead. They were not at the park very long when suddenly Lance had to go to the bathroom very badly and so Lance and I rushed home.

Saturday—October 12th—Ruth had contacted a lot of Lance's Aunts, Uncles and Cousins for a birthday party for Lance. There were about 15 relatives and friends that we squeezed into our small apartment living room. Ruth had the dining area decorated with green and yellow streamers and served chips and dip, a fruit plate, a vegetable plate and small pizza snacks. Ruth had also ordered a special birthday cake, with candles, for Lance. Lance needed help in blowing out all the candles. Tim and Shaun acted out a skit for everyone. Todd and Elis Taylor shared with us their ministry involvement in their respective churches. Special guests were Nana (Estelline) and Grandpa Tom Bennett. Tom had been a deacon at the First Assembly of God Church in Ellensburg, Washington which Ruth and I had pastored in the middle 1970s. Lance and Lani had adopted them as their special grandparents. We had kept in close touch with them over the past 20 years and had maintained a close friendship. Lance was so thrilled to have them there! Since

Lance's eyesight had deteriorated to the point that he was unable to read. Estelline read his birthday cards for him. Lance was as quick witted as ever and seemed to have a smart comeback for everything that was said. He was the "life of the party" and kept everyone laughing. Lance enjoyed the challenge of being in a crowd and the opportunity that gave him to make everyone laugh. His sense of humor just never failed him, and everyone enjoyed his wit. Before everyone left, Grandpa Tom had special prayer for Lance. Everyone had a good time, although the party was bitter sweet for us all. Everyone realized that this would probably be our last celebration with Lance. Later that evening Lance shared with a friend in California about his birthday party, and said that he finally felt that he had celebrated his birthday.

Lance made an interesting comment to Ruth after the party. He said that his goal for the past several years had been to reach his 30th birthday. However, now that his birthday was past he didn't have any goal to look forward to. Ruth suggested that he set a new goal. He didn't seem interested in setting any new goals; in all probability because he knew that the time he had left was very limited.

Monday—October 14th—Lance wanted to go and visit Hal Heine who was still at Bel Air. So I offered to take him. We were proceeding down 19th Street and had just gone through the 19th and Mildred intersection when the front left wheel came off of an oncoming truck driven by the owner of a used RV dealership in Puyallup. The wheel struck my 1988 Oldsmobile at the left front side of the car, just in front of the wheel. The jolt really shook Lance who would later complain of pain to his neck. The owner of the truck never did pay for damages and was finally able to "skip out" on his obligations to us. The truck he was driving was not insured because his business was in financial difficulty and he had not insured his vehicles. I finally had to get his own insurance company to pay for the damages because the other fellow was such a flake. He and Lance went on to see Hal.

One day Lance shared with Ruth that he had gotten up during the night to go to the bathroom. His sight, by this time, was limited to lights and shadows. With the hall light on all night, Lance simply walked toward the light to find the door to the bathroom. However, on getting ready to go back to his bed, because of his loss of eyesight, he said he had been unable to find his way out of the bathroom. It had been some time before he was able to find the door and get back to his bed. Another evening, in the middle of the night, Ruth heard a loud bang, as if something had fallen. She jumped out of bed, ran into his room and turned on the light. There was Lance sitting on the floor in the left-hand corner of the room and leaning against one of my file cabinets. Ruth asked him what had happened. He explained that he was coming back from the bathroom and thought that he had reached his bed. When he went to sit on the bed, he was disoriented and had ended up on the floor instead, about six feet from the bed. Ruth inquired if he was hurt. He said he didn't think so and asked where he was. Ruth helped him up, led him to his bed, and tucked him in. She emphasized again that all he had to do was to call for us and either she or his Father would come to his aid. However, it was very important to Lance to maintain whatever limited independence he could muster. So he very seldom called for help during the night.

Even though Lance and Rose were divorced, they kept in touch with each other by phone. Rose often called Lance and shared particularly her financial problems with him. In one of these conversations Rose informed Lance that she was going to have to move from their house, where she had been living, because she could not afford to continue paying the rent. This news was very upsetting to Lance. First of all, because there was nothing financially that he could do about it. And secondly, because, in addition to all the other things he had lost he was now going to lose the home that he and Rose had shared together, and all the special and happy memories that the house represented. It also meant that if Lance were to get strong enough to go back to California he would now have no place to go. After receiving this news, Lance became despondent and had to go back on his anti-depression medication. At one point, I'm not sure when it was, Lance remarked to me that he was surprised at how hard it was to die and at how much difficulty he was having with finding a way to die, just to quit and die.

Monday—October 21ˢᵗ—Francine, from the State of California Department of Fair Employment, called and stated that she was now ready to begin the investigation of Lance's complaint against GODIVA. She said that they had a very heavy caseload. However, because of Lance's physical condition they were going to give priority to his case over others. She had called to talk to Lance concerning any witnesses he might have who could verify his charges against GODIVA. Lance gave her the name of several GODIVA employees who had worked under Lance. Francine said that she would follow up and talk with his references.

On Lani's last visit with Lance they discussed the possibility of Lance going up to Lani's apartment to spend Halloween weekend with her. This gave Lance something to look forward to. Ruth cautioned Lance that he would have to miss the Ganciclovir treatments in order to do that, and that permission from Lance's doctor would be needed before he could follow through on those plans. Ruth also cautioned him that if his schedule was not strictly followed that this could set him back physically. His response was that it was just a matter of time anyway and that this was important to him, whatever the consequences. Ruth also emphasized with Lance the importance of taking all his medications according to the schedule the doctor had set for him. Dr. Demaio said that if that was what Lance wanted to do that it probably would not hurt to miss just a couple days. So the plans were formulated and Lance looked forward to spending some time alone with his Sister.

Wednesday—October 30th—Ruth gave Lance his Ganciclovir treatment the first thing this morning, and wrote out all the necessary instructions for Lani to follow concerning Lance's care. She also packaged up Lance's medications according to their individual schedules, with the time for taking the medication noted on the package. She also sent up juices and other drinks, plus foods that Lance could eat. Ruth emphasized with Lani the importance of Lance having food on his stomach before she gave him his medications. Otherwise, Lance would have a problem with nausea. Ruth helped Lance pack his clothes. And then I took him up to Lani's place in Seattle, about 2:30 that afternoon. Lani's friend, Stephanie, who is a beautician, cut and bleached Lance's hair for him. Ruth and I called them daily to make sure that Lance was doing well.

Saturday—November 2nd—I drove to Seattle to get Lance and bring him back to Tacoma. Lance had been vomiting and was having difficulty keeping his food down again. From this point on he really started going downhill with his physical condition.

Sunday—November 3rd—Dan and Barb arrived back from California and came to our apartment to visit Lance. I was feeling very despondent because we did not have any money to pay our bills and had no idea how we would make it financially through the rest of the year. God had miraculously provided so that, up to this point, we had been able to keep up on our monthly payments in such a way that our credit rating was not damaged. Because of Lance's care it had been some time since we had been to church. I decided that I needed to experience the Presence of the Lord in a special way and felt the need to hear some good Gospel singing and the preaching of a sermon. Consequently, I attended Life Center in Tacoma that evening, in hopes of finding some healing and encouragement for my soul as I sat in the Presence of the Lord and participated in a corporate worship service with God's people. However, my emotions were such that I fervently hoped that no one would speak to me or ask me how we were doing. I really didn't trust my own emotional state or reactions. For this reason my intention was leave the service as soon as the last Amen was said and hope that no one would speak to me. I did not want to burst into tears while trying to talk to someone.

Pastor Buntain preached that night on the Kindness of God. I remember that sermon as one of the finest sermons he had ever heard Dr. Fulton Buntain preach. By the end of his message, Fulton had spotted me in the audience. There were somewhere between one thousand to fifteen hundred people in attendance that night. Because of the celebration of the Holy Communion at the end of the Message, and certain other events after the Holy Communion, the entire Pastoral Staff, as well as the Deacon Board were all on the platform. Pastor Buntain explained to the congregation that he had an evangelist friend in the audience that night that was really hurting because of the impending death of his Son from AIDS. Fulton asked me to come to the platform. My impulse was to bolt for the door (because of his extreme depression that evening). Instead I walked to the platform as requested, and Pastor Buntain began interviewing him on the subject of AIDS. I was able to answer a few questions and then broke emotionally and began to sob before the entire church. The Board and Pastoral Staff gathered around me, laid hands on me and prayed for God's strength and help. Pastor Buntain, at that point, decided to give the congregation an opportunity to help Ruth and I financially and said that they were going to take an offering. Pastor asked the ushers to stand at the door and said that the people should give whatever was on their heart to give as they left the auditorium. The thought that went through my mind was that by taking the offering that way there would probably be only a few hundred dollars, at best, in the offering. Nevertheless, my spirits were lifted and ministered to that night by all the outpouring of love and concern. Why Pastor Buntain had chosen to be such a compassionate and caring friend to me was always a mystery. But, in part that could be understood by the fact that Fulton was a compassionate friend to everyone in need. One of the most caring people we ever met!

Pastor Buntain called the next day to let us know how much had come in from the offering for us on Sunday night. I was not home at the moment and so Pastor talked to Ruth and told her that $4,015 had been given the night before. A few days later, when I went to the mailbox a check was there from Life Center. This amount would help us make it through November and December. What was equally amazing was that early in January, I would go to the mailbox to find another check from Life Center in the amount of $2,000. Thus God miraculously provided for our financial needs all the way from July 1996 through the end of January 1997. Ruth and I would return to traveling in seminar meetings in the churches the first part of February.

Tuesday—November 5th—Lance had an appointment with Dr. Demaio. Because he was having trouble keeping anything on his stomach, and had become dehydrated, Dr. Demaio ordered Lance back into the hospital. Bel Air called and said that we could come by and pick up Lance's TV and telephone.

Wednesday—November 6th—Because Lance was missing his kitten, which he had been unable to bring up with him from California Ruth decided to find him a substitute. Before going to see him at the hospital she visited several stores before finding him a white, fluffy stuffed kitten that played music. On arriving at the hospital Ruth presented it to Lance and he was thrilled with it and hugged it to himself, kissed it and thanked Ruth. Lance was still finding it difficult to keep anything on his stomach. The vomiting robbed him of what little strength he did have. Ruth stayed with Lance the remainder of the day and evening.

I had called Dester earlier in the day to ask about how to handle Lance's death if he should die in our home. Dester said that I should call the Pierce County Medical Examiner and ask to have Lance placed on the "Coroner's List". The Medical Examiner's office would ask for Lance's doctor's name and verify with him that Lance is terminally ill. They would then place Lance on the "Coroner's List". This will make it unnecessary for the Medical Examiner to come out to the home when Lance does die. We will simply be able to call Dester who in turn will notify the Coroner for us and the come to our apartment to pick up Lance's body. This way, neither the doctor nor the Medical Examiner will need to be involved at time of death. We planned to let Dester know how many copies of the death certificate we would want. The cost would be about $11 apiece. So Ruth and I also needed to talk about where we wanted Lance buried. Dester said he could get prices for us from other cemeteries if we don't want Lance buried at Haven of Rest. I also called Tom and Estelline Bennett and told them about Lance's condition, so they could go see him.

Up to this point in time, Lance was mainly determined to fight for his life as long as he could. The exceptions were when he went through periods of depression because of his continued loss of independence and his continued need for assistance. Ruth and I had often encouraged Lance to fight and not give in. However, at this point Ruth felt the need to have a difficult but necessary talk with Lance. Ruth let Lance know that she was aware that he was very tired of the struggle. She let him know that it was okay if he wanted to give up the fight. She told him that it was his life and that it was his decision. She went on to assure him that we would support whatever decision he made. She also let him know that he did not need to worry about us, that we could handle it emotionally if he wanted to just turn loose and die. Ruth reassured him of our love and let him know that we would be with him to the end and that he would not have to worry about dying alone. After Ruth had expressed all this she was surprised at the fact that there was no response from Lance. Ruth felt that it was very important that we verbally release him and give him permission to die. Thus there would be no guilt feelings on his part. Although she was crying during the time she was sharing these thoughts with Lance, Ruth knew (as did Joseph) that we needed to let go and let him die with our love and support.

Thursday—November 7th—Dr. Demaio made the decision to take Lance off of all his medications since they were only causing more nausea and vomiting and were not prolonging or improving his quality of life. The doctor told us that he thought Lance had only two or three weeks to live.

Friday—November 8th—I spent quite a bit of time on the telephone calling family and friends letting them know that the doctor had informed us that Lance had only two or three weeks to live. Lance had been assigned a "Buddy" from the AIDS Foundation in California. Her name was Claire Humphrey and her daughter, Christy. Over the last couple years they had become very close with Lance. Lance referred to them as his "California Mom" and "California Sister". In fact, Claire shared with us that Lance and Christy even argued like brother and sister. Ruth had been in touch with Claire by phone and felt that it was time to call her and give her an update on Lance's condition and the doctor's prognosis. On calling them that evening, they asked if it was okay if they flew up to see Lance. We assured them that they would be welcome, and gave them the necessary information on how to get to the hospital. They said that this was going to be a very difficult trip but felt they needed to come to help them in the closure of their relationship with Lance.

Sunday—November 10th—Claire and Christy Humphrey flew up from southern California and spent several hours with Lance that afternoon and evening before flying back to California.

Monday—November 11th—I called and talked to Rose at her work. She promised to send Lance's cuckoo clock (that he had gotten from Grandma Taylor) and whatever else she believes we would want as momentous from Lance. I also told her she was welcome to fly up there to see Lance one more time if she wants, but also observed that she had already said her "goodbye" and that she didn't need to put herself through that again if she didn't want to do so. I said that we would understand and not feel badly toward her if she decided not to come up. I also told her that she would always be special to us. She replied by saying that we would always be special to her as well. I told her that we did not want to lose contact with her after Lance's death and she agreed that she would not let that happen. I also told her of his conversation earlier that day with Tom in which he had made it clear that we would prefer to have this time alone with Lance without people outside the family intruding upon us at the time of Lance's death.

I then called Lani at work and told her that if she wanted to see her Brother while he was still able to recognize her and talk to her that she needed to come tonight to see him. She said that she wanted to do that and that she would rather come that night than take her days off to see him.

Tuesday—November 12th—I talked to Lani again today. She said that she would be coming the next day (Wednesday, November 13th and asked me to come pick her up at the bus depot). I then confirmed a meeting with Pastor Dester Cummins for 11 AM this morning. The purpose of the meeting was to meet with him and Tom McKee regarding the disposal of Lance's body, as well as to visit Three Cedars with Dester. Tom was on the Board of Three Cedars and also knew someone else who was on the Board. They agreed to put Lance's name at the top of the list. However, there was no immediate opening.

Wednesday—November 13th—Today Lani said that she had a migraine headache and had vomited and didn't want to come down until tomorrow. I called Ruth at the hospital. Lance had been moved to another room so that he was now right across the hall from the nurse's station. Just before Lance was moved, Pastor Dester Cummins came in and had a long talk with him about his soul. Ruth said that Lance had given all the right answers and Dester had prayed with him before he left. Tim Cox also came in from Life Center that day and talked to Lance about his relationship with God, and had prayer with him. Dan Johnson Jr. (who was in with Danny Thomas the other day) came with a friend of his and they had prayer with Lance. Barb also had prayer with Lance before she left. A few days before this, Sister Mayfield, wife of the former pastor of South Tacoma Assembly, had come in to visit with Lance and had also discussed with him his relationship to the Lord. She had also prayed with him.

Thursday—November 14th—There was once during this time that one of the pastors from Life Center had come in to see Lance and then asked to spend some time visiting with us. So we went into a small conference room close by and spent about ½ hour with him, leaving Lani alone with Lance. When we came out, Lani was out of Lance's room and greatly upset because we had left her alone with her Brother. She was having a hard time dealing with Lance's condition. Plus she didn't know where we were and was worried that I might not return in time to take her to her bus that she had to catch in order to get back to Seattle, and work the next day.

It was probably on the 14th of November that hospital social services began talking to Ruth and I concerning Lance's departure from the hospital and the question of whether or not he would return home with us. Up to that point we had wanted to continue honoring Lance's request to die at home rather than somewhere else. We had thus planned to continue caring for him. However, Ruth began feeling that we should consider putting Lance in a facility where others could focus on his physical care. This thinking was because of the long hours required to care for Lance and the lack of sleep she and I were already experiencing; there were also other stress points that were factors in this decision. This would free us up to focus all of our attention on him personally and the emotional and psychological factors involved with his death. We wanted to "be there for him" at an emotional level. Dester Cummins had previously told us about Three Cedars AIDS hospice in Tacoma but Three Cedars had contacted the hospital and said that it would be a couple weeks before they could possibly have a place for Lance.

Friday—November 15th—The hospital Social Services worker, by the name of Audrey, was trying to get Lance into the Orchard Park facility because Lance had been very emphatic about not ever wanting to go back to Bel Air again. The Orchard Park Health Care Center normally did not take certain categories of patients, including AIDS patients. They did not take patients who needed intravenous feedings or special pain control. However, they agreed to accept Lance on a trial basis. One reason they were hesitant to take Lance was because the home care facility that delivered the medications that were needed had to come all the way down from Redmond, Washington. There were times that they experienced a 24 hour delay in getting medications down there. This was because they first had to contact the doctor to get permission to use a particular medication, and then the doctor had to send in an Rx prescription, and then Orchard Park would contact the home health care facility to order the medicine. By this time it might be the next day before the medicine could be delivered and that would be whenever the driver worked them in on his route.

Monday—November 18th—On the morning of the 18th, I had called Englewood Assembly in Englewood, New Jersey to talk to Bob Parlante who was now on staff there, and still Secretary of the Board. I gave him an update on Lance's condition and thanked them for the church's gift of $500. Bob told me that the church choir frequently had prayer for Lance and our entire family. Lance was transferred from Tacoma General Hospital to Orchard Park Health Care Center. When Lance first got there they did not have a private room for him and the man in the other bed was continuously talking and groaning out loud. His noises greatly disturbed Lance. Ruth called me from the hospital and I met her there at the Orchard Park Health Care Center. The two of us went into the office to take care of the paper work while Lance was getting settled in his room. They said they were trying to find another room to move the man who was already there so that we could have the room to ourselves as a Family. Ruth and I began each taking 12 hour shifts in staying by Lance's bedside. They told us that we were welcome to use the second bed for taking naps as we had need. By that first evening the man was moved out of the room and put in with another patient in a different part of the facility.

That afternoon I made calls to family and friends and let them know that Lance was now at Orchard Park Health Care Center. At 5:21 PM, I had called Dolly Smith (pseudonym) and left a message on her recorder asking her to call before she comes up here to see Lance. Dolly called me back and I informed her that she was not welcome to come see Lance, and that we wanted to have this time alone with Lance without outside interference or confusion.

Wednesday—November 20th—Ruth called me this morning to let me know that the Hospice case worker wanted to meet with both of us at 2:30 that afternoon. Rose had called Ruth that morning at Orchard Park. She was upset and wanting to know why her Mother was not being allowed to come see Lance. Ruth let her know that when we had freely invited them to come up two months earlier in September that they had used the occasion to encourage Lance not to come back home and had caused a lot of problems and confusion. Ruth told her that we were dealing with enough emotional trauma at that moment, trying to care for a dying Son, without having to worry about any more discord and confusion that they might cause if they came. Rose denied that they had anything to do with what happened in September. Ruth told her that it was hard for us to believe that it was a mere coincidence that Lance was begging us to come home just the day before they came up, but then the day before they left had changed his mind and decided that he didn't want to come back home. Rose was very angry and started making accusations. First of all she said that the only reason we cared about Lance was to help alleviate our own guilt feelings for never having been there for him his whole life. When Ruth informed her that Lance had told us on many occasions, the opposite, and had even put in writing that we are the only people who have always been there for him, she changed her tactics and accused Ruth of only wanting to take care of Lance because of the money we were getting from social services. Ruth explained to Rose that it was Lance and the social service people that informed Ruth and encouraged her to take pay for being Lance's care giver. Ruth added that she would have still gladly cared for Lance even if she had received no pay at all, because Lance is our Son and we love him and that is what love is all about. Ruth also told Rose that if she had been doing it for the money that $2,000 for five months of round the clock care was not very good wages and that she wouldn't have taken the job on that basis. Plus, she did not get paid during any time Lance was in the hospital or health care facilities, but that she and I still visited with Lance many long hours of every day possible. Rose was saying that her Mother had a right to come and see Lance and Ruth reminded Rose that she was no longer legally Lance's wife because she had divorced him more than two years before. That really made Rose even angrier and, at that point, Rose began to bring up other issues. Ruth simply let her know that this was not the time or place to be discussing those things, but that, if at a later date, she could talk calmly and kindly she (Ruth) would be glad to discuss them with her. Then Ruth let her know that she had a Son that was dying and needed his Mother and that she had to go. Ruth said goodbye and hung up and returned to Lance's room.

Just before the meeting with the social worker that afternoon, Suzanne from the AIDS Foundation came to visit Lance. At the time she got there Lance was medicated to the point that he was unable to communicate with anyone. She inquired as to whether Ruth had talked to Rose lately or not. Ruth told her that, yes, she had talked to Rose just that morning. She then asked Ruth if Rose had said anything about coming up for a visit with Lance. Ruth told her that Rose had said nothing about coming up and that, in fact, she had just moved out of their house and still in process of moving into her new apartment, plus working part-time and going to school part-time. Ruth said she thought they had already said their goodbyes when they were up in September. Suzanne seemed surprised about what Ruth had just communicated, but then inquired about how Lance was doing. Ruth told her that Lance had deteriorated and that the doctors suspected he only had a matter of days left to live. Suzanne stayed about 15 minutes and then left.

It was at the meeting, later that afternoon, with the Hospice caseworker that a comment was made concerning our unwillingness to allow Dolly to come and visit Lance. They had received a phone call from a social service worker, from either the hospital or AIDS Foundation, concerning a complaint from Dolly. We briefly explained to them our reason for not wanting them to come because we felt like they had betrayed our trust when we had gladly invited them to come and visit Lance in September. We also let them know that we did not want to accept any more phone calls coming into Orchard Park from anyone calling from Southern California. The Hospice caseworker promised to cooperate with our wishes and added that we had the right to make any decision that was in the best interests of Lance and his immediate family. Another thing that was said in that meeting was that the hospice would pay for all Lance's expenses from then on. They explained to us their procedures for caring for a dying patient. They talked about the wisdom of gradually cutting back on the hydration so as to avoid the possibility of Lance's lungs filling up and causing him to drown in his own body liquid. In fact they said that if they discovered his lungs starting to fill up that they would cut off the hydration all together. They assured us that because of all Lance's pain medications, etc. that as they began to cut back the hydration that Lance would not feel any discomfort from the lack of liquid in his body. We expressed to them our desire for Lance to have enough pain medication so that he was not in pain. However, we were concerned that they not over medicate him so that he was not lucid or able to communicate with us.

By this time Lance had been off of the Ganciclovir and all other medications (except pain medicine) for almost two weeks and the CMV virus was causing intense intestinal pain. On Wednesday, in the early evening, the pain became so severe that Lance was thrashing around in his bed and trying to get out of the bed. Ruth found it necessary at times to physically restrain Lance and hold him in the bed. Tim Taylor had come for a visit that evening, as did Barb and Dan Taylor. Barb sat beside Lance and talked to him and tried to calm him down.

Another problem about this time was that the nursing staff found it advisable to insert a catheter in Lance. They had previously had a condom like catheter on him so that he could urinate freely. But the catheter kept coming off, as Lance would feel for it before allowing himself to urinate and in the process inadvertently pull it off.

Thursday—November 21st—Ruth and I brought some soft, soothing and peaceful gospel instrumental music and had it playing softly in the background day and night. Many of the nurses and visitors who came remarked about the peaceful atmosphere they felt when they walked into the room. With all the prayers and hymns going on, Lance's room had become a spiritual sanctuary. Lois Hanson came by to see Lance today. Somehow she had heard about his condition. Lois Hanson is the Mother of Cheryl Hanson Langford who had been my Secretary at the First Assembly of God Church in Ellensburg, Washington many years before. Cheryl had also babysat Lance and Lani during that time. After I came, about 6 PM, Ruth stayed on until about 8 PM and then went home. She got a bite to eat and went to bed. I called her about 1 AM that next morning to let her know that the nurses were not expecting Lance to live through the night. So Ruth came back down to Orchard Park and we both spent the rest of the night with Lance. Lance was so medicated that he was not able to communicate with us. The Nurses were also coming in about every hour to put drops in his eyes.

Friday—November 22nd—I returned home for a brief time and made a number of phone calls to family and friends concerning Lance's imminent death. The nurses had told us that morning that they did not expect Lance to live even until noon. Lani came down by early afternoon. Pat Taylor, Bill and Marilyn, Esther, Karen, Kenton Lee, Elis, Pastor Dester Cummins, Tom & Estelline Bennett, Jacque and Ralph Simmons, Tammy, Dan and Barb, Paul Shelton, Cathy Taylor came to visit Lance. We informed everyone when they came that although Lance could not respond to them, he could hear what they were saying. We encouraged them to go to Lance and share any last thoughts they cared to share. Many people did that. We all stood around the bed and sang choruses. Some people shared memories about Lance when he was growing up. Elis shared that when we were in Africa he had gone up to Grandma Taylor's attic and found Lance's battery operated helicopter. He had gotten it out and played with it and thought it was the neatest thing. Elis acknowledged that he had gotten into Lance's box of toys and asked Lance to forgive him. "Nana" and Grandpa Bennett shared a few thoughts about Lance. Tom Bennett talked about the little boat he had made for Lance and that often, when Nana was babysitting the kids, Lance had taken the boat to the creek and sailed it. Lance had told Grandpa Tom that he still had the boat packed away in the toy box. Ralph Simmons read some Scripture to Lance and shared a few words about the Scripture. We all stopped and had a word of prayer at that time. Dester Cummins had also read Scripture and had a word of prayer with Lance and the entire group.

We were all out in the hallway when a call was received at the desk from Rose, who was asking to speak to Lance. Since there was no phone in Lance's room it seemed at first that it would be impossible for her to speak to Lance. In talking with the staff at the desk I indicated that it would be okay for Rose to speak to Lance if we could find a cordless phone for her to call back on. Someone mentioned that the lady in charge of Lance's hospice care had such a phone. We approached her and she offered to allow us to use her phone. She thought Rose was calling from Seattle. In speaking with Rose, I emphasized with her the need to keep the call positive and not say anything to get him upset. I told her that Lance was not expected to live more than a few more hours. When I told the Hospice Case Worker that Rose was calling from the L.A. area she said that the call probably wouldn't go through because her cell phone was limited to western Washington. She made the statement that it would take a miracle for that call to come through from Southern California. Arrangements were made for Rose to call back on her number. So we went into Lance's room and waited for her call. To our amazement, the phone rang and Rose was on the other end of the line. She was able to talk to Lance for a brief few minutes.

While we were still in the hallway Ruth asked Lani if she would like to have some time alone with her Brother. At first, she didn't feel she could handle it emotionally. Ruth pointed out that she felt that the private time for just the two of them would be very meaningful to Lance. However, Lani said that she did not want to spend the night there with Lance. Ruth tried to encourage her to stay because these would be her last hours with her Brother and Ruth felt sure it would be very meaningful to Lance to have her with him at the end. Lani let Ruth know that she did not want to be with him when he died. She just didn't feel she could handle it. At that point Barb and Dan offered to take her back to Seattle that evening, since they had previous engagement in that area. Lani then went in and spent some time alone with her Brother before the rest of us came back into the room.

At noon, a Staff Member from the office came and informed us that they had prepared lunch for us and that the table was set up in the conference room. There were a few that had to leave but the rest of us went in and ate lunch together before going back to Lance's room. Paul Shelton had offered to stay with Lance while the rest of us ate so that Lance would not be left alone. However, Tammy let Ruth know that she wanted to stay with Lance. So Ruth told Paul that Tammy had requested to stay with Lance and have that time alone with him.

Ruth was so exhausted from two days with almost no sleep that shortly before lunch she laid down on the other bed in Lance's room to try to get a short nap. It was while Ruth was trying to get some rest that the nurses came in and told us that liquid was filling Lance's lungs and that they needed permission from us to turn off the hydration so that Lance would not drown. They wanted to know who the immediate family member was. At that Ruth got up to respond to the nurses, but moved so quickly that she became dizzy, lost her balance, and almost fell over on her face. We gave permission for the hydration to be terminated and this was immediately done. The nurses then asked us all to go out in the hallway so they could take care of Lance's personal needs.

A lot of the family and friends stayed until about 10 or 10:30 that night. It was about 11 PM before Richard and Patti were able to come. They spoke to Lance briefly and then visited with Ruth and I until midnight.

Ruth and I decided that we would take turns being with Lance while the other tried to get some rest on the other bed. The agreement was to take two hour shifts and I took the first shift, while Ruth laid down for a rest. It was at this moment that I began to have my last Father/Son talk. I told Lance that I loved him and that he was proud to have had him as a Son. I also told Lance that I wanted to see him again in Heaven and said, "Son, I know that a lot of things have happened to you down through the years that have disappointed you and hurt you." I then asked Lance to forgive me for anything I had said or done as his Father that may have wounded him. I went on to say that I knew Lance had some feeling that his life had been a waste, and that he really had not accomplished much of anything important with his life. But I told Lance that I planned to share Lance's story with other teenagers and to use his story to warn them about the importance of making right choices so as to avoid evil consequences. When I made the statement that I would share Lance's story everywhere I went and that I would try to make sure that Lance's story accomplished some good in other people's lives, good that would ultimately count for eternity, at that, a big tear rolled down each of Lance's cheeks. At this point Lance was not only paralyzed and blind, but he was also unable to close his eyes. This was true in spite of the fact that nurses had been keeping his eyes moist with hourly eye drops. What was even more miraculous about this was that Lance had been off of hydration for at least 10 to 12 hours and must have been completely dehydrated.

It was about 1:30 or 2 AM when I laid down for a rest and Ruth got up to be with her Son one final time. Ruth planned on reading a Psalm to him, which she had been doing on a daily basis. But instead Ruth felt impressed to just share from her heart with Lance some happy memories from his childhood. Ruth began by recalling how he loved to sing different Sunday School choruses when we traveled in the car. And when he couldn't remember any more choruses he would make up his own and sing about his love for Jesus. Then Ruth went on to comment how at some time later a gulf came up between he and his relationship with God. Ruth began to express that she didn't understand what had happened, but then the Holy Spirit showed her what had caused the gulf between Lance and God. So Ruth explained to Lance that the gulf was caused because of his struggle with pride and self-centeredness, and the question of who was going to be in control of his life. Ruth emphasized with Lance the fact that each of us go through that same struggle on a regular basis, and that we each must choose who we are going to allow to sit on the throne of our life. Ruth expressed to Lance how sad we were that he had made the decision to make his own choices in life without regard to God and His Word. She also explained that God is all-knowing and everywhere present at the same time. Therefore, God knows what each day holds as well as what the future holds for us and that since He created us He alone knows what is best for our lives. Ruth explained to Lance that it is pride and arrogance for any of us to think that we know what is best for our lives, instead of trusting God, Who knows everything. By this time Ruth was feeling an ever increasing anointing and Presence of the Holy Spirit. It was as if she were standing back and listening with amazement at the words that were flowing out of her mouth. It had to be God! Ruth did not have to stop and think about what she was saying but was rather trying to keep up with the flow of thoughts the Holy Spirit brought to her mind.

Ruth explained to Lance that pride and arrogance were the first sin that was ever committed, and was done by Lucifer, who later became the devil. Lucifer's pride caused him to rebel against God, because he wanted to control his own life, instead of allowing God to be in control of his life. Then Ruth told Lance that the only answer to pride and arrogance (which is sin) is to repent. Ruth emphasized that repentance is not simply saying, "I'm sorry", but that the word "repentance" in the Bible means to turn away from and to change direction. Therefore, if one truly repents of their sins they will turn away from that sin. It also means that they will cease from following the Broad Road of sin and instead choose to follow the narrow road that leads to God and Eternal Life. Ruth further explained that if one has not turned away from their sin and changed the direction of their life that they are not really saved.

Ruth also shared with Lance about what it means to love God. That when we truly love God we will want to live our lives in such a way as to please Him, as well as to live in obedience to His Word. Also, when we say we believe in God it does not mean that we are simply acknowledging the fact that there is a God. Scripture tells us that even the devils believe and tremble. The word "believe", in the Bible, has the meaning that one will always choose to live their life according to what one really believes. Therefore, if I believe in God, I will choose to live my life in agreement with his commandments.

Ruth used the illustration of Lance's desire to go back to California. She explained that he could get in a car and begin driving but if the car was never headed away from Tacoma he would never end up in California. That he first had to drive away from Tacoma and specifically head toward California if he hoped to reach his destination. Ruth explained that it is the same way in our relationship with the Lord. That we must first turn away from our sin and our willingness to allow Satan to influence our decisions and choose as an act of our Will to serve God and to live for Him.

Ruth then shared with Lance that he was standing at the door of death and that he could pass through that door into eternity at any moment. "The question is", Ruth said, "will you be ready to meet your Creator when you pass through that door into eternity." "If you are not sure that you are ready", Ruth continued, "you can take this opportunity to made sure that you are ready." "That can be done by confessing your sins to God and committing your life to Him." Ruth explained that she knew that he could not pray verbally at this time but reminded him that God knows the thoughts and intents of our heart. Ruth said that she would pray for him and that if he wanted to invite Jesus into his heart and commit his life to Christ that he could pray after her in his heart. Ruth told him that if he was sincere and really meant it that God would save him, because God has promised that if we repent of our sins and turn to Him that he will be faithful to forgive us our sins and to cleanse us from all unrighteousness. Ruth explained to Lance also the importance of not only acknowledging his sins but also confessing them and renouncing them, which means that he lets Satan know that he is turning away from them forever, and that he will never go back to them.

Ruth then led out in prayer, confessing and asking God's forgiveness for his self-centeredness and for thinking that he knew what was best for his life. She than began to name and ask forgiveness for every sin she could think of that she knew Lance had ever struggled with. Then Ruth proceeded to renounce those same sins one by one, stating that as an act of his will he (Lance) chooses to turn his back on them. Ruth then stated that as an act of Lance's Will he chooses to surrender his life to Christ and to serve Him for the remainder of his life.

Since Lance's arrival in Tacoma five months earlier, Lance had usually reacted negatively when either one or us spoke to him about the things of God. Particularly, if we related it to his need for a personal relationship with God. Lance would usually become very agitated or even angry. We were very careful not to discuss the subject unless he brought it up. Therefore, when I overheard Ruth talking to Lance so forcefully concerning death and Lance's spiritual condition, I became very concerned, and somewhat fearful of what Lance's reaction might be. I jumped up from the bed where he had been resting and peered around the curtain that separated the two beds. Ruth told me later that she had immediately noted the look of shock and concern written all over my face. However, that she also knew she was not speaking her own thoughts but words that were directed by the Holy Spirit. By the time I came around to Lance's bed and stood by Ruth's side, I began to also realize that something extraordinary was going on here. I was still somewhat concerned, but felt a check (which I recognized to be the Holy Spirit) and so refrained from interfering with what Ruth was saying and instead began to support her with quiet prayer.

At the conclusion of her prayer Ruth suddenly realized that we had no way of knowing whether Lance was awake, asleep or had gone into a coma. It was essential that we know beyond a shadow of a doubt whether or not our Son had recommitted his life to Christ. The only thing Ruth could think to do was to ask Lance to blink his eyes if he had prayed that prayer that prayer in his heart along with her and recommitted his life to Christ. Ruth realized at the time, Lance had been unable to close or blink his eyes over the last two days. Therefore she realized that she was asking for Lance to do something which, in the natural, was impossible for him to do. After asking Lance to respond with a blink Ruth and I looked down into his two open but blank and staring eyes. As we anxiously waited, there was absolutely no movement or response. Our hearts sank and we immediately thought that in all probability he hadn't even heard us. However, Ruth would not give up. Once again she explained to Lance that this was very important to us and asked him again to blink his eyes if he had prayed that prayer with his Mother. Ruth and several of her friends had been praying for a couple of months that God would give her a sign that would indicate if Lance was ready to meet the Lord. There could be no peace for us without the assured knowledge that we would once again meet our Son in Heaven. Once again we gazed into those vacant eyes, when suddenly there were two quick, forceful and definite blinks. It seemed that he had just made a supreme & successful effort to blink his eyes! We immediately turned and searched each other's faces to try to determine if the other had seen the same thing. We both burst into tears of joy and rejoicing as we realized that God had answered our prayers. We were both filled with a great sense of peace and assurance that Lance had truly made his peace with God. In spite of the fact that Lance had repeatedly stated to many different people that he was ready to meet God, that peace and assurance had been lacking for us, his parents. What made the difference this time was the fact that Lance's confession was not just another expression of desire to agree with what he thought someone wanted to hear. His confession this time was actually confirmed by the miraculous sign from God of blinking his eyes, which in the natural, at that moment, was physically impossible.

Ruth continued to weep as she began to express to Lance what was in her heart. She assured him that we had seen those blinks and that God had forgiven and cleansed him of his sins. It was now 3:15 AM of Saturday—November 23, 1996, just six hours before Lance would pass on from this life into the Presence of his Savior. Ruth reminded him that now when he stepped through that door of death the arms of our Lord would be there to greet him. She also reminded him that the family members who had gone on before would also be there. Ruth specifically mentioned his Grandma Taylor who he had been very close to, as well as Grandpa Taylor, Grandma and Grandpa Meyers and his Aunt Grace and Uncles Joseph and James. Ruth also shared with him that one day she and his Father would also join him for a happy reunion.

Ruth then shared with Lance that she knew that he probably felt that his life had been a waste and that all that would be left would be a heap of ashes. Ruth let him know that God could take the broken pieces and ashes of his life and make something beautiful out of it. Ruth made a commitment to him that everywhere we went we would share his story and warn other young people about the serious consequences of wrong choices. We fulfilled that commitment in the months and years to come as we took his ashes into the public school system up and down the West Coast, from Alaska to Montana, Idaho, and California. Ruth also stated that we would use his story to encourage other parents concerning the Grace, Mercy, Love, Faithfulness and Forgiveness of our Heavenly Father. And that we would emphasize that they should never give up on their children, for God has never given up on any of us.

While Ruth was speaking, the Lord suddenly brought to her mind the answer to a question that had plagued her and I for several years. The question was, "If God knows everything, why did He allow us to adopt a child that He knew ahead of time would end up turning his back on God?" As Ruth was sharing with Lance, suddenly the Holy Spirit revealed to her that God had placed Lance in our home "for such

243

a time as this", and that 30 years earlier God had known the choices Lance would make concerning the direction of his life. God also saw a young couple who was longing for a child and upon whom God could depend on to be faithful at times that Lance would need them, and to personally show him the pathway to God. Lance had, on several previous occasions, made a statement to others that he didn't feel that his parents deserved the two rebellious kids they had adopted. Ruth felt that it was very important that she share with Lance what the Holy Spirit had just revealed to her. This she did and told him that our action of adopting him was an expression of God's love and provision for him, way back even before he was born. God had a plan for the lives of the two people who would be his parents, and that was to be channels through which God could shine His Light on Lance's pathway, to lead him back to God. As the fullness of that concept impacted Ruth she was overwhelmed with the knowledge of the trust and confidence that God had placed in us. We also realized that without God's enabling power we would have failed.

Lance would later have two grand mall seizures six hours and leave us to go into the Presence of His Savior and God. After our time of prayer with our Son and the victory that followed I laid back down for a short nap. Several hours went by and I finally woke up and told Ruth that I wanted to go home for a quick shower and to change my clothes. She begged me not to go, but I felt confident that it would only take me less than an hour to shower and get back to Ruth's side. I hurried as fast as I could. But it was on the way back that I had a strange experience or sensation. It was as if a wind blew through the car. When I entered the room where Ruth, and now our good friend, Paul Shelton were waiting by Lance's bedside it was to learn about Lance's Grand Mal seizures and the fact that he had breathed his last shortly before I walked into the room. I was not there to hold my wife in my arms and comfort her when Lance died. My friend, Paul Shelton, did that for me, but Ruth was not happy that I had not gotten back in time to be with her at that critical moment. Don't blame her! And I did feel very bad about not being there. Lance passed into eternity on November 23, 1996 at about 9 AM, a little more than one month past his 30th birthday.

Our good friend, Rev. Dester Cummins, took care of Lance's body removing it to McKee Funeral Parlor in Tacoma where he was cremated.

Lance's memorial service was held in the chapel at Life Center First Assembly of God in Tacoma, Washington. His three wonderful, beautiful Aunties, Karen Taylor Jordan, Renee Taylor-Seeley and Julianne Taylor-Senff sang as a trio at his Memorial Service. I doubt there was a dry eye in the building at that point. Dr. Warren Bullock, District Superintendent of the Northwest District of the Assemblies of God brought a powerful Memorial message.

I need to keep my word to my daughter and relate that Lance was probably "Gay" from his teenage years forward. I had suspected that to be the case at the time, but whenever I tried to draw Lance out in discussion of any area with which he might be struggling as a young man, he refused to discuss those kinds of issues with me, and I just didn't know at the time how to handle the situation. Furthermore, we have no certain proof as to when Lance contracted the Human immunodeficiency virus, better known as AIDS. What is important is that Lance admitted that his lifestyle (whenever it started) was wrong. At the end of his life he renounced that lifestyle to me personally, as his Father, asked God for forgiveness and confessed Jesus as his Lord and Savior. I believe that Lance is in Heaven with his Mother and Grandma Taylor and so many others. Someday I intend to join them all. These are the things that matter. Whether Lance was Gay early in life or later, after he met Peter, is irrelevant simply because it is irrelevant to God. The fact that he renounced that life-style, repented of it and surrendered his heart to Jesus Christ, those are the issues that have eternal relevancy!

Chapter Seven

The Storm (Wind) of God's Spirit in our lives during Twelve Years of Ministry as Itinerant Seminar Speakers across the USA and western Canada

I can't wait! Here is the list of Ruth's Seminar Topics which she wrote without books or resource materials (except the work of the Holy Spirit in her heart!). I believe these were awesome teachings from the heart of God through the human vessel of the woman I was privileged to know as a Woman of God, and also to whom I was married! What a talented and Godly Lady God gave me to be my life's companion and my most wise human advisor in life and ministry!

1. Discerning Truth: Tests to determine if something is of God, Satan or Self
2. Exposing Pathways to Deception: Spiritual Deception in the lives of Believers; its Causes and Cure.
3. Spiritual Warfare: Recognizing and overcoming Strongholds
4. Vessels of Honor: A Study in Brokenness, Humility and Christ-likeness
5. Women of Grace: Biblical Foundations for Love and Marriage
6. Fresh Bread from Heaven (Ruth's Messages to Women)

I was privileged to be her typist and editor but this was her material, placed in her heart and mind by her Heavenly Father.

The following are several of the twelve Seminars I wrote and taught.

1. Biblical Keys to Covenant Forgiveness & Secure Relationships: The Healing of Injured or Broken Relationships and How to Establish Healthy Relationships
2. Get Your Dynamite—And Create A Meeting! (A seminar on Intercessory Prayer)
3. Biblical & Historical Principles for a Spiritual Awakening (Revival)
4. Spiritual Warfare: Preparing the Warriors!
5. Biblical Restoration: Its' Function & Power in the Life of the Believer
6. The Essence & Expression of Biblical Worship
7. The Path to Relational Wholeness: A Crucified and Ascended Life
8. "Between The Eternities": A Study in Theocracy, Free Will & Salvation History
9. Destructive Elements to Relational Wholeness: The Deception of Perceptions

When, in 1988, Ruth and I came home from Africa we thought it would be a furlough during which time we would visit the churches that supported us, raise additional funds ($50,000 cash plus additional monthly support) and then return to Africa. Instead, for various reasons, we found ourselves at the end of our missionary career and without a clue as to what we would do next. During the first few months while we were still thinking we would return to Africa, we stopped in to a Mitzel's Restaurant that specializes in chicken and turkey pot pies. Ruth bit into something that she thought was just a small bone or gristle but turned out to be several small pieces of glass. She swallowed the glass which got caught sidewise in her throat. Later in the evening she tried to swallow

247

an antibiotic pill to help with a problem with infection located else-where in her body. The antibiotic pill got caught on top of the piece of glass lodged in her throat causing additional harm to her vocal cords and the inside of her throat. The doctor allowed me to look inside her throat and see the ulceration that had occurred. We thought we would soon be returning to Africa and settled with the insurance company more quickly than was wise. All current medical bills were paid but Ruth's beautiful soprano voice was ruined by what the glass and antibiotic dissolving in her throat did to her. There were other complications that lasted the rest of her life. Ruth could not long endure being outside if it were windy. Sitting under any kind of draft (like air conditioning outlets in restaurants) would cause a sore throat with varying degrees of severity. And so, when we went anywhere I always got her as close to the door of where we were going so that she did not have to walk across a parking lot. Ruth had always been physically fragile (beautiful but fragile—and we nicknamed her, "China Doll"). But this latest development only added to her general fragility. Amazingly, she was far healthier out in Africa than she ever was in the USA or Canada.

Our income stream from the Assemblies of God World Missions Division lasted through the end of February, 1990 and then we were on our own. But God was at work for us although no angelic choirs announced His involvement. We were learning some new lessons on trust and dealing with worry and fear (which is the opposite of trust).

Fulton Buntain, Senior Pastor of the Life Center Church in Tacoma which counted some five thousand members and adherents in its Congregation had just moved out of his old office suite and into a brand new office. I had preached for Fulton many times over the years and for some reason he had taken an interest in our ministry. Fulton invited me to move into his old office suite and use the phones to schedule meetings in churches. I also became aware of a Law Firm in the area that had helped Fulton's Son in-law incorporate free of charge as a 501 © 3 non-profit religious organization and was able to obtain their services for the same purpose for myself. It was then that Church Renewal Ministries was born, complete with a Board of Directors and the ability to give tax credit receipts to donors.

I had returned from Africa on the verge of a physical and nervous breakdown. So emotionally drained was I that, in spite of the obvious blessing of the Lord to help us get started in a new ministry, I would lie on my bed at night and pray for God to take my life. During the day, in the offices Fulton had provided for me, I would pick up a phone to call a church with the purpose of lining up a speaking engagement; after dialing the number I would often hang up and burst into tears. The reason for my emotional breakdown was the stress of the last couple years out in Africa. At the time we left Africa, the combined three sets of Financial Accounting Books for which I had sole responsibility were out of balance by $5,000. In other words, $5,000 was missing and I had no answers for the discrepancy. It was that, as much as anything, that had thrown me into a deep depression. After working so hard [62] I had been surprised by the financial discrepancy but convinced I could resolve the issue. Since the bookkeeping system worked with three currencies and each deposit and expenditure had to be entered according to the

---

[62] From earlier in the book: "My work day began about 2 AM every morning and ended at 10 PM that night. As Interim Director, Academic Dean and Business Manager, plus Professor of Bible and Theology, all rolled into one person I was on a path toward a physical and emotional collapse. I was also the Field Fellowship Secretary-Treasurer and Christian Education Representative to the National Church. I arose at 2 AM to write my class lecture notes in English. For me it was easier to write in English and translate into French in my head as I lectured later in the day."

"As Field Fellowship Secretary-Treasurer I not only recorded the Minutes and decisions of the Field Fellowship in business session, but also gave regular financial reports as part of my duties. Basically, I kept financial records in three currencies (dollars, French Francs and Ivoirian Francs). The difference between Ivoirian and French Francs was a settled 50 to 1 but the differences, when dealing with dollars, or French Francs, fluctuated from day to day. Thus each transaction (deposits and expenditures) has to be meticulously recorded with the proper exchange rate notes for each transaction. That also was part of my duties. To top it off, I had the same responsibilities for the Bible Institute finances and my own "work funds" as I did for the MFF. (Missionary Field Fellowship). In regards to my position as the national Christian Education Representative I was responsible for making sure that all 200 Assembly of God churches in Ivory Coast were supplied with their "Sunday School" literature for their individual church and to do that on a monthly basis. I was further responsible for a report to the National Church at their annual business meeting. My duties as Academic Dean were to keep track of the academic grades and accomplishments of each student, keeping them on track toward graduation and making sure they were each taking the required courses. I passed out grades at the end of each semester and signed them each up for the appropriate classes during the following semester. As Interim Director I was responsible for the overall smooth operation of the entire college, including hiring the appropriate support workers, like African professors, cooks and grounds maintenance and making sure there was enough money to pay them once a month. I had a cash box for each area of financial responsibility. And when we were short of cash, to pay the workers, for instance, I would put an I.O.U. in another cash box and take out the money to pay the workers, etc. And so, of course, when balancing the books I had to pay back the I.O.U. from the cash box that had borrowed money to the original lending cash box. It got complicated when there was multiple I.O.U.s in the various cash boxes."

exchange rate for that day, I was sure the problem was somewhere in the records of exchange rates for deposits or expenditures, and that I would be able to find it & restore the books to balance. But we ran out of time and departed from Africa, not with a sense of victory and accomplishment but with shame and a sense of failure. A special auditor was flown to Africa for the purpose of auditing my records. Eventually my name was cleared although the discrepancy was never completely resolved. I did receive a letter from headquarters stating that they were satisfied as to my integrity and would not hold me responsible for the missing funds.

It was for the above reasons and my total physical and emotional exhaustion that the thought of talking to a pastor (or anyone for that matter) was just too much to handle. But gradually things began to come together and the demands in the churches for our ministry increased. God was blessing. Ruth and I wrote and self-published 18 different seminars complete with study guide notes which were made available to the audiences in the meetings. We would go into a different church each week and begin our week of meetings by teaching the Adult Sunday School Class and the Morning Service. Sunday evenings began the schedule that would be held to throughout the week: two hours of teaching with a coffee break in the middle of the evening. No music, just teaching. At the end of the meeting we would invite the folks to come to the altar areas for a time of prayer, reflection, introspection and new levels of dedication of their lives to God. I would always begin my remarks, especially on Sunday mornings and Sunday nights, by saying, "I am not here to see your emotions stirred but, with the aid of the Holy Spirit, help you change your thinking" about whatever the subject matter was for that week. The demand rose for increased exposure to the teaching & so cassette albums were recorded and sold at the end of each service. Those sales were a big help toward our financial survival. For several years we also held morning services of 2 hours length on a different topic, complete with study guides. It was a grueling schedule and slowly Ruth, who now did 50% of the teaching, began to buckle under the strain of it all. We eventually had to stop doing the morning classes.

Earlier, near the beginning of our twelve year ministry as itinerant seminar teachers across the United States and western Canada I thought I heard the voice of the Lord within me saying, "You need to make room for Ruth in the teaching schedule." I went to Ruth with the message I felt the Lord giving me concerning her. The reply? "Well when God tells me the same thing I'll let you know." I chuckled to myself and let it drop. It was while we were in meetings at a little church in Montesano, Washington that Ruth said, "Why don't I ever get ten or fifteen minutes in the Sunday morning Christian Education hour (Sunday School) to have something to say?" I replied, "I've been waiting on you to believe the Word of the Lord." (I was only trying to tease her!) Gradually Ruth began pushing me to give her more and more time. Eventually she was teaching a full hour every night, Sunday through Wednesday, and also for an hour in the morning sessions. I would teach the first hour and Ruth would teach the second. And then the switch was made so she could have "top billing", teaching the first hour which was followed by her gradually encroaching on my teaching time. I got what was left over when she finished. At first this created a little problem between us, but not for long. For I quickly began to see that this was of God, and that my sweet China Doll was being powerfully used of God to touch many lives. Her teaching was supremely simple and direct, practical with pungency covered over with the honey of sweet words. I used to tease her by saying, "You sure know how to stick the knife in your audience's minds and emotions and get then them to accept it because you cover it with so much honey!" And that was my Sweetheart!

Ruth would labor endlessly, with tears and frustration, during the day over her studies and handwritten lesson notes and then we would work together to develop the study guides from those notes, type them and print them out from my computer and portable printer. My efforts to persuade her to use the PC Study Bible program on my laptop computer met with her resistance. The thought of learning a new software program was too intimidating for her. She was a hard taskmaster on herself and her husband even though her refusal to learn to use my Bible Software program added greatly to the challenge of preparing her own lesson notes. However I thoroughly enjoyed this part of our ministry together. And so the hours in each day were split between my own studies as well as helping Ruth with the development and printing of her materials. We were a team! And our marriage was made stronger by this whole process.

But we were both working feverishly to develop our own materials as the Spirit of God moved upon us and brought new understanding of the topics covered. Ruth's series on "Doorways to Deception: Spiritual Deception in the Lives of Believers, its Causes and Cure" was especially popular. And pastors, if they were aware of this series, would insist that Ruth teach it when we came to their church.

Here are a few of the main points of the first four pages of her First Lesson (a lesson that is actually 17 pages in length) on Doorways to Deception: [63]

---

[63]   Ruth was careful to provide many Scriptural supports for all her statements but most of those Scriptures not included here.

Title: What the Bible says about Deception

First Main Point: Understanding Spiritual Deception

A. What is Spiritual Deception?
1. Biblical Definitions of the word "deceive";
   a. New Testament Greek definition from "planao" [(plan-ah'-o);[64] meaning, "to roam (from safety, truth or virtue).[65]
   b. O.T. Hebrew definition from: "kachash" (kakh-ash) [66] meaning, "a failure of the flesh"; i.e., emaciation, a wasting away (like someone with AIDS); figuratively, hypocrisy because of the wasting away of the inward character; thus deception is that which leads to a deterioration of spiritual, moral or ethical health. KJV translates this word as, "leanness, lies or lying".

---

[64] (Biblesoft's New Exhaustive Strong's Numbers and Concordance with Expanded Greek-Hebrew Dictionary. Copyright © 1994, 2003, 2006 Biblesoft, Inc. and International Bible Translators, Inc.)

[65] References where the same Greek word is used: Matthew 18:12-13 (gone astray); 22:29—"ye do err"; John 7:12—"he deceives"; II Timothy 3:13—"deceiving and being deceived"; Hebrews 11:38—"they wandered"; I Peter 2:25—"going astray"; II Peter 2:15—"are gone astray"; I John 2:26—"seduce you"; Revelation 2:20—"to seduce"; same Greek word is used 39 times in the NT with various translations, all to do with: error, deception, seduction, going astray (like dumb sheep)

[66] References where the same identical Hebrew word or its stem is used: Job 16:8—"my leanness"; Psalm 59:12—"lying"; Hosea 7:3—"and with their lies"; Shades of meaning from the Theological Wordbook of the O.T.: "to disappoint, fail, grow lean, deceive, undependable nature of a person or choice, dealing falsely with someone to that person's detriment" (Leviticus 5:21-22; prophets forecast a grim harvest due to the climate of deception and unfaithfulness in which Judah & Israel lived: Hosea 4:2; 7:3; 10:13; Also, "to deny" or "fail to face facts"—Genesis 18:15; Job 8:18. Failure of health or loss of necessary fat, become gaunt—Psalm 109:24; Job 16:8; Habakkuk 3:17; Life choices that have these results. All refer to the character of "deception" or, "to be deceived".

(1) Deception is a Process; it leads away from truth and thus away from God.[67]

(2) The Root of Deception starts in the heart.

   (a) What is in a person's heart reveals their true inner Character.

   (b) Following one's heart is the result of focusing on self (desires & opinions) rather than on truth.

(3) Satan's strategy is to persuade us to follow our heart.

   (a) Following the Heart is the greatest danger and common ingredient to becoming deceived.

(4) How to guard against following our heart:

   (a) the need to search and examine our heart and allow God to examine it by His Word.

   (b) The need to bring every thought into obedience to Christ.

   (c) Make sure that the meditation of our heart is pleasing to God.

(5) Scripture warns against the danger of self-deception.

   (a) We deceive ourselves by relying on human knowledge, reason and wisdom.

   (b) The wisdom of this world is foolishness in God's sight.

(6) We deceive ourselves by refusing to apply the truth of God's Word in our daily lives.

   (a) Truth that is not acted upon (applied in our daily lives) leads to disobedience, deception and rebellion.

   (b) We deceive ourselves by neglecting to acknowledge God as the Source of our life, strength, talents, spiritual gifts and accomplishments.

---

[67] Deuteronomy 32:4; Psalm 31:5; Isaiah 65:16

(7) We deceive ourselves if we think we can escape God's justice.

(8) We deceive ourselves when we fail to recognize and acknowledge sin in our lives.

(9) We deceive ourselves by believing we can live as we please and still inherit the Kingdom of God.

(10) We deceive ourselves by believing that bad friends will not influence & corrupt good character.

(11) We deceive ourselves by making self and our own interests our priority and focus.

(12) We deceive ourselves by believing that baptism in water or a profession of faith makes us a Christian.

    (a) By their fruit (Christlikeness) you will recognize them—Matthew 7:16;

    (b) Not everyone who says to me, "Lord, Lord" will enter the kingdom of heaven, but only he who does the will of my Father who is in heaven." Matthew 7:21.

(13) We deceive ourselves by believing we can be spiritually mature and not control our tongues. (James 1:26)

There are four lessons in this series, but I shared only a little from the first four pages of Lesson One.

And then an invitation came from a pastor in Englewood, New Jersey. He was previously familiar with our ministry and so contacted us to come hold a week of meetings at his new pastorate in Englewood. This would require a trip across the USA from the West Coast. But it was a meeting in the early summer months when it is generally hard to get meetings. It was an act of faith to accept the invitation because I had no meetings lined up in churches along the route back east. However, I accepted the invitation and went to work trying to get meetings lined up for us on the way back east. I was trying to build an itinerary the wrong way, but felt that if God was in this it would work. We arranged to stop off in the Chicago area, on the way back east, and stayed with our dear friends, Paul and Loretta House, who live in Oswego, Illinois (near Wheaton where Ruth's Father had lived as a boy). Ruth wanted to search the archives for Taylor Family records. We did manage to find the old house owned by Ruth's Grandfather and Grandmother and where her own Father had grown up. And I remember the first time we drove into the Old Town part of Wheaton and saw the cobbled stone streets Ruth started to tremble and then burst into tears. She said that she felt as if she were making a connection with her Father who had now been dead many years. She knew better than to believe in any sort of connection. It was just an emotional reaction to being on the very street where her Father and Uncles must surely have walked, laughed and talked. We were looking at the very stores where maybe they made purchases.

So every day I dropped Ruth off at the county courthouse (or wherever she wanted to be) as I went on into Wheaton to do research at the Billy Graham Center, Wheaton College Graduate School of Theology. My research would be in the area of the Great Spiritual Awakenings of early Colonial America in the 1600s, 1700s and 1800s, particularly what is known as the First and Second Great Spiritual Awakenings and centering on the ministries of Jonathan Edwards and George Whitefield, Charles Finney and others.

It is amazing how these things work out when God is in it. Let us look first the problem and then God's solution.

We got back to New Jersey and the Pastor had completely forgotten about the arrangements we had made earlier in the year. I had written him the normal series of letters to make sure communication was adequate, but he had been busy and neglected to even open my correspondence. So when we arrived, he was shocked to find out that we were there to preach a week of meetings. Circumstances in the church were such that he could not honor the previous arrangement. He did invite me to preach on a Wednesday night. But that was all. So we started back out to the West Coast without any meetings.

The Solution: I had mentioned to the pastor that I was working on a book I hoped to write on Principles for a Spiritual Awakening in America and before we left Englewood, New Jersey Pastor Temple asked me for a phone number where he could reach me when we stopped off in Chicago. Arriving back in Chicago I received a phone call from Pastor Scott asking us to return to Englewood, and agreeing to have me preach every Wednesday night and Sunday morning and evening for the rest of the summer. He had gone to the Official Board with a request to have us return and fill the pulpit for the rest of the summer. The offer was to pay us $5,000 for the summer and I could work on my book during each day. I was also able to go to work trying to establish other meetings back east. This was successful and we had meetings into the Fall in Parkersburg, West Virginia as well as Calvary Assembly of God in Elkhart, Indiana and the rich in history Indiana town of Tippecanoe; also in churches near Columbus, Ohio.

It was while preaching in Englewood, located just across the river from New York City, that we received opportunities to visit Brooklyn Tabernacle where Jim Cymbala is Senior Pastor and Times Square Church where Dave Wilkerson was Senior Pastor. Our experiences at these two churches were outstanding and eye-opening!

Jim and Carol Cymbala's daughter and her husband were on staff at the Englewood Assembly of God church where we were preaching for the summer. This young couple was able to take us to the Cymbala home, and also to get Ruth and I front row seats at a Tuesday night prayer service. There were at least 1,500 people present that Tuesday night with an additional 300 plus standing in the foyer looking in. The prayer service was powerful! That kind of attendance is normal for their Tuesday night prayer services. Many people have their lives transformed by the power of God and often delivered from drug addiction weekly in those meetings.

Ruth and I also attended a Sunday evening meeting at Time Square Church. What was notable here was that as people began arriving at least 30 minutes before service they would either bow in prayer in their seats or, as most of them did, go forward to pray in the altar area until the beginning of service. An interview with Dave Wilkerson had been arranged for after service. I had developed an extensive outline for the book I hoped to write on Principles for A Spiritual Awakening and was hoping that Brother Wilkerson would take time to study the outline and get back to me with suggestions. Instead, he glanced quickly through the outline and handed it back to me with this comment, "We don't talk about Revival or Spiritual Awakenings at Time Square Church anymore because the very word encourages unbiblical beliefs in some people. We talk about the Manifest Presence of Jesus instead of Revival." He went on to say that every Revival in history has ended in confusion, disputes, disunity and further coldness of heart." Needless to say, I was shocked! He was saying that every special move of God in church history had ended very badly. I knew that the word, "renew" or "revive" were both in the Hebrew text of the Old Testament and even once in the New Testament. And I also had historical records to Spiritual Awakenings that changed entire nations, like the renewal movement in England which was the birth of the Salvation Army organization, feeding the poor, putting an end to child abuse and the use of children to work the factories, thus being a catalyst for the institution of Child Labor Laws in England and eventually in America. The Sunday school or Christian Education ministries came out of those Spiritual Awakenings. Also the attack on alcoholism came from Christian influence. Later, the Anti-Slavery or Abolitionist Movement both in England and early America was largely the work of Christian people. Pastors thundered in their pulpits against the evils of slavery. Later, a woman's right to vote and women's rights in general would come from religious teachings. Most of these things came out of the atmosphere of the First and Second Great Spiritual Awakenings (late 1600s through the 1800s).

And so after my disappointing interview with Pastor Dave Wilkerson, disappointing because a man whom I greatly admired had told me something I wasn't prepared to hear, we finished our teaching ministry for the summer.

It had been near the beginning of the summer when we first began to be aware of the seriousness of our Son's health condition and the possibility that he might have AIDS. Our Son had been calling us complaining about his health. He once said to me, "Dad, I am tired of being tired and not feeling well. I am sick all the time. And so it was about then that I took Ruth to the JFK International Airport and flew her back to the West Coast (Manhattan, California) to see if she could help our Son. For some reason, our Son did not receive his Mother well, and approximately 2 or 3 weeks later Ruth flew back to be with me and finish our meetings New Jersey and in the South.

We then decided to visit Ruth's Uncle and his wife who lived in Mobile, Alabama. Also, Brownsville, Florida was not very far from Mobile and we were able to attend one night at the then famous, Brownsville Revival. The Brownsville Revival Movement was, by that time, world famous. Pastors were coming from around the globe to be part of these services where hundreds were coming to Christ, marriages were put back together and parents and children reconciled. Great miracles of healing occurred nightly and the most obvious were often documented by medical doctors from the audience.

Briefly, here is what we saw that night at the Brownsville Assembly of God Church. The auditorium, that seats something more than 700 people, was packed. Extra chairs had been brought in and people were standing around the exterior walls. No place to even put our back to the wall. We were ushered to a side room where another 100 people were watching on closed circuit TV. The service had started at 7 PM and we were only a minute or two late when we arrived. Testimonies were given by several teenagers or young adults about how their own hearts had been changed by God and they had been reconciled to their parents. Parents had similar testimonies about improvement to their parenting skills, patience and Christlikeness in dealing with their children (healing from anger problems) and reconciliation with their children. There were personal testimonies of husband/wife relationships healed and homes where there were only bitter, angry words now filled with love, respect and compassion for each other. Those kind of psychological and spiritual healings don't come because of hype or emotionalism. That takes a miracle from God and willingness on the part of people to change their attitudes and behavior.

At first, Ruth and I could not hear what was going on in the main part of the service and so slipped back into the main auditorium, finally finding a place to back up against the wall and listen. The preacher, Evangelist Steve Hill, preached a simple message. In fact, the thought went through my mind, "This guy can't preach his way out of a paper bag." But I was soon rebuked by what I witnessed as more than 200 people came forward to the altar area to commit their lives to Jesus Christ. And then the service continued on and lasted until midnight. For the skeptics, there has got to be much more than hype or emotionalism to get people of all ages, young & old, teenagers & grandparents to stay and participate in a church service for five hours.

On the way back to the west coast, Ruth and I stopped off again in the Chicago/Wheaton area for further studies. Once again, our friends, Paul and Loretta House, were gracious hosts to us as we each pursued further studies: Ruth did further research on her family tree and I went back to the Billy Graham Center/Wheaton Seminary with two questions in my mind: (1) Was Pastor Wilkerson historically accurate in what he had said to me; and, (2) If so, why? This second question was one for which Pastor Wilkerson had offered no insight.

I spent most of my time in the Rare Books section which was under lock and key and closely monitored when people like me asked to use books from that section. So it was a privilege to be granted unlimited access to that section of their huge library. I would spend 6 to 10 hours per day with those irreplaceable rare books from past centuries. The answers to my two questions should have been obvious in my original research but somehow I had missed even the issue of bad endings to Spiritual Awakenings. Before we left town I managed to Xerox 2,000 pages of notes from the rare books section before I was finally told that what I was doing was against the rules. However, I was granted another privilege by being allowed to keep all the work I had done. I had decided to use the period of the seventeenth, eighteenth and nineteenth centuries (1600 through 1800) in England and Colonial America as my historical model. Even during that time, and probably especially during that time because those years included the two Great Spiritual Awakenings, there was ample evidence of what God seemed to be doing in people's hearts and lives sabotaged by unchristlike actions and attitudes expressed through God's Children. It makes me think of the sadness that must come to the hearts of human parents when their children destroy by their actions the reputation of their family name.

There was also the Welsh Revival in Wales, the Wesley Revival in Great Britain and Revivals many others in other parts of the world, like the South Pacific. So not even 2,000 pages of Xeroxed notes were adequate, but it was all I had time to pull together and analyze. Already, I was beginning to see that, if my historical model was truly representative of church history, Pastor Dave Wilkerson was probably correct in his assessment of historical revival movements. This should not have been a surprise as Dave Wilkerson was himself a student of the history of Spiritual Awakenings. Furthermore, I thought I was beginning to see a pattern that would show the reason for the bad ending to all these Spiritual Awakenings over the centuries.

What I eventually found was that the eventual demise of most all Spiritual Awakenings in Church History has been caused by people not getting along with each other. Arguments over non-essential doctrines are symptoms of spiritual pride and are destructive to any genuine work of God. Baptists, Pentecostals, Presbyterians, Lutherans and many other Christian groups may differ over doctrines about Worship and Liturgy, Bible Prophecy, Divine Healing, the Holy Spirit Baptism and other doctrines that are not essential to their New Birth into the Family of God but those disagreements over doctrines not essential to salvation should not create an excuse among Godly people for breaking fellowship with each other.

Protestants and Catholics can disagree over doctrines not essential to salvation and eventually meet each other in Heaven. The essentials are Faith in Christ as the Son and Sacrificial Lamb of God, as well as His atoning work on the Cross, as well as surrender & obedience to His Sovereignty. The Virgin Birth, plus, of course, belief in the fact and meaning of Christ's Resurrection from the dead and ascension into Heaven are also essential doctrines. If we don't belief in the Virgin Birth we would of necessity need to believe that Jesus also was born with a fallen sin nature and thus not qualified to be God's Sinless Sacrifice to cover all our sins. That, of course would be heresy over which there could be no compromise. The process of inner transformation into Christlikeness is natural, and essential, subsequent to a genuine Born Again experience. Jesus said, "Not everyone that says to me, 'Lord, Lord' will enter into the Kingdom of Heaven but *("ONLY" implied from Greek text, emphasis mine)* those who do the will of my Father in Heaven."

People not loving each other according to the pattern in First Corinthians 13:4-7 or not genuinely forgiving each other or accepting each other on the basis of the shed Blood of Jesus give germination to the destruction of God's Work.

James 1:19-21 states, "Understand this, my dear brothers and sisters: You must all be quick to listen, slow to speak, and slow to get angry. Human anger does not produce the righteousness God desires. So get rid of all the filth and evil in your lives, and humbly accept the word God has planted in your hearts, for it has the power to save your souls."

Church fights do the Devil's work for him and he just sits back and laughs at our immaturity as well-meaning but spiritually and/or psychologically immature people wreak havoc in the Church, the Body of Christ.

The Book of First John 4:20-21 teaches, "If someone says, "I love God," and hates his brother, he is a liar; for he who does not love his brother whom he has seen, how can he love God whom he has not seen? And this commandment we have from Him: that he who loves God *must* love his brother also."

The Bible, which is God's Revelation of Himself and His Will, is the only reliable and authoritative Source of Truth! There is no other source! And one of His most important commandments is that we love each other, as well as the unregenerate of the world for which Christ died. Here are a few results of my further studies in Wheaton at the Billy Graham Center which constitute the Graduate Studies buildings. The purpose was to study Spiritual Awakenings using my historical model of the 17th, 18, & 19th centuries (1600 thru 1800s). Some of this I already knew, but the further studies began to bring at least tentative answers to my questions following up on the interview with the much respected Pastor Dave Wilkerson.

One of the leaders of the First Great Spiritual Awakening (early 1700s) in colonial America was Jonathan Edwards. Benjamin Franklin once said that Jonathan Edwards was the most intellectually brilliant and thoroughly educated man of the first generation born in Colonial America. Young men with a thirst for learning were often in college by the age of 17, but Jonathan Edwards entered Yale College (now Yale University) just prior to his 13th birthday. The entire student body at Yale, at one time, was required to communicate with each other outside the classroom and on campus only in Latin. So at the age of 13 Jonathan Edwards was already fluent in conversational Latin. Jonathan was also interested in natural science and atomic theory, light and optics. He would later become a Puritan Preacher, a philosopher, biologist, botanist, linguist (Latin, Greek, Hebrew), and astronomer. His studies convinced him that the laws of nature proved the wisdom and care of God along with God's concern about our daily lives. When we sin, when we need God's Regeneration, Deliverance, Forgiveness, Cleansing, Healing or encouragement, etc., we need to know that God is near, [68] rather than some philosophy like Deism, believed by many at the time. Deism teaches that God wound up the universe like a clock and left it to tic on its own; the consequence being that God is not interested in our daily lives and could care less what we do or say. Jonathan Edwards reached the conclusion that God is very much interested and involved in our daily lives. Deism teaches that God is transcendent in power, but nevertheless not imminent so as to bring Himself into personal involvement with either the universe or the human race which He created. Jonathan Edwards studied Physical Science and Philosophy as other men did, but rejected Deism, coming instead to diametrically

---

[68] See Psalm 119:151 where the word "near" contains the idea of "approachable" based on kinship. The same concept of Psalm 145:18; 148:14; Luke 10:9, 11; 21:28, 31 "near" with idea of "approachable"

opposed conclusions about the God of the Bible. He taught that God is very much compassionately interested in and concerned about our daily lives. Edwards believed that the convicting and cleansing power of God the Holy Spirit, plus His willingness to heal our sick bodies and deliver us from the daily attacks of the Enemy of our Souls described the actual activities of BOTH an Imminent (close by) and Transcendent (above all) God. This imminent God does indeed hold us accountable for our thoughts, words and actions!

Edwards was one of the leaders of the First Great Spiritual Awakening in Colonial America that began in 1742. Several years later, after having just been appointed to be the new President of the College of New Jersey (Princeton University), he would die of complications from a new development in medical science called the small pox vaccination. He was 55 at the time of his death. One can only ask, "God, why such an untimely death by one of your greatest servants of that era?"

Probably, Edwards' most famous sermon is, "Sinners in the Hands of an Angry God". It has been observed that Pastor Edwards was near-sighted and that he wrote out his sermons in manuscript form and read them word for word as the paper was held closely in front of his face. What is known for sure is that, as that sermon was delivered, the conviction of the Holy Spirit settled upon the congregation with such force that moans and groans began to be uttered until finally, in frustration, Pastor Edwards asked the folks to be more respectful and just listen without all the moaning and groaning. At the end of his message the congregation fell on their faces before God in stark fear of the possibility of going to Hell and in repentance for their sins.

A comparison between two families, living at the same point in history, those of Max Jukes and Jonathan Edwards, Puritan Preacher, Scientist and College President, is instructive.

Mr. Jukes was a backwoodsman who showed no interest in education or matters of religion. He was a drunkard who married a godless young woman. Of their descendants, 310 died as paupers, 150 were criminals, 7 were murderers, 100 were drunkards, and more than half of the women were prostitutes. And 67 of the 709 descendants were reported to have syphilis, 300 of the descendants died an early death, not living the normal life span for their time. It is said that these 540 descendants who were criminals cost the State one and a quarter million dollars, and 130 of his descendants spent 1 year or more in jail. Of the 20 who learned a trade, 10 learned it in a state prison.

However, Jonathan and Sarah (Pierpont) Edwards produced a different lineage and heritage. It has been said that their family alone produced a disproportionate impact for good and righteousness upon early America. More than 100 lawyers and 30 judges came directly out of their union, plus 13 college presidents, more than 100 professors, 100 missionaries, pastors and professional teachers of God's Word. Also, among their direct descendants were 80 people elected to public office including 3 mayors, 3 state governors, several members of congress, 3 Senators, 1 Vice-President of the United States (Aaron Burr), one comptroller of the U.S. Treasury and one First Lady, Edith Roosevelt, wife of President Theodore Roosevelt (1901-1909). Sixty of their descendants were famous authors who produced 135 books of significant importance.

I am currently reading a book entitled, "Anchor Man: How A Father Can Anchor His Family in Christ for the next 100 Years" by Steve Farrar. [69] Obviously, Jonathan and Sarah had the principles outlined in Steve Farrar's book pretty well "down pat" 260 years before the book was written.

Jonathan Edwards was a brilliant man whom Benjamin Franklin greatly admired. Edwards was extremely hard working, spending 13

---

[69] Thomas Nelson, Publisher: Nashville, Dallas, Mexico City, Rio de Janeiro, Beijing; 1998, 2000

hours per day in Bible Study and/or his other studies in Physical Science (Astronomy, Botany, Biology) and Philosophy, as well as pastoring a church and leading the First Great Spiritual Awakening in early colonial America. It was said [70] that "much of the capacity and talent, intensity and character of their more than 1,400 descendants were due to the influence of Jonathan's wife, Sarah. Sarah came from a family of well-known pastors and Christian Leaders. Her own father was the founder of Yale College. One source says that her disposition was like sunshine. She was cheerful and of a practical disposition, a good housekeeper and hostess to their many guests. Sarah is said to have been an exemplary wife, and mother of Jonathan's eleven children. One might wonder how they ever had time to produce babies or enjoy marital love, let alone raise all eleven children to be bright, respectful and, in adulthood, successful individuals in their own chosen careers. All of their children were committed Christians and respectful to their parents. I once read a copy of a letter which Jonathan Edwards wrote to his own father. It began with the words, "Dear Honored Sir". I think most parents today would give up a lot just to be treated respectfully and with honor by their own children.

Jonathan Edwards gave similar respect to his wife by trusting her to direct the household, and teach, develop and discipline the children, with no effort on his part to interfere, dominate or control her as she administrated the household. Sarah, in turn, was a I Peter 3 kind of wife, giving honor and respect to her husband as the Lord and Head, under God, of their Household.

Contrary to popular opinion, the Puritan philosophy on human sexuality was far healthier than that of our own contemporary culture. Sex was seen as something to be enjoyed by two married people,

---

[70] From a book by Richard Dugdale with comments on a WEB site, http://www. rfrick.info/jukes.htm accessed on January 9, 2014.

partially for the purpose of raising godly children for the benefit of God's Kingdom on earth and doing that within the limits of marital fidelity. Believe it or not, the Puritan concept of sexuality was that God intended the bedroom to be the play room for any married couple, and that they were free to enjoy each other's bodies as they wished. [71] The Puritan teaching was to have all the sex you want, just keep it within the marriage covenant! And women, especially, were to be modest in dress (I Peter 3:1-7) so that their sexuality was emphasized only for the view and enjoyment of their husband. The husband, in turn, was to show good manners and compassionate care for his wife, not being a controller or bully, but treating her with gentleness, respect, and understanding of her own unique, individual needs as his wife. Every woman is different and has unique strengths and weaknesses and should be honored and cared for accordingly by her husband. Here is a question for each husband to consider, "What are my wife's unique strengths and weaknesses and how can I be the best possible husband to her, taking that uniqueness of hers into full accountability?"

I read an account in J.I. Packer's biography of Jonathan Edwards wherein, sitting around the dinner table with a guest preacher during which time the topic, "God's Goodness", was being discussed. Sarah had such a strong emotional (moving of the Holy Spirit upon her?) reaction that she swooned and had to be carried to her room where she remained in worship to God for some length of time, totally oblivious to what was going on with their guest or elsewhere in the home. Jonathan Edwards considered physical manifestations such as these to be incidental to the real work of God, "but his own mystic devotion and the experiences of his wife during the Awakening (which he gives in detail) make him think

---

[71]   I Corinthians 6:15-20; 7:1-5

that the divine visitation usually overpowers the body, a view which he supported with Scripture".[72]

The Revival Movement led by Jonathan Edwards, I would learn later, splintered into 100 different church mini-denominations, all of them critical of each other usually over some minor point that, in the light of eternity and/or the requirements of salvation and personal transformation, was really non-essential. Jonathan Edwards was not part of all the infighting. Those were awful results coming out of the original Spiritual Awakening. And obviously there was an absence of enough knowledge of Scripture and the Ways of God to understand the sinfulness of their argumentative attitudes which brought so much chaos to what God had done. The original, knowledgeable & well trained Godly leaders at the beginning of the movement were also criticized so as to diminish their influence. Such "goings-on" are really the result of pride, and immature people who are overly opinionated, without sufficient training in Scripture and without gracious Christian love that is patient with other people's opinions.

The reason I have taken the time and space to recount a few details of what I learned in my studies at Wheaton is because much of my own teaching in our Seminars had been in the area of Principles for A Spiritual Awakening. Furthermore, I need to distinguish between "A Spiritual Awakening" and "A Revival" or "Renewal Meetings". A Spiritual Awakening is what happens to those who are unsaved, spiritually dead, totally self-centered, carnal and given over to lust and the satisfaction of their fleshly desires, unregenerate with no relationship to God, their Creator. These people are on a path that will end in Hell Fire and will surely go there, unless something is said or something happens,

---

[72] http://en.wikipedia.org/wiki/Jonathan_Edwards_(theologian)#Works accessed January 9, 2014

that awakens them to spiritual realities and brings them to a place of complete surrender to Jesus Christ as their Savior and Sovereign Lord.

When a Spiritual Awakening is focused on the Person of Jesus Christ and His Word (the Bible) the Spiritual Awakening will lead them down a path to Eternal Life. According to Jesus, the Christ of God, all other religions are demonic counterfeits! [73] Jesus said, of Himself, "I am the way, the truth and the life". The presence of the definite article in the Greek text for this passage (John 14:6) demonstrates that there is no other way, no other truth or no other source of life. Jesus is the one and only way, the one and only Source of Truth and the one and only Source of Life. In fact, He IS Truth and He IS Life!

In the case of "Revival", also known as Spiritual Renewal the need of Revival or Renewal indicates that a Child of God is near death and needs to be revived or renewed to a status of Spiritual Health. The signs of a "near death" experience are: "no hunger, no thirst, no activity that comes with life and health". What is true physically in this regard is also true spiritually. If there is no hunger [74] for Spiritual Food: the Bread of Life, prayer (conversation with God), personal Bible reading and study during the week, hearing the Word of God explained by a Pastor on Sunday mornings, etc., little or no desire to be with God's people, or no thirst for the Water of Life the absence of spiritual hunger and thirst are an indication of a dangerous, near death spiritual experience! Emergency action is needed to correct this condition or spiritual (eternal) death will occur. The remedial actions of Awakenings and Renewal to Spiritual Health are what happened in the 1600, 1700 and 1800s.

---

[73] John 10:1-10; 14:6; Ezekiel 22:28; Genesis 3:1-15 with Romans 16:20 and Revelation 12:9 & 20:2; Second Peter 2:1-2;

[74] Matthew 5:6; Luke 6:21, 25; Psalm 42:1-2; 63:1-2; 84:2; 107:9; John 6:27; Amos 11:8-13;

During the middle 1990s there was a lot of controversy concerning certain activities in churches experiencing a Spiritual Renewal (fresh hunger for God in the pews among common ordinary people). The physical manifestations that came as a result of God's felt Presence were unsettling to some and exciting and reassuring to others. I was being invited by pastors to come teach and share my insights concerning these matters. I had come to the conclusion that these physical manifestations of crying, laughing, shaking, trembling, etc. are supportable by Biblical example [75], but, I likewise felt that the outward manifestations could be a distraction from the real work of God in a person's life. What God really wants to accomplish in each of us is the inward transformation of character, values, or attitudes, along with freedom from anger, unforgiveness, resentment, bitterness, depression, cynicism, and a myriad of other mental and/or emotional problems. Dealing with those issues is the real work of either Spiritual Awakening or Renewal. The word "renewal" comes from a Hebrew word which means, "to cut back, prune, dig around, plow up, cultivate". Both Renewal and Awakening are just that! It has little to do with the number of people coming to Christ for salvation, nor the outstanding demonstration of the supernatural, as in physical healings. All those things are desirable and, hopefully, will be present, but that is not either Spiritual Awakening or Renewal. Revival is the process of transforming the fallen human nature from being earthly (with carnal, fleshly values & reactions) to being heavenly with the values of Spirit Beings who already live constantly in God's Presence of perfect Love. The hope of Heaven is that one day each of us will find ourselves to be sinless, and living beyond the possibility of having evil desires or doing or thinking anything evil. We will be like Jesus in every aspect of our personality and nature! No

---

[75] Daniel 4:19; 7:15; 8:16-18, 27; 10:8-10, 15-17; Habakkuk 3:16; Numbers 24:4; Isaiah 28:19; Jeremiah 9:1; 23:9; Acts 9:3, 6, 9; 16:25-29; Philippians 2:12;

anger! No resentment! No fear! No depression! No unforgiveness! No lust! No self-centeredness!

Can you picture yourself being that kind of person? That is the future of all who surrender to and are renewed by our Heavenly Father! [76]

My own outline which formed a foundation for my teaching is as follows, but the main outline of my teaching on Principles for A Spiritual Awakening is four pages long, single spaced. The following is foundational to the rest of the outline and each line is a separate lesson.

A. The Process of Revival
    1. A Process of Divine Judgment for Sinners & Fiery Trials to purify the Saints
    2. A Sense of Desperation coming out of Judgment & Testing (Fiery Trials)
    3. Brokenness & Humility: The Plowing of God's Spirit in Human Hearts (see parable of soils, Luke 8)
    4. New Spiritual Hunger: A Desperate Desire To Seek & Know God
    5. Anointed and Powerful Praying
    6. Inward Sanctification & the Practice of the Examined Life (examination in the light of God's Word of the inner life of Thoughts, Emotions, Desires and Priorities)
    7. The Knowledge of the Holy: Preoccupation with the Mind & Ways of God
    8. Human Vessels: Dedicated, Committed, & Anointed to Serve God
    9. The Joy of the Lord: Walking in Genuine Faith, Hope and Love
    10. Outpourings of Spiritual Refreshments

---

[76] Hebrews 12:7-10;

B. The Price of Revival
1. Purification: The Inward Cleansing of the Temple (human spirit & soul: emotions, thoughts, desires and priorities)
2. Prostration: The Meaning & Lifestyle of Humility
3. Prayer: The Lifeline and Maintenance of Revival
4. Pilgrimage: Perseverance & Progress in Holy Living

C. The Product of Genuine Revival: A Divine Visitation
1. Renewal of the Life and Nature of Jesus in the Daily Lives of individual Believers
2. Renewal of Spiritual Perceptiveness among Believers
3. Renewal of God-centered priorities in the lives of those who claim the name, "Christian".
4. Renewal of the Sense of God's Glory and Holy Presence
5. Renewal of the Demonstration of God's Power and Blessing
6. Renewal of a God-consciousness in Human Society

I need to wrap this chapter up by simply stating that, as a result of what I learned at Wheaton about the problem with Spiritual Awakenings in the light of history my preaching/teaching changed from an emphasis on Renewal to an emphasis on interpersonal relationships: how to get along with people; understanding different personality types, dynamics of forgiveness; also, The Deception of Perceptions and much more.

Ruth and I began to do Marriage Seminars and also some teaching on parenting skills. Rules and skills for getting along with people in the church and how to work with a pastor and church leaders and do so with humility and patience; these all became our points of emphasis as we continued on our travels until the year 2001.

It isn't that we no longer recognized the validity or need for Spiritual Awakenings for Sinners, and Spiritual Renewal (Revival) for Saints, but rather there is a certain preparation of the human heart that encourages the Awakenings and Renewals that are needed. And so our teaching changed over to the broad topics that will allow that heart preparation, particularly the topic of Interpersonal Relationships. This would include how to bring healing to broken relationships, how to avoid causing damage to relationships (just because you disagree with the person you care about on some issue, while it may not be minor it is still not worth losing or damaging the relationship over that issue). How to build healthy relationships that almost automatically will withstand the strain and pain of misunderstandings that do come just because that happens in this broken world where false perceptions are easily and unknowingly created.[77] We also did Marriage Seminars, and teaching on how to get along with other people in group settings; being polite, gracious, quick to forgive, etc. There are two kinds of people: the kind of person that walks into a social setting and, by their words and body language say, "Here I am everyone!" And then there is the person that quietly, humbly walks into the same situation and says by their words and body language, "There you are! I am so glad to see you again!" In other words, the self-centered person or "other person centered" individual.

But this is also true in a family. Does the Husband and Father look at his wife and children as being there to serve him (self-centered) or does he see himself as present to serve and attend to the needs of the wife and children(other people centered)?

So it is with the wife and children, each should see themselves as the servant of the other members of the family. And so if the wife says something like, "Honey, you go sit down and rest, I've got this covered and you have already worked hard enough today" then the husband is free to let her finish the work, and maybe even bring him his favorite beverage if she offers. If that doesn't happen then Husband or Dad needs

---

[77]   Exodus 22:10-34; Matthew 17:7; Luke 17:1; Romans 16:17; I Samuel 2:17; II Samuel 12:14; I Timothy 6:1; Titus 2:5

to take the absence of that kind of thoughtful release by the family as the signal that his attention and involvement is needed. Someone has said that intimacy in the bedroom begins in the kitchen. An interesting observation!

Such an "other person centered" household of family members surely produces well-balanced and harmonious family relationships where each person feels loved, respected and valued. Jesus said, "Let the greatest among you be the servant of all." So, if Dad wants to be respected as "Head of the House" he will make himself servant to all. The wife also should want to minister to the needs of her husband and children, not thinking of herself, but simply being an example of unselfish giving. At the end of a meal, no member of the family should be relaxing while the Mother and Wife still toils in the kitchen (unless that is the way she wants it). Each should have their appointed tasks and then all can relax together when work is done. Here is the example of a Family of Christ Followers!

I recently read a personal testimony somewhere (maybe in Readers Digest) about a man who was stressed out as he tried to labor through the process of finishing a writing assignment for a certain publisher. He and his wife decided to rent a cabin at a lake side retreat in the mountains so that the gentleman could focus on getting the writing assignment finished.

One evening, in order to alleviate the stress & anxiety her husband was feeling, his wife planned a romantic evening for the two of them, candle light dinner and all the romance to follow. Later, in the middle of the night, he awoke to see his wife nursing their new born child whom they had brought with them. Exhausted from all her activities of the previous day, her head was nodding as she tried to stay awake long enough to finish nursing the baby. The thought went through the husband's mind just before he drifted back off to sleep: "Now there is a real saint! She has just used her entire body to minister to the needs of her husband and child and is paying the price of utter fatigue as part of the result." Sainthood, it seems is much more than staying free from sin, or worshipping God. It can also include unselfish living as we give ourselves for the greater good of others. So let us consider together the Word of the Lord as translated from James 3:17-18 in the Living Bible

> *17 But the wisdom that comes from heaven is first of all pure and full of quiet gentleness. Then it is peace-loving and courteous. It allows discussion and is willing to yield to others; it is full of mercy and good deeds. It is wholehearted and straightforward and sincere. 18And those who are peacemakers will plant seeds of peace and reap a harvest of goodness.*

Chapter Eight

The Storms & Challenges faced in Ministry Throughout Southeast Asia

As I think back over the past few years, especially from 2001 to the present, I am reminded of one Scripture in particular that states that each of us should "delight yourself also in the Lord and He will give you the desires of your heart".[78] Actually, there are several important words mentioned in verses 3-5 that hold the key to the fulfillment of that promise. The words are: trust, do good, dwell, feed, delight and commit, and again the word, trust. The words "trust" and "do good" (acts of righteous compassion that is a benefit to others) and "commit" are self-explanatory. But "dwell in the land" and "feed on my faithfulness" might need a little explaining. "Dwell in the land", is the place to which God has taken you as your place of life and work for Him. Stay there! Don't cut and run when things get tough! Focus on God's Will as you understand it to be for your life, and feed (be nourished physically, psychologically and spiritually) to whatever extent and in whatever way God provides for you. Be content! [79]

God did not lead the Children of Israel to any other country but Canaan (Palestine). And it was there they were to settle down and

---

[78]   Psalm 37:3-5 but see also, Psalm 43:3-5; 104:34; 145:19-21; Isaiah 58:10-14; I Peter 1:6-9; John 15:7; Jeremiah 17:7-8; Proverbs 3:5-8

[79]   Philippians 4:11-13; I Timothy 6:8; Hebrews 13:5-6. "Be content" comes from a Greek word meaning, "the sailing away of self"! Put self in a boat and send it away from the shoreline of God's Will for your life; the place where you stand. Say goodbye to self and say hello to Him & His Love!

accomplish God's purposes for their personal and national lives. The idea of feeding on His faithfulness is the idea of being content where God has placed us and with the provisions He brings to us. One interesting fact about Canaan (Palestine) is that it is mostly desert, uninhabitable and not at all the place one would expect God to place His People as an expression of His Love and Care. But the descendants of Abraham, Isaac and Jacob were expected to turn the desert into a garden. Through much toil, suffering and danger they would realize finally how gracious was their God. [80]

The Children of Israel (12 sons of Jacob and their descendants) were expected to fight for every inch of the Promised Land. God didn't wield the sword for them! They had to go into battle, make themselves expendable as they did the will of the God Who had called them and promised to be with them, provide for them and protect them. Being a Follower of Jesus Christ has the same requirement. One must fight for victory over the carnal nature we each still possess. Kill it! Crucify it! And yield to the God Who wants to build within each of us a Christ-like nature, one so opposite to the value system of this fallen, broken world. And in each generation, each century in history, the cost and requirements of discipleship are different. Foxe's Book of Martyrs is all about the cost of Discipleship! [81] Although the cost does not always end in martyrdom, Jesus made it clear that to be His Disciple required the daily taking up of one's Cross (symbol of suffering, total commitment including death, and most of all, the death to the self-life or the unique requirements of God's Call and expectations in our own personal life). Current statistics prove that even in the 21st Century an average of

---

[80] Deuteronomy 7:13-15; 15:1-6; 28:1-14

[81] Look for this book on Amazon.com or at www.ccel.org/f/foxe/martyrs/home.html

150,000 people per year still lose their lives for the cause of Christ! Sometimes death to our own self-will can be harder.

Jesus described the Kingdom of God as a Treasure hidden in a field. [82] Thus, the Treasure must be searched for and then removed by effort to a safe place.[83] The application for us, in the 21st century has to do with removing ourselves from those who own the field (the culture, society). You can't buy the Treasure if you continue to live & participate in the activities of the Field with its ungodly lifestyles. We must come out from among them in order to be received by the King of Heaven. Do not be unequally yoked together with unbelievers in life or tasks that will require you to participate in things contrary to the Heavenly Culture, represented by The Treasure. "For what fellowship has righteousness with lawlessness?" The lifestyles of this fallen world are equated to lawlessness because they are contrary to the laws of your new identification as a Citizen of Heaven. This is why a church auditorium is called "a Sanctuary". It is a place where one meets in safety from temptation with those who have also become Citizens of another World (Heaven/God's Kingdom). Furthermore, possession of the Treasure will cost the Finder everything he/she owns. And that "everything" will be different for each person and generation. So it is with God's blessings here on Earth and in Heaven. Like Paul, [84] we know what it is to abound (be successful, have more than enough, extra provision of all kinds) and we know what it is to suffer want, struggling for finances, health, and loving relationships, often experiencing the hurt of not able to count on the reactions of others.

But one should never compare themselves to others! I have visited the gravesites of martyrs in West Africa. These were people who had

---

[82]   Matthew 13:44

[83]   II Corinthians 6:14-18

[84]   Philippines 4:12

lived for a short span of time and were either killed (chopped to pieces or beheaded with machetes) or died of some tropical disease after sowing the seed of God's Word and the Love of Jesus and Hope for Eternal Life for only a short period of time. But Ruth and I were able to minister in the same areas that hadn't changed all that much as far as danger and risk is concerned but to do so without harm to ourselves. The Gospel Seed, planted earlier, sprouted and took root, and we, and others with us, were able to come along at a later time when systems of protection against malaria and other dangers were in place so that we did not suffer or die for the privilege of sharing the Gospel but were able to water and care for what was already planted and be instrumental in the hands of God to help His Gospel Garden to grow and flourish even more. We lived in a nice mission house built on the edge of the jungle, mostly protected from snakes, mosquitos and bandits, and thus did not face the same risk to our health or from angry people resisting the Gospel. There was some suffering involved, but nothing that we may not have also suffered here in the USA in the course of normal living (with the exceptions of bouts with malaria, or sleeping for days and weeks in mud huts and eating snake, rat, dog, fish heads and eyeballs, and monkey meat or taking bucket showers in the same thatched facility, only partially private, where people also urinated).

The advice 'not to compare ourselves to others' is difficult to follow, especially if one is a hard worker with a desire to do one's best, as well, maybe, as the tendency to think, "well I am trying to do my best to please God, why do I not have some of the desirable circumstances or opportunities that this other person seems to enjoy?" The need is to focus on doing God's Will and being faithful to Him. The pastor or deacon or Sunday School Teacher in a small place of service, when faithful and obedient, will receive as great a reward as the person in a large place. Faithfulness and Obedience to God is the two fold measuring stick by which we will all be rewarded on Judgment Day.

For the Believer, Judgment Day is the Reward Seat (as at the Roman games) where crowns (NOT punishment) are handed out. The words coming from our King and Heavenly Father, "Well done thou good and faithful servant" are equivalent in Heaven to winning Olympic Gold on Earth and will bear eternal reward and recognition. It is normal to wish for our own idea of significance, and it is normal to want to do well and be recognized by others for having done well. But we are cautioned in Scripture that where there is bitter envy or self-seeking in our hearts that such "wisdom" is earthly, sensual, and demonic . . . for where envy and self-seeking exist there is confusion and every kind of evil that is present. [85]

However, the promise of the Bible is that God will give us the desires of our heart. The Hebrew word for "desires" can also be translated "requests". So it is the "requests of the heart" that God has promised to those who trust, commit, dwell and feed on His faithfulness, meaning that He will look into their heart and know the requests, even if unspoken, of the emotions and thoughts of the heart and that He will act to give us those emotional and mental, even if unspoken, requests that are within the prevue of His Will for us. By feeding on His Faithfulness is meant, also, that one harbors no feeling that God has been unfaithful just because circumstances are not what we would like them to be; no accusations of the heart toward God.

The Bread Ruth and I cast on the waters, by means of all God has allowed us to do in His Name, took years for some of it to be received back into our lives. In the beginning, it literally cost us everything! And yet, in the process of committing all our lives, strength and possessions to God, holding nothing back, considering ourselves to be expendable for the Cause of Christ and His Presence in people's lives, and at times working long hours beyond our endurance to the point of suffering

---

[85] James 3:13-18; 4:1-10

chest pains and depression, we fed on His faithfulness and continued to serve Him out of love rather than a desire for some recognition or reward. As part of that, our focus needed to be on cooperation with the Foreign Missions Leadership of our church denomination, being a Team Player to the point of not insisting on our own rights or even that promises made to us earlier are kept. Why? Because we recognized that the overall strategy of the Missions Outreach by the Team as a whole was more important than the desires and felt call of the individual, and so we tried to consider ourselves as expendable. Those were the rules we all played by, and were expected by our leaders that we work by, knowing that if God had a special Call or Task He had placed in the heart of an individual it would eventually come to light and be honored. The opportunity to do what our heart was telling us to do would eventually come to us, which for me would be to teach at the West Africa Advanced School of Theology in Lomé, Togo.

So, in the long run the Bread we cast on the waters did come back and eventually we also received the Blessing of the Lord according to the promise of God's Word. Consequently, we do know what it is to travel to exotic parts of the world, to see sights and have experiences that many people would pay small fortunes to experience, and we have done it all, mostly all expenses paid, or at least with comparatively small cost to ourselves.

Ruth once asked me, "Which do you like most, the ministry found in what we do, or the adventure of events along the way?" For instance travel in foreign places along with the events during those travels? It was a valid question because I had often talked of the adventure part and Ruth had listened patiently over and over again to all my stories as sermon illustrations of one kind or another.

But I tell of these things not to boast on where Ruth and I have traveled or the sights we have seen, but to boast on our precious Lord who saw the secret desires of my heart and granted my wishes above & beyond what I could have even thought to ask for!

First Example: [86] While still living in a small, government subsidized apartment in Tacoma, Washington I received an invitation from my friend Micah Smith to join a team of 13 people he would lead to Vietnam for the purpose of the official opening of an orphanage north of Hanoi and just a few kilometers south of the border with China. Ruth and I prayed about the matter and decided to put out an appeal to our family and Church Renewal Ministries mailing lists to see if God would provide the funds for me to join the team going to Vietnam. It was sure thing that we didn't have the funds. In fact we were struggling just to keep our rent paid and food on the table. This was about August of 2003 and the team would leave in December of that same year. The cost would be somewhere around $2,500, including air travel to and from

---

[86]   See: Ecclesiastes 11:1; Proverbs 11:24-25; Isaiah 32:8. We visited places in France, Italy and Switzerland where many people pay out huge sums of money to visit for just a short period of time, but where we traveled all expenses paid because being there was required of us for ministry or training for ministry (language studies, etc). It was part of our work! We were close to the Matterhorn in Switzerland, The Eiffel Tower and Versailles Palace in France as well as actually living in the French Alps while we were in language school learning French, and so visited these places. Living in the Swiss Alps while I studied Bible and Theology at a Swiss Bible College so that I could gain the needed Biblical vocabulary in French provided other opportunities at little or no cost. A trip one Christmas to Southern Germany, Austria & Italy to visit several famous castles like the Neuschwanstein (made famous by Disney World); the Vatican Museum in Rome, The Sistine Chapel, paintings by Michael Angelo, The Statue of David in Florence; & the Leaning Tower of Pizza. Also the Chateau de Chillion on Lake Geneva for which the famous autobiographical poem, "The Prisoner of Chillon" was written by Lord Byron. We were able to visit many places in Alaska, India, Cambodia, Thailand & Vietnam (Hanoi & Saigon; The Hotel Hilton in Hanoi where American prisoners were held) all for a fraction of the cost others would have paid, and often, with no cost at all. I visited a 13th century Muslim Mosque in Berkina Faso (formerly, Upper Volta, W. Africa) and visited churches & African Church Leadership in Ouagadougou, a walled city up on the Sahara Desert of North Africa. Comparatively few people experience those kinds of adventures!

Vietnam as well as lodging and food. Twenty-five hundred dollars round trip from Seattle via Japan and Thailand to Vietnam was an unheard of low price. Of all the places we had traveled in Europe and Africa, even years later in Alaska, it was mostly in the context of a lot of hard work being done on our part. So much so that there was little time to "do the tourist thing". That was not always true, but normally was the case. But this time, I would travel just to share in the excitement of opening this Orphanage at Center of Hope in LocBinh, North Vietnam. The balance of funds needed did not come in until just before the deadline, but the fact is that God did provide and I was able to make the trip without using any of our personal funds.

In the process of making the trip we would stop off in Bangkok, Thailand to visit Pastor Somnuk and his wife, Lilly, who were pastoring in that city. Somnuk and Lilly are both fluent in the Thai language as well as one or more dialects of Chinese. This was one of many interesting parts of the trip. One evening a special social event was put on for our Ministry Team during which we were able to meet people from various ministries throughout Southeast Asia. One couple I remember in particular was from southern California. Both the man and his wife had graduate degrees in education and had, at one time, been school teachers. They had given up their well paid jobs and a comfortable lifestyle to come to Laos and become chicken farmers so they could share the Gospel with the people of that country. The government of Laos is Marxist and very anti-Christian and anti-Democracy. Since 2002 Laos has been ruled by the Lao People's Revolutionary Party, a Marxist Government. It was necessary for this couple to enter Laos on work visas and portray themselves as chicken farmers. Their efforts to spread the Gospel were fraught with danger, especially for the citizens of Laos who came to see them. They used an old mimeograph machine to publish the Bible on sheets of paper in the language of Laos and to pass out samples of the Bible text, one sheet at a time. People came to this social event from as far away as the Golden Triangle in and near Burma where much persecution of Christians occurs. All of these folks and others I met at that social event literally put their lives on the line daily for the sake of spreading the Gospel of God's love into various countries of Southeast Asia.

From Bangkok our team flew directly to Hanoi, Vietnam. Going through customs was an interesting experience. Each of the people who were engaged in processing us was gruff when speaking to us, but mostly silent and seemed to be angry that we were there, certainly not at all welcoming. It was apparent to us that they were waiting for a bribe before they would expedite our entrance but we had been instructed to resist the temptation to offer them money to do their jobs. After lengthy delays our passports were stamped with the requisite visa and we were on our way to our motel which was about a mile from the downtown area of Hanoi.

The next morning, I showed myself to be a rookie traveler in a communist country. Emerging from my room and descending the steps into the lobby I spotted Pastor Somnuck and greeting him with a cherry, "Good morning, Pastor!" The room fell immediately silent and, without saying a word, Somnuck turned, walked out of the lobby and stood outside. I immediately realized that I had pulled a major "no, no!" and had actually put his life at risk! We were in a Communist country where Christianity is outlawed and Christians are regularly imprisoned for their faith. Somnuck had been bringing supplies and hosting trips into Vietnam for a number of years. I had just jeopardized his life, or at least all his future trips into the country. I later apologized to Somnuck and he was very gracious to me. But I had made a serious error in judgment and he could have been arrested and jailed that day. By God's Grace and protection nothing ever came of the incident, for which we were all relieved. My error could have also jeopardized each of us on the team. We could have all been arrested. It probably wouldn't have gone so hard with the Team because we all had American passports. But Somnuck lived in Bangkok and had gained regular entrance into Vietnam, frequently meeting up with the Underground Church. All that would have needed to be done was to follow us while we were there or when he came back into the country on a later trip. Up to that point it was not suspected that he was a pastor. To my knowledge, the people at the desk in the motel where we stayed must not have heard my remark, or chose to ignore it. I say that because there were never any adverse consequences to my terrible error in judgment. We were all thankful for God's favor and protection.

The next day I walked the half mile or so into town and was able to visit the Hanoi Hilton, as the G.I.s who fought in Vietnam called it. The Hanoi Hilton[87] had actually been turned into a museum to showcase the atrocities perpetuated by the French against Vietnamese Freedom Fighters as the French were conquering and colonizing Vietnam and before the Americans got involved in the fighting. But it was the same facility the Vietnamese would later use to mistreat American soldiers. It is where Senator McCain and so many more of our men were held and tortured. I walked slowly past the cages or small rectangular rooms where the prisoners were held and also visited the torture room and saw the instruments of torture that were used. Two guillotines were in the inner courtyard where the prisoners were allowed to get some exercise. These were purportedly used by the French to execute some of their more notorious prisoners but I don't believe they were in the courtyard or used while our American men were incarcerated there. At least I never heard them mentioned in the news reports during that era.

I believe it was the day after I visited the downtown area of Hanoi, including the lake into which some of our downed pilots had parachuted

---

[87] Official name: Hỏa Lò Prison which means, "fiery furnace" or "hell's hole". Seems appropriate!

and were subsequently beaten to death, that we drove north about 115 kilometers to LocBinh where the Center of Hope orphanage was located. This was what we had come to Vietnam to do.

The following is the record of an interview I conducted by email between Micah's smart phone and my laptop computer. Micah Smith, Founder of Global Gateway Network (GGN) and a close friend of mine had invited me to travel with him to Vietnam but was at the moment of this interview traveling to a speaking engagement in Idaho. Here is most of what was exchanged between us as I contacted him:

Micah: What I have observed through the years of travel is that both in the spiritual sense and physical realm, there are large parts of the world that cannot reach the things I still enjoy and sometimes take for granted here at home. This is where one can make a beautiful difference for people who believed certain things were out of their reach. With God's help, you simply prove to them it was not out of their reach. What God seems to be saying to us in 2014 is that when we spot something out of our reach and reach for it anyway, our arm will stretch and extend as God helps us reach His goal, dream and miracle.

Micah: First a bit about Center of Hope in LocBinh, North Vietnam. One GGN Board Member, Robert Armstrong, flew to Hanoi with me on March 3, 2003. We met with the Peoples' Committee and negotiated for a piece of property that Robert and I had prayer walked previously (prayed as they walked around the property, claiming it for God's purposes). The government agreed to give us the land and bring utilities to the property if we would build the buildings and maintain support for the children. The buildings for the home for children were completed in September 2003. As you may recall, (I was there) we dedicated the facilities and 47 children in December 2003. For 10 years, GGN (Global Gateway Network) and our supporters supported, maintained and cared for 38 to 50 children at Center of Hope. We concluded our monthly support in March 2013. Center of Hope is now standing on its own. We helped many of the children forward to obtain secondary schooling or some trade craft. Some of them are friends on Facebook now. There was a short window from 2006 to 2008 when we were allowed to give (the children) gospel materials. The government of Vietnam continues to take the old line communist position and there is still a lot of persecution against Christians.

Joseph: What was the background of this trip (in 2003)? How did God impress this on your heart? What were some of your initial steps in getting the project moving forward, like prayer and financial support and getting your team in place?

Micah: God spoke to my heart during Amsterdam 2000 (A Billy Graham event) to adopt three unreached people groups. The first was the Kim Mun hill tribe in North Vietnam. I took a team of 12 men up close to the border of China in August 2001 and we hiked into the mountains to make first contact with the Kim Mun people at that time.

Joseph: What were some of the challenges you faced in planning and organizing the 2003 trip? In contacting Vietnamese officials?

Micah: As noted, the Vietnamese government officials are hardline communists. I don't believe there was one exception that we did not have Secret Police following us. Including the time you traveled with me. In the 10 years we worked at COH (Center of Hope) we must have sent at least 30 teams. Largest was a 35 member international medical team. Although our working relationship with the government grew a bit smoother, there was never a wide open door. COH is located about 6 km from the Chinese border. This is a hyper sensitive region and control is very tight.

Joseph: I remember that the buildings were already in place when we arrived. So was it necessary for you to get those constructed or were they already on the property when the decision was made to establish the orphanage?

Micah: GGN paid for all the construction, infrastructure, paved roads up the hilltop, security wall, farm and garden, maintenance, bicycles, furnished rooms, educational materials, hygienic training and supplies.

Joseph: I remember that you were in long meetings with the communist officials and that we were required to take some of our supplies down the hill to another school. What would you like to share with me about all that?

Micah: The school below Center of Hope is a government run high school. We wanted to build good neighbor relations with them. However, it was necessary to build a security wall. (Please note the implication of this last statement.—Joseph)

Joseph: How is the orphanage doing now? How many children are there and how big is the staff?

Micah: The staff is made up of three local people, and obviously our "hands on management" was very loose because of time, distance and government control. However, our team did pray with 21 children and one staff member to become Christians.

Joseph: I think I remember that some effort was made to rescue girls from the sex trade up on the border with China, north of the orphanage. Is that true? And, if so, what can you say about that?

Micah: I didn't see any evidence of a professional sex trade in this particular rural region; however any girl is very vulnerable to abuse, especially orphan girls.

After leaving the orphanage we returned to Hanoi and the next morning were driven to the airport where we caught a flight to Ho Chi Minh City (Saigon). We got a hotel (I believe it was the Rex Hotel) in the downtown area so as to better enjoy the city. The 2003 Southwest Asia games (like our Olympics) was to be held in Vietnam during the week we were in Ho Chi Minh City and we would also each have time to visit the Vietnam War Memorial just a few blocks from where we were staying plus do some shopping in a huge shopping center that covered several city blocks. And I did some shopping there, buying gifts for family and special donors who had given the most to make this trip possible. But it was in a little shop on the way back to the hotel that I found my most prized treasures, four paintings on velvet backdrop and inlaid with exquisite mother of pearl. They were beautiful! I received a special bargain when I bought all four.

The next day I went to the Viet Nam War Memorial Museum but was sickened and saddened by the hatred being spewed into the ears of a group of high school kids about American atrocities during the war. I was not the only white man present there that day or I might have felt uneasy. I was probably, however, the only American present at the Memorial. There were American atrocities committed during the war and I saw pictures of some of them. There were also atrocities committed by the North Vietnamese against their own countrymen in the south and against Americans. That happens in war. But to pass on the hatred and anger to the next generation was what bothered me the most.

That night I watched from the window of my hotel room as literally millions of motor bikes filled the streets in celebration of the fact that Vietnam had been declared the overall winners of the 2003 Southwest Asia Games. A tremendous honor! And I rejoiced with them for their victories.

Before leaving Ho Chi Minh City (Saigon) we took one final excursion. The Team was driven out of town in a large van. It seemed like we drove a very long time. Suddenly, the van reversed direction and headed back into town. What had happened was that we had successfully evaded the secret police that had been following us and were able to return to our destination which was only a short distance from our original point of departure.

We quickly disembarked and quietly walked through a small restaurant to the rear of the building where we entered another door and went up a flight of steps into a room where about 90 people were waiting for us. These were part of the fabled underground church known as the Midnight Bride of Christ because of their habits of meeting at midnight for worship in remote places out in the Vietnamese Jungle somewhere, and away from the prying eyes of the Communist Secret Police. I would learn later that evening that every one of these folks had been jailed for their faith. Many of them, men & women, had spent years incarcerated just because they were Christians. The Vietnamese authorities will tell you that there is religious freedom in their country. And, I suppose if you say that religious freedom is expressed by the one Catholic Church in the middle of downtown Ho Chi Minh City, where weddings can be held and people can attend a brief Catholic Mass on Sunday mornings, then, yes, there is religious freedom. And I did witness a wedding in the downtown Catholic Church in central Ho Chi Minh City.

But the folks I dined with that evening knew nothing about religious freedom. Evangelical Christians are considered to be outlaws of the State (as were the First Century Christians in the Roman Empire) and can be arrested if they are found in a group of more than five people. Each member of our Team sat at a different table with a group of these Vietnamese Evangelicals. There was one Vietnamese person at each table who spoke at least broken English, and this allowed us limited communication. I found myself choking with emotion, and tears welling up in my eyes as I listened to their individual stories.

I could not escape the feeling of being seated on "holy ground" in the presence of God's special Saints. None of them are able to work for a living because of their faith. No one will hire them because of their "outlaw" status. These folks are completely dependent on family and friends to house, feed and clothe them. They have no other way to survive. Forget about medical care. They have none! Their faith & trust in God for healing when needed is all they have in the way of medical care! Getting married, or having children if they are married, is a real problem for that only adds to the burden of those who care for them.

As we left that night I could not stop the tears that coursed down my cheeks, knowing that I would never again see, this side of Heaven, these precious Brothers and Sisters in the Lord. I was humbled by the honor to have been in their presence. It was quiet in the van as we drove back into the center of town. I think we were all overawed by what we had just experienced! We had each left in the hands of Pastor Moses as much money as possible from our own personal funds.

I can imagine that the Vietnamese Christians we had just spent the evening with, in the natural, feel very weak and helpless. But in their weakness they are God's Mighty Ones in the Spirit. We who are strong, financially self-sustaining, healthy and living in a land of freedom, full of hope for the future left that evening feeling our own weakness and emptiness alongside the spiritual giants with whom we had just dined and conversed. I wonder if that is what Jesus meant when He said, "But many who are first will be last and the last first"? [88]

Second Example: when, in 2006, my wife, Ruth and I were asked to come to Soap Lake, Washington to pastor a small country church in the high desert of eastern Washington State we were offered housing and a salary of $1,200 per month. That was the best the little congregation could do. I had previously been complaining about the necessity of

[88] Matthew 19:29-30

working at a "secular" job as a loan officer for a mortgage company. I wanted to get back "into the ministry" not realizing at the time God had given me the opportunity to increase my Social Security benefits and that I would need those benefits in just a few short years. In it all, God was providing for my future financial well-being even when I didn't realize it.

Ruth and I did agree that it was God's will for us to accept the financial package which was about one third of our monthly budget at the time. We knew that it is always safe to act within the parameters of God's Will and rest in trust that He will provide what is lacking. And God has proven His faithfulness over and over again during these intervening years.

We came to Soap Lake to accept the pastorate here in August of 2006. In September, our District Superintendent, Rev. Les Welk, called me to say that Dr. Roger Butz would be leading a four man team on a seven week trip through Thailand, India, Cambodia and Vietnam. The trip through India would be the most extensive part of the trip and one of the most important stops on the trip was in Nagaland, located in northeastern India. A great deal of political unrest was going on in Nagaland and our proposed train ride across north India would take us through territory held by some 50 terrorist organizations. For that reason, it was required that our team be composed by at least four persons. Three men had agreed to go but they were having a hard time getting the fourth man. Rev. Welk asked me if I would like to be that fourth man and I told him that I would have to discuss the possibility with my wife. I reminded Rev. Welk that Ruth and I had just arrived in Soap Lake to begin our pastoral ministry there and that, as much as I would like be part of the missions team, it might not be a good idea for me to leave my wife at that moment to go running around the world. It would require Ruth to be pastor in my absence and carry the full brunt of speaking on Sundays and Wednesdays, as well as taking care of getting unpacked (our living room was full of boxes) plus carrying day to day pastoral duties in my absence. But somehow my heart was warming to the idea and so I did not immediately turn down the opportunity but told my Superintendent that I would make it a matter of prayer and discussion with my wife. I did say that unless she was 100% in agreement with me going and felt like it was God's will that I would have to back away from the invitation. I thanked Les for thinking of me and went to mention the matter to Ruth, not expecting at all that Ruth would be in favor of me accepting the invitation. We spent a couple days discussing the pros and cons of my going off on such a venture, and certainly made it a matter of prayer. Without any pressure from me, in fact I think I was doing my best to discourage the idea, Ruth threw her enthusiastic support behind the idea and so I called our Superintendent to accept the invitation. My acceptance was conditional on God providing the necessary finances. This would be a seven week trip across Thailand, India, Cambodia and Vietnam and the cost would run something around $4,500 for travel, lodging and food for seven weeks across four countries in Southeast Asia.

Little did we suspect at that moment that our faith would be tested even more before I would leave the USA. I don't know the exact date but Ruth underwent a major medical crisis with a ruptured appendix, but I do know it was sometime in the Fall of 2006 and just weeks before I was to fly out for Southeast Asia. My teammates were flying on different airlines than was I, and so we had arranged to meet up with each other at the airport in Bangkok, or if we missed each other, to meet at the Ariston Hotel, downtown Bangkok, across the street and down the block from the new 11 story shopping mall. That was the best we could do. Another complication was that the number three man on the team (I was number four) had suddenly withdrawn from the trip. With these three complications in view, the entire trip was suddenly again in question. So what happened in all this?

First, Ruth's appendectomy was originally botched at the hospital, spilling more infection into her body, but then corrected and my concerns for Ruth's recovery were somewhat alleviated. However, I was very uneasy about going in spite of the fact that Ruth insisted that I had given my word and should not be the one to cause the whole missions trip to fall apart. People all across Southeast Asia were counting on us.

But our living room was still stacked with unpacked boxes and Ruth was facing several weeks of recovery with no one there to care for her. She was told not lift anything heavier than ten pounds. So what would happen to all those boxes stacked in the living room and other places? I would learn years later that our daughter, Lani Rochelle, came over from Seattle and did most of the work for Ruth in lifting and unpacking the boxes. What a blessing she was! Well, I finally did leave for Asia and left my wife at our new home to recover from her surgery and pastor the church in my absence. I was ready to back out right up to the last minute but Ruth would have none of it. I had given my word, the trip was in God's timing and will and, in her mind I had no choice but to go. What an amazing woman!

Two or three weeks after I left for Asia, one of the Brothers in the Church in Soap Lake, Abe Littleton, would collapse onto the floor in the morning service as Ruth stood up to deliver the Sunday morning sermon. The entire service was interrupted as people went to prayer on Abe's behalf and as the ambulance was called for. Abe never regained consciousness and was pronounced dead a short time later. He was taken to a hospital some 55 miles distance, and Ruth did not feel well enough to make that long drive to visit him. I was told later that she really felt guilty, and felt that she had failed me by not going to visit him. She told someone, "If my husband had been here he would have gone and been with Abe (and his wife, Betty Littleton) at the hospital."

The three of us on the Missions Team, Dr. Roger Butz, Pastor Mike and I flew out of Seattle on separate flights with connections through Japan. I met them at the taxi curb at the brand new airport seven miles outside of Bangkok, after having gone through customs, and we proceeded to the Ariston Hotel. Dr. Butz had arranged for us to meet Santiago (Sonny) Largado and his wife, Dahlia to obtain future contacts and sources of information about the multi-faceted ministry to which they give oversight. Sonny is the Director of Ethnos Asia. We were to sit down for interviews with him and several ministries who work in cooperation with him. Sonny is a high energy, hard driving Christian Leader who requires very little sleep and seems to work around the clock (like someone else I know who made the same mistake, and neglected his wife until God just took her home to be with Him in Heaven because she was too lonely to be left here on earth). Ethnos Asia serves a larger organization known as "The Church in Access-Restricted Nations of Asia" (ARNA). Nagaland, which we would visit later, was in that category of being too dangerous because of political unrest for most foreigners to be granted access into the country. A couple other leaders we were privileged to interview was Phon Netneramit, a Laotian native who was imprisoned in past years, but for a couple of decades has been both pastor of a small Laotian congregation in Bangkok, and the full-time Indo-China coordinator for Ethnos Asia Ministries. We were joined also by Tuja Lazum, pastor of a large Burmese congregation in Bangkok and full-time coordinator at Ethnos Asia Ministries for the Indo-Burma area.

We sat down for a day long interview with first one then another of the ministry leaders and listened to their heart rending stories and impassioned pleas for prayer and financial support. Almost every one of these people daily put their lives on the line to spread the Gospel across Southeast Asia, a very dangerous part of the world in which to live and work as a Christian Leader. Especially difficult to listen to were the stories coming out of what is known as the Golden Triangle. The Golden Triangle touches small bits of land in three countries: Thailand, Burma

(Myanmar) and Laos. This is a very dangerous part of the world where people disappear and are never again heard from. Whole villages are wiped out by mercenaries working for one government or another, or by bandits and government soldiers. Especially at risk are people from the Karen (pronounced, "kah-wren") ethnic group. This tribe has been almost completely won over to Jesus Christ. Most of them are vibrant Christians.

While still in Bangkok we visited a ministry to children. This team of talented Christian Thai youth is engaged in writing comic books with a distinct appeal to surrender one's life to Jesus Christ. While visiting their offices, complete with computers and printers and the ability to publish the comic books, we learned that approximately 300 children profess Jesus as Lord and Savior every month. Thailand is 99% Buddhist and it is a commonly accepted belief that the only way Thailand can be reached for Christ is by reaching the children. There is severe persecution and rejection from family and relatives for those children who do convert to Christianity.

After completing these interviews and investigations of ministries while in Bangkok we boarded a plane and flew to New Delhi, India. Arriving around 9 or 10 PM, we were met by Pastor Varghese Thomas, Director of "Mission to the Unreached" in India. New Delhi is a city of 20 million people with one of the worst air pollution problems of any city around the world, but comparable to Calcutta (Kolkata), Peking (Beijing), and a few others. On the way to our motel the church van experienced mechanical problems and we were stranded alongside the road for several hours. The air pollution was so bad that, even at midnight, we all began to get sore throats due to the pollution. It was hard to breathe. We were finally able to get a gentleman to open his auto-repair business and work on the van long enough to get it running so as to deliver us safe to our motel. This was a low cost, low class motel and I shared my bed with a few cockroaches, but thankfully, no bed bugs! I was thankful for the Air Conditioning. I stepped outside the next morning just in time to see a large Brahma Bull walk by and also notice some playful monkeys just across the street. I was warned not to approach them as they would likely attack me, and most assuredly would be carriers of rabies, thus rabid!

Pastor Varghese oversees a Bible College in which one can earn a B.A. and M.A. Degrees in Bible and Theology. I accepted his invitation to be an Adjunct Professor for the undergraduate level of studies at the Bible College but have never had the finances to return to India to fulfill those obligations. They also have a Christian School, grades 1 through 12 and then a number of extension schools that meet in small rooms throughout the slum areas of New Delhi. I remember visiting some of these schools in the slum areas. One school in particular was a small, dark room with very inadequate lighting, hot & humid but packed with children anxious to learn.

Also, I remember, as I approached some areas, having to be careful to avoid large Brahma Bulls that are prone to want to charge and gore people. The Hindu religion forbids animals to be killed because it is believed that they represent the reincarnated souls of many of their ancestors. Consequently, large cities like New Delhi are overrun with rabid monkeys plus Brahma Cows and Bulls. Especially the large bulls, crazed by thirst because of a low availability of water for them, often go berserk with thirst and kill people throughout the city. This happens almost on a daily basis, but in a city of 20 million people events like that are hardly noticed.

I had a close brush with a cow while gazing at the sights like a typical tourist and failing to pay attention to what was going on around me. I suddenly noticed Pastor Varghese staring at me from some distance and then, instantly, became aware of a large white Brahma cow walking past me just inches from my body. I could have reached out and swatted her rump but fortunately resisted the urge! These animals are unpredictable.

It might have kept walking and ignored me, or it could have turned on me and killed me before I would have hardly known what hit me. Was the devil putting it in my head to swat that cow and God protecting me from the consequence of my impulse? Or was I afflicted with a moment of unwise mischievousness? It was probably the latter. If I had swatted that cow and then she attacked me, there probably wouldn't have been enough left of me to say, "The devil made me do it!" Nothing was said later by Pastor Varghese but I do remember the concerned look on his face.

Another sight that caught my attention and spoke so graphically to the poverty of these people was the sight of ladies bending over "cow patties", getting their hands right into the manure to shape the patties so they could dry them in the sun and use them later for fuel for cooking over an open fire.

Pastor Varghese's vision for getting the Gospel to the unreached peoples of India is awe inspiring. And he doesn't just have a vision, he gets the job done! Our team was privileged to teach and preach before many of the students at the Bible College and then visit extension churches throughout New Delhi.

A few days later our team left New Delhi for a quick plane flight to a place called Siliguri, West Bengal (India)[89] where we disembarked for several days of ministry in the foothills of the Himalayan Mountains. We also, high up in those foothills, visited the Darjeeling Tea fields and walked down a steep hill to visit a pastor friend of Dr. Roger Butz. Our hosts told us about how the villagers had attacked and burned their church, just because it was a Christian Church and not Hindu. But that they were in the process of rebuilding.

---

[89] For images of Siliguri, West Bengal, India: enter into the Bing search engine these words: "Siliguri, West Bengal & it should take you to a whole page of photos for Siliguri and the surrounding area.

Everything in this area is either up or down. There is no such thing as a flat spot. And difficult as is the climbing, and as high as this is, it is still just the foothills. One needs to have a strong heart in order to sustain the strain of climbing around some of that area!

On Sunday of that week our Team each went our separate ways to preach in various mountain churches, all of them very small with a dozen to two dozen people present. I remember preaching on Divine Healing and praying for the sick. Again, some challenging hikes just to get to church, but the efforts were worthwhile.

After returning to Siliguri late in the day from our preaching assignments we took a day or two to relax in the famous Bidhan Market before leaving to go back up the mountain, and beyond where we were on Sunday, all the way to the Ancient Kingdom of Sikkim.

Sikkim is a landlocked Indian state located in the Himalayan Mountains. The state borders Nepal to the west, China's Tibet Autonomous Region to the north and east, and Bhutan to the east. The Indian state of West Bengal lies to the south. Sikkim's Monarchy was established in 1642 and for the next 150 years they suffered frequently from Nepalese invaders from the north. In the 19th century they allied themselves with the British Protectorate of India, until eventually they became a British protectorate. The size of this ancient kingdom, now the smallest state in India, is only 2,740 square miles. In spite of its size, Sikkim has 11 official languages. By name, these languages are: Nepali (which is its lingua franca), Bhutia (from the country of Bhutan, just north of Sikkim and east of Nepal), Lepcha, Tamang, Limbu, Newari, Rai, Gurung, Magar, Sunwar and English. English is taught in schools and used in government documents. The predominant religions are Hinduism and Vajrayana Buddhism. Sikkim's economy is largely dependent on agriculture and tourism, and as of 2012 the state has the third-smallest GDP among Indian states, although it is also among the fastest-growing in population.

The Sikkimese Monarchy was abolished in 1975 and the Indian army moved in to take charge. Being the nostalgic sentimentalist I am, I felt sadness in my own heart because of the final plight of this ancient mystical and beautiful kingdom. I had read about the Sikkimese Kingdom as a child and remember romanticized tales of their culture. The beauty of this entire region from Siliguri up to the Darjeeling area and then to Sikkim has a wild and breathtaking beauty all its own!

The road we traveled from Siliguri to Sikkim was steep, rugged and dangerous, however, and with many spots where it would be easy to tumble over the edge of the road and down the side of the mountain a couple thousand feet. And all along the way, after we got past a certain section of road that was barren and treeless, the road (mostly dirt and mud) was lined with hundreds of monkeys and their families. Surprisingly, the higher we went the more trees and verdant vegetation we encountered and it was there the greatest number of different monkey species were encountered. It would have been dangerous to get out of the car as we would have undoubtedly been attacked by these tremendously interesting creatures. They would not have been happy about any attention we may have paid them, even small attention like taking their pictures, so when we did stop for a break, we stayed in the car and took pictures from that vantage point of safety.

Mount Everest, with a peak at 29,029 feet, is north of Sikkim on the border with Nepal and China. So that tells you something about how high up into the Himalayan Mountains we had gone. In the Darjeeling area, a considerable distance before we arrived in the Kingdom of Sikkim, we were already at 7,000 feet above sea level. In the small town in Sikkim where we stopped to do a Pastor's Conference we were much higher than Darjeeling and everything was literally built on a slant. One was either walking up or down, but never on the level. I teased someone, saying, "I'm surprised that cows and people don't have one leg longer than the other just to help you keep your balance as you walk in these mountains."

Pastor Asinlo Khing is Director of Mission to the Himalayas. On the way up we had passed the place in the road where he had lost control of his car a couple years before and had fallen some distance down the side of the mountain before a group of trees coming out of the side of the mountain or small ledge (not sure which) stopped his descent toward certain death. He declined to show us the exact spot where this happened and just kept driving. It must have been so very traumatic and he never told us about why it happened or how he was rescued. Pastors, all of them under the leadership of Asinlo Khing, had come from some 90 different churches located throughout the Himalayas between us and Nepal. Our Team Leader, Dr. Roger Butz, I and Pastor Mike each taught for a couple hours during the day and then enjoyed a beautiful church service each evening for a week. Of course we were teaching through an interpreter. My subject matter had to do with forgiveness and keys to building solid interpersonal relationship within a church congregation. The material seemed to be appreciated and we enjoyed some powerful times of prayer in the altars. Dr. Roger Butz is an interesting speaker that preaches without notes. His ministry was particularly well received. (Dr. Butz, is a retired Medical Doctor and retired army General. Without him the trip would not have been possible.)

Eating meals with the pastors was a challenge as most of the pastors and their wives did not speak English. But we did our best to mix and fellowship with them. Over all, it was a powerful week of Bible Study and prayer. The pastors & church leaders seemed to really appreciate contact with fellow pastors from the outside world and the increase in their understanding of worldwide Christianity that the week provided. Between the three of us, our Team had pretty well subsidized the meeting and their travel expenses. This had provided a welcome break for inspiration, new ideas and rest from their local ministries. I have gifts of handmade leis (made from silk, and different than Hawaiian leis made from flowers) to show their gratitude for us coming to spend the time with them.

All too soon it was time to say goodbye and head back down the mountain in order to catch a two day train ride across the rest of northern India and into Nagaland. This would necessitate traversing an area in north India under some degree of control from 50 different terrorist organizations. We heard later in the week that the train that came after us the next day was stopped by a terrorist group and one or two people killed. We were thankful for God's mercy & protection during that trip.

Ministry is always done in the context of culture and politics. That fact of life is unavoidable, and our ministry in Nagaland was highlighted by cultural and political unrest. Nagaland is a mountainous state, an extension of the Himalayan Mountains, in the far northeast of India, and borders Burma on its own eastern boundary. The Naga Nationalist Movement is alive and well to this day and was the cause of a good deal of social and military turbulence taking place as our Team arrived for ministry. Attacks on Indian government and army installations have been frequent for many years and this had also occurred just prior to our arrival.

Dimapur is the largest city in Nagaland (the 16th State in India) and was the center of political unrest at the time of our visit. The question of secession and a national identity separate from India was once again plaguing Nagaland as it has repeatedly done for over a hundred years. The history of violence in Nagaland goes back to 1816 when they were invaded by Burma. Before that time there is no written record of Nagaland except that it was populated by sixteen tribes of a very warlike people eventually known as the Nagas. The Konyaks, Angamis, Aos, Lothas, and Sumis are the largest Naga tribes. Much could be written about their traditional colorful dress and ancient warlike dances.

These are on display particularly during the time of the annual Hornbill Festival (named after a colorful tropical bird found in large numbers in the forests north of Dimapur) which takes place between December 1-7 each year and which I would personally like someday to attend!

The Naga people are a vibrant, colorful people and I would love to return there before I get much older just to preach in more of their churches and see the culture of the people up close. Pastor Angami, who was also the Nagaland Assemblies of God District Superintendent, said to me, "Pastor Joseph, Dimapur is not the real Nagaland. You need to come up north and spend some time with me and let me show you around to our churches and people. The climate is much cooler less humid, and the countryside is beautiful and mountainous."

I would imagine the north of Nagaland would be very similar to the Himalayan Mountains and countryside around Darjeeling and Sikkim from which we had just come the week before. But the culture of the Nagas would be even more intriguing as they are a lively, vigorous and sometimes warlike people.

According to one source I consulted, Nagaland is mostly a mountainous state with most of the countryside varying from about two thousand to six thousand feet above sea level. About one-sixth of Nagaland is under cover of tropical and sub-tropical forests. Elephants, leopards, bears, many species of monkeys, deer, oxen and buffaloes range over a large area of Nagaland.

British rule established in 1892 over this area brought a temporary end to massive bloodshed stemming from the Burmese invasion. Its native inhabitants are the Naga tribes and were referred to in the Burmese language as "Naka" which means "people with pierced noses." On December 1, 1963 Nagaland became the 16th a state within the Indian Union. But their desire has long been to form their own national identity and that desire had once again come to some kind of ferment shortly before we arrived. In addition, various terrorist organizations were vying for dominance in order to take advantage of the political unrest.

Nagaland is predominantly Christian and is the only state in India with that distinction! Of its just under 2 million population, 90% are Christian and 75 percent of those are Baptists. Most of the remainder is Pentecostal and Revivalist (Charismatic). Hinduism and Islam are the two minority religions and claim about 7.7% of the remainder of the population.

We arrived in Dimapur (the largest city in Nagaland) in the late evening, and were met by Rev. Moses Murry, pastor of the Lotha[90] Assembly of God Church in Dimapur, and his lovely wife and family. We were then taken immediately to the police headquarters at the train station to surrender our passports for the duration of our stay in Dimapur (always a scary thing when police or government officials in a foreign country demand to hold your passport while you are in the country). I had noticed, as we disembarked at the train station, that the place seemed overrun with armed soldiers, and could immediately feel a certain tension in the air.

Rev. Murry was almost immediately engaged in an animated conversation with the police that went on for over two hours. Finally we learned that our papers were not considered to be "in order" because there were supposed to be four men on our team and we had shown up as a team of three. Especially in light of the operation of terrorist organizations across a broad area of northern India, to show up with one man missing, when we had previously registered as a team of four, looked suspicious. They wanted to know the location of the fourth man (which had stayed home in the USA) and where we may have dropped him off in India, etc. We were detained by the police overnight giving them a little time to determine what they would do with us. We were,

---

[90] Reference to the name of one of the larger Naga tribes in the region.

however, treated with respect and sensitivity and allowed to sleep on couches in the Officer's Quarters. As I recall, we each received a bottle of water and a few crackers to eat and then were left under lock and key in the officer's quarters. We spent some time in prayer for God's Will to be done concerning our fate (whether we would be jailed or deported or released). And then lay down to sleep. I think we all felt peace in our hearts although we had no idea what the outcome might be.

We knew that we had come to Nagaland as another important part of our seven week missions' odyssey throughout Southeast Asia and that God certainly had a purpose in all this. In the morning we learned that the policeman in charge of our case was also a member of the Lotha Assembly of God church (and probably a member of the Lotha Tribe) and so was naturally more inclined to believe his pastor's explanations and had cooperated with him to assure our release and issue us the required Restricted Area Permit for our stay in Nagaland. We were released and taken to Pastor Murry's home where the evening meetings would be held. The home was surrounded by high walls topped with barbed wire and was large enough to house over 200 children. Many of the children were orphans and others were sent there by their parents to get a good education in the context of a Christian world view. But danger from terrorists and bandits was an ever present problem and it was necessary to take all precautions to protect the children.

Rev. Murry and his wife, who operated the school, also lived there. It was one smooth, well organized operation the like of which I have never seen in my life. It would be a great model for private schools in our own country! And, wow! Could those kids sing and pray! It was powerful, especially their praying. When it came time to pray, those children, all 200 of them, were either on their knees or stretched out on their faces on the ground before God bombarding Heaven with their supplications and praise. They were obviously trained intercessors and would undoubtedly put to shame most praying Christians (including myself!) or prayer services in American churches. In the light of the political, criminal and terrorist realities all around them, their lives depended upon their ability to reach Heaven through prayer!

As we entered through the large gates to the compound of the home we saw stretched before us a grassy lawn and also a large canopy (like an open tent) with several hundred chairs already in place in anticipation of the week long Pastor's and Leader's Conference for which we were the featured speakers. All this expansive space was in front of a residential home filled with 200 children! We walked through the area and up the steps to the entrance of the home. We were then seated in a large living room area and served food and beverages before being taken to our hotel accommodations where we could shower and change our clothes before the evening service.

I need to mention that we were locked in our hotel every night and could not enter or exit after nightfall or before dawn. An exception was made for us if the evening service went too late and they had already locked us out of the hotel for the night. This only happened once, however, and we were allowed to enter after the curfew. The large iron gates were hurriedly closed in order to protect everyone in the hotel from being taken hostage by some terrorist group, or from injury due to stray bullets & violence which came to a head every night throughout Dimapur. I lay in my bed and listened to bombs exploding and gunfire every night throughout the night and then read about the results in an English newspaper the next day.

The ministry and worship time we shared with these wonderful people was punctuated by powerful singing and praying, and they testified to the blessing and encouragement to them personally of the hours of teaching/preaching ministry throughout the day and into the night.

I write the following with a good deal of sadness. I had checked with the India Times Newspaper while writing the above record of our travels and saw this news bulletin: "Ethnic killings: more central troops for Nagaland. In the wake of the execution of nine Karbis last week, the Centre plans to rush additional para-military troops to the trouble torn area." And I solicit the prayers of the reader for Nagaland, an area of the world for which I have developed some affection. You may have a hard time understanding that. But I grew to love those people.

The Christian culture MUST supersede all other human cultural loyalties. Our former Team Leader, Dr. Roger Butz, informed me even as I work on this paragraph, that Dr. Wati Aier, the President of Oriental Theological Seminary in Bode, India where we went together in 2006, has spent a great deal of time working on reconciliation between warring factions in Nagaland and has done so with some success. And I understand that the Baptists in Nagaland have been working for peace between ethnic groups for more than thirty years. So there is reason for Hope. The situation would undoubtedly be worse if there had not been that effort.

If one is a Christian, then the culture of God's Kingdom on earth trumps whatever ethnic background that Follower of Jesus Christ might have. We each must be a Child of God before we are anything else! For instance, if one is a Follower of Christ then their loyalties to Christ should be held higher than any allegiance one has to political or ethnic ties. Those kinds of priorities should be true and faithfully expressed in Nagaland or any other place on earth!

So our team flew out of Nagaland down to Calcutta (the real name is: Kolkata) where we spent several days before flying back to Thailand. There we spent a two full days going through the Assemblies of God Church Sanctuary (it is huge with many classrooms!) and Hospital, mammoth structures with numerous ministries throughout the city of more than 20 million people. One hundred thousand are fed every day. There are clothing outlets for the poor and ministry to people that live on the streets with no more than cardboard boxes, newspapers or tarp to protect them from rains. Ministries of love and compassion extend throughout Kolkata.

Once we were back in Thailand, our team split up and Dr. Roger Butz and Pastor Mike went to Vietnam while I went alone to Cambodia to teach for three days in a Bible College in Phnom Penh.

One of the first things that happened was that I was taken to the Tuol Sleng Genocide Museum, but did not have time to visit the Killing Fields which is a four and one-half hour tour. I did walk through several two story buildings full of crushed or bullet riddled skulls of all sizes (men, women and children). Quote from Wikipedia on Cambodia, "Ideology played an important role in the genocide". The desire of the Khmer Rouge was to bring the nation back to a "mythic past", and stop foreign aid, foreign cultural or foreign financial influence from entering the nation from abroad, (which in their eyes was a corrupting influence) and restore the country to an agrarian society, plus the manner in which they tried to implement this, was one factor in the genocide. "This new agrarian society was to be based on Stalinist and Maoist ideals". From all I have read elsewhere, this is an accurate, although limited assessment. The decade of the 1970s was, as one Cambodian victim described it, "hell on the earth". War, genocide, and starvation devastated the country to a degree that has few parallels in modern times. The most recent estimates of killing and death run from one million, five hundred thousand to one million, seven hundred thousand as people were forced out of their homes, particularly in cities and towns, and were forced at bayonet point to go into the countryside to become farmers. This was done without giving them food to sustain them or tools with which they were to work. Large numbers of the population simply starved to death. While they were starving, people ate worms, roots, leaves from what trees were left after the violence, and even ate each other. Women and children suffered the most.

I flew out of Phnom Penh with somewhat of a heavy heart regarding Cambodia. The work of the Gospel there is both rewarding and difficult. It was in the news while I was there of a resurgence of popularity of the Khmer Rouge party, which would be devastating to Cambodia as the Khmer Rouge are the once guilty of the genocide & ruination of a once beautiful, happy peaceful nation. While there I had visited some outlying areas, including crossing a lake to preach at an Island church. The Buddhist Temples are sad reminders of the outward beauty and emptiness of all Satan's deceptions, and the museum of skulls of a horrific past that has greatly scarred the lovely and formerly exuberantly cheerful Cambodian people.

But there is hope for Cambodia as evidenced by the work of Christian churches and Bible Colleges and active, cheerful, hard-working missionaries & national pastors. There are several Bible Colleges in Phnom Penh. One in which I was privileged to teach for three days. I believe it was the Phnom Penh Bible College where I taught.

Arriving back in Bangkok I joined back up with Dr. Roger Butz and Pastor Mike and we took a train north to Chiang Mai where we took a couple days to do some sightseeing while Dr. Butz made arrangements for two truckloads of supplies which we would be taking into the Mae Rah Moo Refugee Camp near the town of Maesariang. This was deep in the jungle just south of the border with Myanmar (formerly, Burma) and about 200 miles north of Bangkok. Dr. Butz warned Mike and I that we would be in jungle and away from all modern conveniences, including emergency medical care. No helicopter would come in to get us if we got hurt or sick. In fact we would be outside of any possible contact with the outside world. Arrangements were made for Mike and I to go to an elephant camp and then a poisoned snake habitat to watch snake handlers perform. We had finally been joined by our fourth man for the team, a young pastor by the name of Rev. Rob Jansons who accompanied us to the elephant and snake farms.

Joseph Meyers

Joseph on left (hat and dark sun glasses) with
Rob Jansons, north of Chiang Mai

While at the snake farm I did get a picture of me with a large boa constrictor wrapped around my neck and body and, at the elephant camp, a photo of me riding an elephant! As I wandered through the snake farm I remember seeing a violently trembling rabbit in a cage with a snake. That poor bunny knew he was providing supper for the snake! I

312

also visited a market place where I could purchase several colorful Thai silk shirts. The boy in this man was beginning to come to the surface as I began to relax from recent experiences.

And then it was time to leave for the Mae Rah Moo Refugee Camp. Dr. Butz had arranged for two trucks about the size of large dump trucks and these were filled with the supplies he had purchased for us to take into the Refugee Camp. Those supplies were to be distributed to about a hundred new refugees that would be contacted and signaled to leave their individual sleeping places in the jungles around us and enter the Mae Rah Moo Camp as soon as we were ready to distribute the supplies we had brought for them. We drove some distance out of Chiang Mai before we turned north toward Burma and headed into the foothills. Soon we began to climb higher and go deeper into beautiful jungle countryside before we topped out, left the pavement and began our descent on a four-wheel drive kind of muddy dirt road going down the other side of the mountain with 1,000 foot drop offs on one side and vertical cliffs on the other. In some ways it reminded me of the road up from Siliguri to Sikkim, only this time we were going down, down, down, slipping and sliding around sharp curves and, in some cases, deep crevices in the road. It was a long and dangerous drive down to the Camp. Before going very far we passed the last village on our right and then it was down into the northern jungles of Thailand toward the Burmese border. We were late (because of earlier mechanical problems with our personal vehicle) and arrived at the edge of Mae Rah Moo just after the armed guards had closed the entrance to the camp for the night. The Burmese soldiers were about an hour away from us but we were protected by the Karen Freedom Fighters on the Thai side of the border. The guard station did have radio contact with the camp headquarters and finally got clearance for us to enter the camp. After entering and driving a short distance, we stopped and parked beside a building next to a fast flowing river, unloaded our belongings (for me, small suitcase and sleeping bag) and crossed the river walking carefully on top of a fallen log which was the only bridge to the camp headquarters where we would be staying. The struts nailed to the side of the log were useless! One slip off that log into the gushing river would not be good! And yet children traversed that log every day going to and from school.

Before the weekend, we had about three days just to relax, do a little hiking, and wander around the camp. This is a refugee camp where people come when they are fleeing for their lives! Most of the camp is made up of Christians from the Karen Tribe fleeing from brutal and merciless Burmese Soldiers under orders to exterminate them. As I walked around camp I met men and women and children with arms and legs missing due to their having encountered exploding land mines or attacking soldiers. I knew that their villages were frequently burned to the ground and that they had undoubtedly lost most of their clothes and other possessions. We were taken on a special tour to a large multi-room bamboo building on stilts to meet young Teenage Girls, many of whom had suffered horribly at the hands of vicious Burmese soldiers. The girls were being carefully cared for by compassionate women who taught them, and did their best to bring physical, psychological and spiritual healing these young women, as well as giving them a reason to live.

The fact is that the people in the Refugee Camp are not citizens of Thailand and not eligible to become citizens or in any way be assimilated into Thai culture and society. They are stuck between their persecutors (the Burmese) and the Thai Government who is merciful enough to allow them to live in one of the five Thai Refugee Camps located away from towns and civilization but not merciful enough to try to assimilate them into Thai society. They live in the camp at the mercy of the Thai Government, the United Nations Relief Agencies and people like us who bring them the essentials of physical existence. That said, the Karen people are a happy and resourceful people, establishing their own education, health and religious programs.

Two final things to mention: There are six churches in the Mae Rah Moo Camp. The Karen people are almost all Christians and very committed to Jesus Christ, to the point of being willing to suffer persecution and death for their Faith. That weekend the three of us split up and preached in all six churches. wewwe

I received a dinner invitation one night from one of the families. It was both painful and enjoyable. Being in their bamboo hut on stilts and doing my best to visit across the language barrier was challenging but fun. I enjoyed the food and the people. But sitting cross-legged on those bamboo slats that were supposed to be a floor was painful. I have never been able to accustom myself to sitting cross-legged on any floor anywhere (even if there is a carpet) much less eating and carrying on relaxed conversation on a floor of bamboo slats. But then, my sleeping arrangements, back at the camp headquarters, weren't any better. If I ever go back (and I would like to do so) I'll be sure to take an air mattress and small camp folding chair with me. Thankfully, I had thought ahead and brought my mosquito netting which provided my greatest comfort as I tried to sleep each night. One doesn't want to travel in these third-world countries, especially in Asia and Africa, without mosquito netting and an air mattress, and your own toilet paper and medical supplies. I have slept on narrow wooden slats out in the mud huts of Africa, but sleeping in Bamboo huts on stilts and laying on narrow, hard bamboo slats was a new experience, and just as uncomfortable. I don't mean to sound as if I am complaining, because I wouldn't trade these experiences for anything, and would do it all over again if that opportunity should ever come back to me. The privilege and adventure of ministry to these primitive, or economically deprived people makes it all well worth any personal inconvenience.

And then it was time to pass out the supplies we had brought with us for the new incoming refugees. I will never forget the opportunity afforded me to be one of the men up front, receiving supplies for the refugees from two men behind me and then passing out what was handed me to each person that came out of their jungle camps. As far as I could see looking down a jungle road there were people of all ages walking toward me. They came, sat down in front of my partner and me, and then, in orderly fashion, rank by rank, filed forward to receive their supplies. Almost every person, especially the older folks, would place their left hand on their right forearm as they reached out to receive the supplies I handed them. This is a sign of respect that I had witnessed many times in Africa among the Mossi People from Berkina Faso (formerly, Upper Volta) but was surprised to see it used in this primitive refugee camp from people coming out of Myanmar (Burma).

There was a bonding that happened that day and it was all I could do to keep the tears from flowing down my cheeks. It was a very emotional and highly rewarding experience! The new Karen refugees obviously felt the emotional connection between us and seemed reluctant to move away. They just sat back down and looked at us. It was then that I almost lost it emotionally! Again, in spite of the joy of having served these precious people there was sadness that I was seeing them for the first and last time.

Later, a group of young men from the camp came to me, saying that they were the official leaders of the youth and young adults in the camp and wanted me to meet with them. Where they meet for their leadership meetings is on top of a cliff overlooking the camp. That cliff was at least 50 feet plus high and perfectly perpendicular! The only way up was on flat stakes that had been driven into the side of the cliff as steps. Once you started up there was no stopping because there was no finger-holds to grasp on to (it was like climbing up the side of a building stepping only on iron pegs driven into the outside wall), and it would be very difficult to restart your momentum if you stopped (although I later saw the young men do just that). With some trepidation, I started up and was doing fine until I neared the top. By then, I was out of breath, my blood pressure had skyrocketed and my heart was racing. I had no choice but to stop! I reached out to the cliff, still breathing hard, and found nothing to hold on to, to help me restart my climb. One of the young men, keeping his balance on the stakes, came back down (face out) to me and helped me to the top.

I immediately fell on the ground at the top of the cliff and it was 15 to 20 minutes before I could get my heart to quit racing, and get rid of the pain in my chest! I really thought I was going to die that day on top of that cliff. Finally I was able to converse with the young men and they shared with me what was on their mind. They, of course, wanted financial backing from me for youth projects in the camp. And then it was time to go back down the cliff (facing outward) and stepping with perfect balance on the stakes as I held on to thin air! I don't know how I managed to successfully and safely descend, but I was finally, once again, at the bottom of the cliff. Momentarily, that felt like Heaven!

Rev. Rob Jansons from Monroe, Washington had joined us on that trip into the Refugee Camp. He was in his mid-thirties and in good physical shape. He just shook his head at me in disbelief and said, "Not even I would have done what you just did." God was good to me, and once more delivered me from possible injury or death because of my habit of rash risk-taking and a desire for high adventure. I guess I must have thought that if those young men could daily go up and down those flat sticks driven into the side of the cliff, I ought to be able to do it once.

Lessons to learn: (1) Have you ever made a bad choice, that could have cost you your life? Like married life, family life, physical health, career life? God is a God that delights in rescuing from the consequences of bad choices those who have a heart after Him (love Him). [91] (2) There is a price, however, for God's help, and that is love for and commitment

---

[91]   Psalm 9:9; 37:39; 46:1; 50:15; 60:11

to Him; [92] (3) We should never make choices for our life or actions just because someone asks us to do something or promises us friendship or reward. [93] Choices should be made because we have prayed and asked God to give us wisdom and show us His will. [94] Not to do this can have eternal consequences for us and our children. [95] Lesson (4): Develop the habit of thankfulness[96]

---

[92]   Psalm 77:2, 4-6, 10, 13; Exodus 20:6; Deut. 5:9-10; I John 5:2-3; John 14:14-15; 15:10;

[93]   Proverbs 13:20; 1:10-15; 4:14-19; 9:6; 12:26; Psalm 1:1-6; 81:11-14; II Peter 2:12-22; I Corinthians 15:33

[94]   Nehemiah 9:19; Psalm 32:8; Proverbs 22:6;

[95]   Deuteronomy 4:40; 5:29; Isaiah 48:17-19; Psalm 19:7-13; 81:13-16; Luke 19:41-42;

[96]   Colossians 3:15-17; Luke 17:15-19; Romans 1:21-32; Philippians 4:6; Ephesians 5:20; I Thessalonians 5:16-18

Chapter Nine

The Seasonal Storms Experienced, Victories Won & Lessons Learned Near the End of our Pilgrimage on Earth

Eulogy OF my wife, Ruth Meyers
September 24, 2011

Job, an ancient wise man from the East, once said, "The Lord gave and the Lord has taken away, blessed be the name of the Lord!" God gave me, to be my wife, the most honest, faithful, committed, loving and selfless person I have ever met. Ruth was beautiful from the inside out. And I am the most blessed man in the world to have had this beautiful creature, this wonderfully gifted person to be my Life's Companion! A lot of the success of my years in the ministry is because of God's Grace (unmerited favor) in giving Ruth to me, to be my life's companion. God must have known that I would need a lot of help, and Ruth certainly was a terrific helper to me in all the challenges I met as we worked together in the Ministry.

Ruth was sweet all the time. Well, almost all the time! Her love for God, her love for me, and for our children was the most precious earthly treasure our family ever had! Of course any family whose primary values is centered on love for God and love for each other, has found the richest of all treasures for this life!

The second greatest characteristic, my wife possessed beside her ability to love unconditionally, was her ability to forgive those who hurt or disappointed her, or those whose actions and choices she could not approve. Her love & forgiveness was unconditional even when her approval was not and that characteristic shown like a Bright Beacon light in our family, as well as to those to whom she ministered. She could scold and speak disapprovingly and still love you unconditionally! I wonder sometimes if our children ever fully understood the difference or the value of those two separate reactions; i.e. disapproval when warranted, coupled with unconditional love! The disapproval was not rejection of the person, but rejection of the behavior. This would be sort of like God's treatment of Adam and Eve. But her unconditional love & forgiveness was always there for the children, as well as for myself.

Ruth, not me, was the disciplinarian of the family, and she thought I was much too lenient with the children. But she loved us, husband & children, with whatever faults she thought she saw in us!

That love was demonstrated to the children by the amount of time she devoted to them on a daily basis, playing with them, teaching them and trying to shape their little lives through her tenderness even when she had to discipline them. Teaching that actions have consequences, but making sure she protected them in their formative years from severe consequences. (Example of 2 ½ year old Lani, crashing crib sides, adventurous climb on top of dresser.)

That brings up a third characteristic of my wife. To her, Truth, as she understood it to be, was not a subject for compromise! The Ten Commandments were not ten suggestions. A daily lifestyle that was consistent with our Christian Profession, was of paramount importance to Ruth. And she knew well the words of Jesus in John's Gospel, chapters 14 & 15, "If you love me, keep my commandments." She was so thorough in all she did, she even insisted I look up for her the meaning in the Greek text of the word, "keep", which means, "guard against loss or injury". She understood, and rightly so, that when we disobey God's Word to us we injure the moral precepts by which God's

Eternal Kingdom is held together, we also injure our ability to be all God intended us to be, we injure our family & loved-ones by setting a bad example, and ultimately we injure our culture, our nation. So the words of Jesus when He said, "If you keep my commandments, you will abide in my love—as I have kept the Father's commandments and abide in His love" were very significant to Ruth. She also understood clearly that obedience to God was a necessary ingredient to one's claim to love Him. One cannot with honesty say, "I love Jesus, and yet defy Him or willfully disobey Him, or ignore His commandments. Ruth held herself, and our family to that strict standard. Anything less amounted to self-deception! And hypocrisy was just not in that lovely woman. She often said that what a person really believes is shown more by their choices & lifestyle than by their words! And she was right!

Another characteristic, all wrapped up in that delicate, fragile lovely form of hers, was her stubborn persistence in fulfilling responsibilities, and commitments; she kept her word (guarded it from loss or injury)! First of two examples: Language school in France was traumatic and hard for her. She had no experience in learning foreign languages, as I had previously done. So her studies were emotionally draining for her, bringing about many effusions of frustration and tears. But Ruth was a perfectionist! She had a deep sense of the need to do what she said she would do, and to do it with excellence. That included learning French so she could minister to women in Africa. And her sense of responsibility to her language studies did not allow her to laugh at her mistakes or make excuses for herself when she did not live up to her own standards of excellence. Characteristically, she persisted, and by sheer will power & self-discipline, she was, by our second term in Africa, a college Professor teaching French grammar to the Pastor's wives!

In addition, she was the Head Librarian of the college where we worked, and was tasked with setting up that Library almost from scratch, cataloging hundreds of books, setting up the classification of books written in French and doing it according to the American Dewy Decimal system. She was also the Book Store Manager and the School Nurse, as well as Professor of Christian Education. She also taught courses on Health, especially pregnancy, birth control & female problems. She even taught a course on human sexuality, and how the women could enjoy that part of life. Such thinking was a novel idea in that culture, causing many embarrassed giggles among the women! But, as a result, the African pastor's wives came to her for counseling concerning all sorts of marital issues. I just don't know how Ruth did it all, but she did what she did, and did it with excellence!

Ruth had no medical training, but spent hours poring through medical books written in English, and comparing symptoms with various prescription medicines. Then she would translate her findings into French before going to the local pharmacy where her white skin was the only qualification she needed to order whatever prescription medicines she felt necessary for the treatment of the students. No questions asked.

Second example of how she fulfilled her responsibilities and kept her commitments: she insisted that I make a 7 week missions trip to Southeast Asia because I had given my word to others that I would do so, & my word must be kept from injury or loss. This was in spite of the fact Ruth had just gotten out of the hospital (emergency appendectomy), the living room was still full of boxes from our recent move to Soap Lake, and Ruth would need my care of her physical well being, as well as help unpacking those boxes.

Yes, I have had the privilege of being married 49 years to a very remarkable woman! Like I said, she was beautiful from the inside out! Oh, we had our spats and disagreements like most couples do and she had her faults, as we all do. The problem for me was that she was more often right than wrong, and liked to tease me about that fact! And of course, that was hard on my male ego even while I was thankful to God for giving me this wonderful woman to be my wife!

Ruth's tendency to cry a lot was interpreted by some as a sign of weakness. But I lived with that lady, and I assure you that behind the tears an iron will was firmly implanted, strengthened by a deep commitment to righteousness and ethical purity, without compromise, no matter what the cost. Her extremely sensitive nature allowed her to know, almost instinctively, the Will of God in matters of daily living and choices. And her sensitive nature also gave her an uncanny ability to know where each person was emotionally, as well as what their motives might be. Wow! Could I tell stories of her ability to advise me, warn me, and even at times, offer constructive criticism to me in matters that concerned my decisions in the various churches where we were pastors.

Ruth was an excellent Bible Teacher! After our retirement from foreign missions service, we spent 12 years as itinerant Seminar Speakers across the USA and Canada. During this time we were together 24 hours a day, seven days a week. You have to really love each other to survive that!

We studied together and wrote and self-published 18 seminars, complete with study guide notes. At first I was doing all the teaching, but Ruth gradually "came into her own", and became a very popular speaker.

I remember when the Lord first spoke into my heart His desire that Ruth start doing some of the preaching/teaching and that He expected me to allow that and make space for her in our scheduling. When I shared that with Ruth, her response was typical, "Well, when God tells me the same thing, I'll do it." I chuckled to myself and said no more. Before long her teaching ministry was developing at such a fast pace that she was in demand by the pastors wherever we went, and to some extent her teaching ministry eclipsed my own. But there was no competition between us. I was as proud as any Husband could possibly be of what was happening. Our focus was on the Will of God for each church where we ministered. It didn't matter who did the teaching.

Her seminar on "Exposing Pathways to Deception: Spiritual Deception in the Lives of Believers, its Causes and Cure" was probably the most popular of her teachings. Other titles were, "Discerning Truth: Tests to determine if something is of God, Satan or Self; Then came, "Recognizing and Overcoming Strongholds", next, "Vessels of Honor: A Study in Brokenness, Humility, and Christ-likeness", followed by, "Women of Grace: Biblical Foundations for Love and Marriage". There were others, but I have mentioned enough to emphasize the remarkable giftedness of this beautiful Handmaiden of the Lord. I am proud of her and thankful for the privilege of having been her husband.

These five years as pastors at Soap Lake Assembly of God have been years of hard work, but some of the most joyous years of our pastoral experience. We have learned to love the congregation deeply, and are thankful that God put this capstone on our ministry just prior to retirement. But God has given Ruth an early retirement, and taken from me the one person who has made more of a difference in my life than anyone else. I feel as if I have been ripped apart inside! But I choose to submit with Praise & Adoration to God's Sovereignty & right to rule our lives!

Three years ago I found my precious wife collapsed in the bathroom. What followed were three surgeries in one day, and it seems to have been downhill from there. Ruth later suffered from what was diagnosed as Vascular Dementia. The small veins in her head became clogged. Not enough oxygenated blood was getting through to her brain. Her ability to recall vocabulary when teaching or speaking to others became increasingly difficult. Finally, she was unable to finish even one sentence without help in completing her thought. Along with the deterioration of her ability to remember vocabulary, came an occasional moment of confusion and she would tell me that I needed to be more careful to express myself clearly and not talk in such a confusing way. Then came a loss of motivation to function in any area. It seemed almost impossible for her to get off the couch. I had, several months ago, taken an interest in learning to cook. And so I started fixing our meals for us, and she was perfectly willing for me to do that. I would take a plate of food to her and wait anxiously for her approval or lack thereof. She actually began to enjoy my cooking and would ask for her favorite dishes.

On Thursday night, July 14, 2011 a little more than two months before the Memorial Service for which these remarks were written, we were sitting together on the couch talking about what, in God's timing, our future might look like. We had, at one time, considered ourselves to be history buffs, with particular interest in the Civil War, and had developed quite a little library on that topic. So I said to Ruth, "Sweetheart, I'll take you anywhere you want to go, including back East so we can visit some of the historical landmarks we had missed last time we were in that part of the USA. And then, in a moment of total male insensitivity I added, "But what I won't do is sit around the house and watch TV with you." I was trying to motivate her to consider a more active lifestyle, which would allow her to enjoy things she had once wanted to do. She did not appreciate my comment at all!

How I have regretted those ill-advised words, and chastised myself many times for saying it! Because watching TV was about all she had left that she could get her mind around. The only exception being once a week when she rallied herself to prepare for teaching the Wednesday morning class to her precious women. Of course, I would have loved her enough to watch TV with her, and I felt terrible after the comment was made because I knew I had hurt her.

Ruth's teaching ministry to the women of the church every Wednesday morning became increasingly difficult for her. But my wife was no quitter, never would be. And she loved those girls who were struggling to dig their way out of the pit of bad choices. She also loved dearly the older, spiritually mature ladies who came each week in support of what was happening. But even that was getting too stressful for her; and, in the privacy of our home she would share with me the stress she felt from the effort each week. I begged Ruth to quit teaching. But like I said, she was no quitter; quitting anything she felt God or others expected of her was foreign to her nature.

Our discussion about what retirement might look like came to an end as we prepared to retire for the night, that Thursday evening on July 14th. Ruth suddenly came rushing back out of the bedroom, pushing me to one side because of her desperation to reach our little green rocker in the living room. There she collapsed. We were out of time for each other, and hadn't realized it.

Ruth had just experienced a major brain hemorrhage and we had just had our last conversation. She must have been in terrible pain. Later that night we would both be admitted as patients in the Providence Sacred Heart Hospital in Spokane, and two nights later, July 17th, they brought her to my room on the seventh floor so we could have a few moments together before she died. The life support was removed. My room was full of family and friends as well as pastors and dignitaries from the Network Offices of the Assemblies of God District Headquarters. We stood around her bed and sang and worshipped God as Ruth slipped peacefully away and made the journey to the Headquarters of the Universe, the very Throne Room of God!

I regret deeply that I didn't climb into the bed alongside her and gently hold her in my arms while the angels took her into Eternity, and into the Presence of Jesus. But I have been told that I was so medicated I hardly knew what I was doing. For me, it would be another seven days in the hospital as a team of six to eight doctors worked to save my own life.

Oh how I wish I could bring another plate of food to my precious wife, wait on her every need, and just sit beside her, to watch with her, her favorite television programs. But it is too late for wishes!

Good night, my Sweetheart, my Love, my Best Friend! I'll see you in the Son-Shine of God's eternal morning!

Save a place for me at the foot of the Throne of God's Glory! God gave you to me and God has taken you from me! Blessed be the Name of the Lord!

Your Loving Husband,

Joseph

Ruth Helen Meyers   Ruth Helen Meyers

Chapter Ten

The Meaning and Purpose of Miracles

The Bible reveals that God has created at least two separate and very different Universes or "Systems of Reality". One System of Reality is described as Visible and the other as Invisible. Each of these Systems of Reality can be said to be a separate Universe, with non-compatible "Laws of Nature" governing each System. A rather complete (though broad) explanation is given in Colossians 1:16 where it is revealed that all that exists was created by Jesus, and that His entire Creation can best be understood in the form of two basic categories: (1) that which was created in heaven (the invisible); and, (2) that which was created on earth (the visible). Furthermore, Colossians 1:16 reveals that there are various levels of authority in each of these two "Systems of Reality".

Because all of the physical universe is available to be observed and explored by those who dwell on earth and because members of the human race are not equipped with the necessary bodily organs by which to perceive & examine the Invisible System of Reality, it seems safe to assume two things: first, "in Heaven" refers to where God and the Angelic Hosts, both good and evil exist in a System of Reality invisible to the Physical Universe and somehow outside of, or not part of, that which is physical in nature or essence. Secondly, that the usage of "on earth" in Colossians 1:16 really has reference to the entire Physical Universe and all that is controlled by "Laws of Nature" and understood through the five senses created by God and given to animal and human creatures. This explanation of the meaning of "Heaven" and "Earth" seems to be confirmed by the prayer of Jesus recorded in Luke 10:21

when He addresses God as Father and then calls Him, "Lord of Heaven and earth" (the two realities!).

What is known as "the scientific method of examination" is used as an exercise of human logic to analyze what we perceive through our five senses. But the scientific method cannot even begin to understand or to accurately analyze the Invisible System of Reality. We know it exists, but we cannot understand or analyze it through means other than Inspired Scripture which we accept by Faith to be our only reliable Source of Objective & Ultimate Truth. This Truth we believe to be inspired (God-breathed) by a Spirit-Being—third Person of the Triune Godhead—called "The Holy Spirit"). To accept and believe the miracle signposts revealed in Colossians 1:16, John 3:16 and, for that matter, all of Inspired Scripture requires a leap of Faith, a work of God, the Holy Spirit in our hearts, and only then are we ready to use Analytical Tools to study and seek to understand Revealed Truth. Faith does not "turn off" our minds, but we need a Supernatural, however objective, Source for the study of Ultimate Truth which reveals an entirely different "nature" or "essence" of all that comes to us out of the Invisible System of Reality.

As a sideline, it is interesting to note that the Visible System of Reality (Physical Universe), includes probably something close to 80 billion galaxies.[97] Earth's Galaxy is known as The Milky Way, but is said to be "in our neighborhood". Within this vast physical universe, there is also the Andromeda Galaxy and the Pinwheel Galaxy detectable by the Hubble Deep Field observation platform, each being an approximate distance of one billion light years in distance from Planet Earth but nevertheless said to be "in our neighborhood".

---

[97] http://www.faqs.org/faqs/astronomy/faq/part8/section-4.html accessed by Joseph Meyers on 12/20/2010

Planet Earth is a small (by comparison) little pea sized object within the Milky Way Galaxy; and The Milky Way can boast of at least 200 globular clusters [98] within our Galaxy.

A Miracle can be defined as the moment when someone (God, an Angel or an Evil Spirit) crosses over from the Invisible System of Reality and enters our Visible System of Reality to perform some action which impinges (forces itself) upon us and changes what happens to us on Earth. The focus of all Miracles is the Human Race. One other explanation may be needed here: i.e., that which is supernatural to us who live in the Visible System of Reality is actually natural in the Invisible Reality. It is when the Invisible System of Reality impinges upon the Visible System of Reality that something ONLY we humans call "Miracle" occurs! The rules and nature of the Invisible overpower the rules and nature of the Visible. The Invisible not only creates, but controls the Visible.[99] And only the Invisible System of Reality will endure into eternity.

A few of the many examples of when the Invisible Reality overrides and controls the Visible Reality that can be cited are: when Jesus walked through a solid wall to meet with His Disciples after the Resurrection and when He went back and forth between the Visible and Invisible

---

[98] The number discovered to date. A globular cluster can be defined as, "a gravitationally bound concentration of approximately ten thousand to one million stars, spread over a volume of from several tens to about 200 light years in diameter." http://seds.org/messier/glob.html (And we have 200 of these clusters within our Galaxy? Wow! The Atlas of the Universe claims that many of these are "scattered in a spherical halo around our galaxy". www.atlasoftheuniverse.com/globular.html And this Physical Universe with all his wonders that challenge the comprehension of the human mind is only one of the two "Systems of Reality" created by our Savior, Jesus, the Christ?!! Colossians 1:16). I wonder what the Invisible System of Reality (The Heavenlies) must be like! These three WEB sites were accessed by Joseph Meyers on 12/20/2010.

[99] Proverbs 16:1,9; 19:14; 20:24; 21:1; Psalm 105:25; 106:46; 121:2; Daniel 4:35; Acts 7:9-10; First Kings 12:15; Isaiah 28:22;

Systems of Reality (Luke 24:31; John 20:19), or when angels frightened tough Roman soldiers so badly that they lost their ability to stand on their feet and ended up on the ground "like dead men" (Matthew 28:2-4).[100] When the rules and limitations of Nature in the Physical Universe, especially on earth, are set aside; i.e., when Physical Science or Medical Science no longer apply so that a bush burns without being consumed (Exodus 3:2), or a dead man is raised from the dead and floats out of his tomb, bound hand and foot so that he could not move, and with his face covered so that he could not see, and yet he comes to Jesus (John 11:43-44), and then is loosed from his grave clothes and later eats dinner with Jesus (John 12:1-2), or when two blind men receive their sight without benefit of earthbound medical science (Matthew 9:27-30; Mark 8:22-25), or when a man is cured of leprosy simply because he obeyed the Man of God and washed in the dirty river of Jordan (Second Kings 5:1-14)—all of these and so much more are examples of supernatural power coming from outside the Visible System of Reality, overpowering Nature and accomplishing what we call, "Miracle"!

And so this book, as you have read it, is a record of my life on earth, and the many times I have experienced God's intervention from outside of the Visible System of Reality in which I live; the times when the laws of nature have been set aside for my benefit, protection and blessing! I would like to be so brash as to declare that if most people (especially those who are God's Servants, Followers of Jesus Christ, Born Again and purified from sin by action of His shed Blood) would take the time to keep a Journal, each would find that God has also frequently overpowered and set aside the Laws of Nature for their benefit as well!

---

[100] I was tempted to describe this scene as "when Beings out of the Invisible Realm caused tough Roman Soldiers to wet their pants!" But I guess that would be pure speculation, wouldn't it?

I am not some kind of privileged child of God. What He has done for me He will do for you, and maybe even more!

The Purpose of Miracles: Developing
Habits of Trust and Obedience

But not only does God bless us by performing the miraculous for our earthly benefit, He also tests us somewhat regularly in two areas: Trust and Obedience! Do I really trust God? And will I, when I can see no miraculous intervention in my current problem or circumstances, obey Him even though the cost is great and the consequences of obedience seem to my perspective to be potentially devastating? In other words, I choose to do what is right and what is according to God's revealed Will simply because it is right and it is God's Will and not because I see any way that those choices will accomplish what I want to see done.

I have come to recognize the still small voice of the Holy Spirit communicating internally in my thought life. I remember distinctly, for instance, when suddenly, with no warning and no predisposal because of thoughts already directed toward God, that I received a communication from the Holy Spirit. The words spoken in my mind were this: "How do you want to be tested throughout your life?" I was shocked by the message. I hadn't even been thinking about God or Spiritual matters. But there it was! No doubt that God had just asked me a question! Immediately after the question, came several options and I was given the opportunity to choose from among them. This happened more than forty to fifty years ago while I was still very young. I do believe it was after my marriage to Ruth, but am not sure. Two options I distinctly remember were "health" and "finances". In other words, was I willing to have repeated problems with my health or frequent financial challenges, either of which would be used of God to test my trust and obedience levels to Him? There were other options but I don't remember clearly what they were so I won't mention them. I chose the area of finances. I would learn to trust and to obey God in the area of financial need. That would be the arena of my testing. And it is obvious that God has honored my choice for the field of testing. But, my choice has also served to protect me from chronic or debilitating diseases or injuries. The voice of the Lord was there once again just recently as I write this book, stating that I would not have to worry about getting cancer. That just isn't going to happen! And so I rejoice in that! So many of God's people that I have cared deeply about have wrestled with cancer. But as I work on the manuscript for this book, I am living on $810 per month plus a few gifts now and then that trickle in. However, I have a roof over my head and food in my pantry as well as a $3,000 dollar laptop computer, and I drive a 2011 KIA that was miraculously provided to me when my 1996 Cadillac twice blew a head gasket and left me stranded in the middle of nowhere. Some bills have had to go unpaid and there are distasteful consequences, but I know that God knows where I am and that He will relieve this pressure point in His own good time!

Abraham was tested by God, even though He expressed both trust and obedience. He had to take his family and flocks on a 1,200 mile hike that must have taken them a year or more to accomplish. The distance was six hundred miles north in the fertile crescent from Ur (in modern Iraq) to Haran, across the top and then six hundred miles south into the Promised Land. The Promised Land was due west of the Ur of the Chaldeans in modern Iraq but between Ur and the Promised Land was the vast Arabian Desert that would have been impassable to anything but Camel Caravans but certainly not passable for women and children and flocks.

The Children of Israel were tested as they wandered through the Wilderness Desert. Deuteronomy 8:1-5 describes that testing. And the testing was for the following purposes: (1) to know what was in their heart (i.e., test their inner character); (2) to test their priorities (would they choose to obey or choose to follow their own desires or instincts); [101] (3) to cause them to know or learn something particular (that they don't need something from this system of reality to sustain life; i.e., not live by bread alone, but by every word that God speaks).

In other words, if God must speak a miracle into existence, something not normally part of the Physical Universe in order to provide for those who serve and obey Him, He will do that (like sending Manna from the sky—see Deuteronomy 8:2-5)! [102]

Daniel was tested when he prioritized his faith in God and habits of prayer over King Nebuchadnezzar's command that no one but the King be worshipped in all of Babylon. As a consequence he faced being cast into a den of hungry lions, which, in fact, happened. But the God to whom Daniel prayed rescued him by giving the lions a case of lock-jaw.

---

[101] This is a vitally important issue that comes up earlier in this book because of our experience with our own Son and because human beings need to know that no matter what physical or hormonal or psychological problem a person may have, they still have a free will; i.e., the ability to make choices. In the case of someone who claims to be bi-sexual, for instance, they still have the option to choose not to gratify their desires. Just say, "No!" It is better to remain celibate than to yield to perverted sexual activity. Go without sex all your life if that is what it takes to live in obedience. We live in a broken world that has been broken since the Garden of Eden days. God did not, nor does not now, nor will not create physical or psychological deformity or dysfunction; all that is the result of the curse that came into this system of reality because of man's disobedience & lack of trust in God.

[102] Deuteronomy 8:2-5 "And you shall remember that the LORD your God led you all the way these forty years in the wilderness, to humble you *and* test you, to know what *was* in your heart, whether you would keep His commandments or not. So He humbled you, allowed you to hunger, and fed you with manna which you did not know nor did your fathers know, that He might make you know that man shall not live by bread alone; but man lives by every *word* that proceeds from the mouth of the LORD. Your garments did not wear out on you, nor did your foot swell these forty years. You should know in your heart that as a man chastens his son, *so* the LORD your God, chastens you."

The Apostle Paul was tested with much physical suffering even though he both trusted God and obeyed Him. In the end, he was beheaded because of his faith in Jesus Christ as the Jewish Messiah.

A personal acquaintance of mine, Rev. John Tucker, went back into the Congo around 1963 after my new bride and I met him in the basement of First Assembly of God in Portland, Oregon. Within a year or two, he was beaten to death by Congolese rebels. Those who killed him were thoughtful enough to save his wedding ring and give it to his wife before dumping his body in the river as food for the crocodiles. These also are tests of faith and faithfulness that require we keep in focus our eternal destiny. When one's spirit leaves their torn, bloodied body it goes into the Presence of their Heavenly Father to await a new and eternal body that can never again die.[103]

I have already tried as best I can to explain the meaning of "miracle" and the purpose of Miracles? [104] And so this Book is my own personal testimony to the faithfulness of God and His frequent miraculous intervention in the middle of much suffering and God-ordained testing.

---

[103] II Corinthians 5:1-4; John 11:13; II Timothy 1:10; some people believe that we all "sleep" after death while we wait for our resurrection bodies (see Matthew 27:51-53). But because of such instances as in and Mark 9:3-4; Luke 9:31 many also believe that after death we will have some sort of spiritual body, although not the same body we will have at the general Resurrection of the Dead and that right after death we will have a conscious and active life, although not with our final resurrection body. So there seems to be some uncertainty.

[104] Matthew 11:20-24; 12:41-42; Ezekiel 3:6-7; Acts 13:34; 28:25-28; I Cor. 2:11-14; 12:4-11; Ecclesiastes 11:5; Ezekiel 37:9; Luke 24:49; Acts 4:31

Chapter Eleven

A Dangerous, Tormented and Searching for Help Kind of Guy

There is a process and pilgrimage to be followed again and again by those who desire to be "soul winners". The souls of human beings (soul being best described or identified by the terms "Will, Emotions and Intellect) are amazingly resistant to God's Love. A "Soul Winner" is one who seeks to bring a Person with all their Thoughts, Emotions and Priorities to the Foot of the Cross causing that Person (Sinner) to seek God's forgiveness for their rebellious Carnal Nature and to surrender all their emotions, thought-life and stubbornness expressed through Choices and Priorities to the Control and Lordship of Jesus Christ.

The Bible states that the Soul that sins will die! And how does a soul sin? Sin is disobedience to the Laws of God at the level of one's Emotional Life, Thought Life and Self-Will (choices, priorities, dreams, goals, aspirations). It has been observed that each day is a new opportunity to decide whether we will obey the One Who created us & loves us so much He died to pay the penalty for our sins, or obey our own self-centered preferences. This process is a long one of necessity because of the requirement to willingly move, on a daily basis, from Self-centeredness to God-centeredness. And that takes time. Human inherited self-centeredness does not easily allow itself to be replaced by God-centeredness! In the case of the whole human race, it has taken over six thousand years to win over enough of a number of Human Beings to be able with integrity to talk about "The Bride of Christ". That Bride (you and I) can be identified by our surrender of our own Will & Choices to the control of our Spiritual Bridegroom, who is Jesus, the Christ. My point is that as Servants, partaking of our Lord's cup, (Matt. 20:23; 26:42) in our efforts to bring someone to Christ, we must be prepared for the process of suffering, disappointment, abuse & rejection by the one we are trying to help. Furthermore, the painful process by which our loved-one moves from self-centeredness to God-centeredness can be a long, drawn out process depending partially on how long it takes a person to acknowledge and repent of their sinful soulish habits (thought life, emotional life and choices). It is in that light that I would like to describe my pilgrimage with someone I choose to call David Deaverson (pseudonym).

David is a man 62 years of age and a Viet Nam War Veteran (Special Forces). I first met David shortly after my wife, Ruth, and I accepted the pastorate of a church in the middle of Washington State. David waved me down as I drove by his house one day, and asked for a ride.

When he got into my car he had several hunting arrows in his hand with the sharp hunting blades attached. I asked him about where he wanted to go and why he had the hunting arrows with him. His reply startled me! He said that he was going out to kill a man that had stolen $5,000 from him & unless this person was able to immediately repay what he had stolen would indeed kill him.

The anger in David's voice as well as his facial expressions made me to know that this 62 year old Vietnam Veteran was not joking or "blowing hot air". Recent conversations with police officers have also confirmed that David is an expert in all kinds of weaponry, from knife throwing to the use of bow and arrows (with intent to kill people or animals); as well as various kinds of modern weapons, and that David would have been physically and psychologically capable of carrying out the threats of that day. But my learning that about David was subsequent to the events of that day. At that moment I had no idea what kind of person was seated next to me in the car and whom I was taking, by his own confession, on a mission of murder. Also, I have recently learned (from the Chief of Police) that David is bi-polar and probably schizophrenic as well. But all that, including David's age and background was information of which I had no knowledge that day. All I knew was that this guy sounded nuttier than a fruit cake, and I was not comfortable with the situation with which I was now entangled due to my efforts to be kind to a man I didn't really know. To any casual visitor where I live is a sleepy little town with not much happening throughout the community. However, a large part of the population is made up of unemployed folk who live chronically in poverty and on prescription and non-prescription drugs. And then there are those whose need for meth and other illegal drugs is so intense that the breaking and entering of homes is common place. Add to that the Hispanic gangs that war with each other (example: recently a 19 year Hispanic boy had his face blown away by a shotgun blast, almost in front my home) and the violence that goes on because of drug dealers, and drug deals gone bad, and you have a potentially explosive situation.

My mind was full of possible scenarios and reactions from David depending on what I said or did at the moment of crisis looming before us. Finally, as we neared our destination, I mustered all my courage, and put aside my fears to say to David, "If there is any violence today, I will back my car out of the driveway as fast as possible and leave you stranded while I call the police on my cell phone, giving them your location and expressed intentions." I had waited until we pulled into the driveway of our destination before I made that declaration, for some reason believing that would increase my chances of surviving this potentially lethal situation. As I waited in the car, the wife of the man David sought came out on the front porch, and she and David talked for a very long time. Finally, David returned to my car without any incident and I took him home.

It was several years later before anything significant happened in my contacts with David. All I knew was that God had placed him on my heart and I longed to introduce him to the Savior I know as Jesus, the Christ. Oh, one thing I do remember was that in one of my earliest conversations with David he had mentioned that he had no respect for my predecessor in the pastorate here. Apparently David had several conversations with the man who came before me, and then had once put a bullet into the offering plate one Sunday morning because, as he later claimed, that was all he had to give. The pastor took that as a veiled threat, called the police and brought charges against David. Apparently there was no "love lost" between the two of them, and David had nothing but contempt for my predecessor. Apparently neither of them understood that communication requires the message sent to be identical with the message received. And also that love, patience, mercy and respect will facilitate true communication.

In late 2012, as I was driving by David's house (shack), he once again waved me down and indicated a desire to visit with me. My wife of 49 years had died the year before (July 2011) and I was dealing with my own pain partially by throwing myself even more intensely into the ministry of helping others. David's comment to me was, "I have been watching you over the past several years, as you walk to the church in all kinds of weather and seem so dedicated to the congregation you pastor." He went on to say, "You are different from the others" and without explaining what he meant by that comment he went on to express a desire to get to know me better. The next day, he was at my front door with his dog, Brownie on a leash and a cigarette in his mouth. I invited him into the parsonage and we began the process of gradually getting acquainted over a long series of conversations that continue to the present day. I mention this fact because of the unique manner by which we have been "getting acquainted".

I don't believe David ever lives through a day without experiencing deep, intense anger and resentment that travels around and around in his personality, and is expressed by violent outbursts of obscenities and vulgarities. Little did I know at that moment that I would be the focal point of these almost daily outbursts! These violent outbursts were often expressed as David paced back and forth between the kitchen, bathroom and living room of the parsonage while shouting and cursing. Words of resentment and promises to rid the world of whoever was the latest object of his anger would flow out of his mouth like a powerful cloud burst of hatred. He seemed to have a particular desire to kill "all the meth heads" and claimed to have an agreement with the local Prosecutor who had promised to look the other way allowing David to kill as many "meth heads" as possible, thus saving the local police, as well as other law enforcement agencies a lot of work. David claimed to have an appointment with the Prosecutor that week to obtain his signature on a document formalizing that agreement. I have learned, with David, to just listen to his claims no matter how insane they seemed to be and quietly make note of them. Also, David said that I made him nervous and apprehensive, making it emotionally necessary to go back outside for another cigarette. Then he would return and begin pacing around the house giving vent to his violent emotions.

I didn't quite know what to do with all this and thought it wise to sit quietly and listen to these gushers of anger until he finally expended his feelings, becoming amazingly calm and rational for a few minutes . . . until either he or myself said something that reminded him of something else which elicited another violent outburst. Finally David would excuse himself and go home. After a number of these episodes, I asked David why he found it necessary to explode and vent his anger in front of me and throughout the house on almost every visit. His response was revealing, when he said, "Pastor, if I didn't explode at you, I would go out and murder the "blankety-blanks". You are my safety valve for my emotions and thoughts. It is better for me to give vent to my feelings this way then to go out and kill someone." Killing people seems to be David's answer to all problems, and he talks about it a lot! David claims to have killed men with his bare hands (in Vietnam) and said that he really enjoyed his experiences in that war. He has also frequently remarked that he is angry about having been born in the first place and that God, if there is a God, should have asked for his permission before allowing him to be born. I have long recognized the work that needs to be done to help him see that murder or beatings or resentment and anger do not resolve problems, the way God would want them resolved; and furthermore that God does not call us to determine (through killing) the eternal destinies of members of His Creation; that is something only Jehovah God is qualified to do.

I remember once when David came to the parsonage to see me. Special "throwing knives" stuck out of several places on his person. (Because of the long string of felonies on his record, as related to me by the local Chief of Police, David is not allowed to own firearms; he can, however own knives.) But on this visit, and around his neck, was what looked to me to be some sort of Indian relic. When I approached him to examine the artifact, he reached up and pulled the lower half out of what turned out to be a knife in its sheath. With one smooth motion the knife was out of its place and the tip of the blade in motion toward my stomach. He looked me in the eye and with a smirk on his face said, "See how easy that would have been?" He then said that he was on his way to kill 20 people that day. Later in the day he came back and claimed to have killed three people ("meth heads" as he calls them) but was tired and would have to save the others for another day. At that point I began to think it was time to talk to the local authorities and/or the mental health unit at the Veterans Administration Hospital about a two hour drive from where we live.

I need to back up a moment and relate that David had previously been attacked by a gang of "meth heads" and beaten so badly that they left him for dead in the shack where he lives. David had been complaining to me about that beating, and threatening vengeance. He remarked several times to me that he was practicing with his throwing knives, with the full intention of throwing those knives into the chests and/or throats of the "meth heads" if they returned. Subsequently David had finally invited me over to his place, a filthy little shack with a metal front door that David obviously used for target practice with his throwing knives. Dave welcomed me inside and seemed genuinely proud to have me there as his guest. As I turned around to look back at the front door, I was amazed to see multiple special "throwing knives" stuck in the metal door.

I had been trying to think of something positive, even complimentary to say. Suddenly my searching mind struck on an idea. I would ask him to give me a demonstration of his skill with the knives. The ones already stuck in the door seemed sufficient evidence that David's effort would be successful and I could then compliment him on his prowess with knives. That would appeal to his ego and get our visit off on a positive note. Upon my request, David seemed pleased and proceeded to rummage around in a pile of non-descript items lying on the floor around our feet. He pulled out what seemed to me to be an old kitchen knife. The knife blade was bent and not at all something that one would expect even an expert to be able to throw successfully. Then David found an anvil and hammer and proceeded to reshape the blade of that old knife against the anvil, with blows from the hammer. David was seated at the moment and without rising to his feet and with a sudden sideways motion of his arm (like a baseball pitcher throwing what is called "a slider") he threw the knife at the door. The knife bounced off the door. With seeming calm assurance David rose to recover the knife and seated himself once more. With the words, "See that small yellow piece of paper on the door? Well

I'll put the knife in the middle of that square piece of paper." From a sitting position, and with the same sideways motion of his arm, he threw the knife with such force that, to my amazement, the blade of the knife pierced the metal door about an inch from the piece of paper. David was not pleased since he had missed his mark, but I was shocked with the obvious force of the throw when, upon examination I saw that the blade of that old knife had pierced the metal door and about a half inch of the blade showed through the opposite side of the door. If that had been the throat or chest of a man, the consequences would have been deadly. The Chief of Police would later state to me that he was not at all surprised at that demonstration, and that David is indeed an expert in all forms of weaponry.

At this point I need to mention that it has taken a matter of months before I could feel safe enough with David's visits not to fear for my own safety, but, at the same time, was not willing to cut off my efforts to gain his friendship or to be able to begin to speak into his life and to endeavor to bring him to Christ. I have invited David over for dinner several times through this process, and once went fishing with him in spite of the counsel of several police officers, and others, that my life might be in jeopardy if I left town with him. It seemed to me that one of David's greatest needs was for someone to care about him enough to be patient with his bad manners, bad language and downright disgusting ideas long enough to help him begin to see life in a different light. David was the first to suggest that we pray together at the beginning of our visits. When I would pray for David to surrender to the Love and Lordship of Jesus Christ, and that God would deliver him from the tormenting spirits who so evidently controlled his mind and emotions, David would in return pray that God would give me patience with him and the strength not to give up on him. I must admit that both prayers pinpointed valid needs.

I need to relate a couple more instances of bizarre behavior to demonstrate the desperate condition of David's mind and emotions, and just how challenging is the need to get him to surrender his life to Jesus Christ.

One event that is worthy of mention happened about 11:30 PM one evening. I had already been in bed about 90 minutes and was sound asleep. (During this time I have been learning how debilitating pain . . . which sends me to bed early every night . . . can be as I suffer with a torn rotator cuff and torn bicep) I was suddenly awakened by the repeated ringing of my door bell and pounding on the door. It took me a few moments to gather my wits about me enough to suspect that it was David making all that noise. But I wasn't going to take any chances. Besides, even if this turned out to be David, I should ask myself, "Who else might be out there with him and what did he, or they, want from me at a half hour before midnight"? So I picked up the phone and called 911. I related that someone may be trying to break into my home and requested immediate police intervention. Suddenly all the noise stopped and a few minutes later the police arrived. They wanted to know if I had any suspicions about the identity of the person pounding on the door. When I mentioned David's name the policeman indicated that the whole department knew David. And that they had experienced numerous encounters with him. So the policeman went directly to David's home. I had also asked the 911 operator who took my call to request that the Chief of Police pay me a visit, which happened that same evening. It was during that conversation that I learned many details of David's life. He is well known by all the local police and county deputy sheriffs.

David likes to drive his automobile at speeds around 80 to 100 miles per hour. Whenever an officer of the law stops him, his background check of David before he ever leaves the police car gives such a long list of felonious activities that backup is immediately called for and the police always approach the car with drawn weapons. David enjoys the excitement of those encounters. Seems the adrenalin rush gives him a thrill he needs and is some sort of satisfaction weakly akin to his war experiences in Vietnam. With great gusto and evident pleasure David tells me about these events whenever they happen.

One more event to share: Recently, there came a pounding on my back door, much shouting and repeated ringing of the doorbell. The time: 3:30 AM! The shouts were loud and clear! "Joseph, don't be afraid! Open the (expletive) door! I hesitated but the shouts were so loud and urgent that I opened, not knowing what to expect or who might be there with David. David stumbled into the utility room, along with Brownie, his pet dog. Blood was running down his face and onto the floor. Apparently, a group of "meth-heads" had taken a baseball bat to his head and body. David was livid with anger and screaming for me to call 911. I didn't need to be urged. When the lady who took the call wanted to know where to send the police, I wanted to give David's street address but didn't know it. David took the phone and began to abuse her with violent and vulgar language for which I forcefully chastised him after a two-day cool down period. When I asked David why he would abuse her verbally while all the poor lady was trying to do is find out where to send the police which we were requesting, his response was again most revealing to his psychological wounds and limitations. "Well", David said, "I wanted her to know how irritated I was." After a couple days cool down time I shared with David my kind, loving, gentle observation, "David" I said, "you remind me of a two year child screaming in a church service or at the grocery store just because the child wants everyone to know how unhappy he/she is!" "Here you are 62 years old and you act like a spoiled brat. The poor woman that took the 911 call didn't deserve your abuse. She was only trying to help us." My comment didn't faze him. His excuse was that he had taken a lot of abuse from his father when he (David) was a child. He replied, "You are right, I am a 60 year old adult with a 2 year old child's emotional maturity. Sixty plus two totals 62 which is my age, so what do you expect? I'm acting my age." So, how do you help a person that uses that kind of rationale? Later, David would say to me, "Pastor, you could never survive in my world!" I said nothing in reply but, in my heart, I knew that he was right. I could never survive in the world he lives in, and that knowledge put a fresh dosage of compassion and Godly love in my heart for this tormented man!

The Police Chief would also confirm what I was beginning to realize: that David needs a different kind of professional help than I am qualified to give him. But if I call the VA Mental Health in Spokane and tell them what I know about David and then David figures out that I am the one that ratted on him, as my daughter who works as an administrator for the VA in Seattle said, "Dad, you'll be dead meat, and I am not ready to lose my Father, the only one I have left in this world. But David will come after you to kill you if he finds out you called the Veterans Administration Mental Health unit." My daughter actually has had successful experiences with these kinds of matters, having talked angry VA Vets who have been threatening to kill someone in off the street and into the VA treatment center for extreme cases of mental health. The concerns I have with that is that anyone who talks daily (no exaggeration) about killing people as a way to resolve problems will sooner or later snap and actually follow through on what has been being said over and over and over again. If I don't call the VA Mental Health to report the danger David poses and then someone besides me gets killed, I would have blood on my hands, and certainly on my conscience!

Following the Police Chief's advice on how best to approach the subject of his own mental health with David, I explained to David that after my wife's death on July 17, 2011 I received a communication from the Assemblies of God District Office stating that they felt I needed to see a psychologist for grief counseling and offering to pay for six sessions. I said to David, "I could have resented the counsel that I need "to see a

Shrink"; that somehow my mental health was not what it needed to be. But I had been told that because of their experience with other pastors having lost their mate and who, refusing grief counseling, had later experienced serious psychological problems, they were offering to pay for me to get some help. Instead of resenting the counsel I admitted that I was not mentally healthy and needed help. From there I asked David if he had ever considered that he might need to see a psychologist. I went straight for the mark and asked him if he had ever considered that he might be bi-polar. I was surprised when David said he was already aware of his bi-polar condition and knew more about it than the psychologists he had consulted with.

David and I are supposed to be studying a series that, my wife, Ruth, wrote on "Doorways to Deception". One lesson deals with "Rebellion and Stubbornness as Witchcraft & Idolatry". The problem is that David's mind always manages to latch on to something that reminds him of something else and throws him into a rage. I do not mean to play down the possibility of various kinds of mental health issues. But getting David to agree to see people who can help him with his mental health issues is going to be a challenge.

My main point is that Divine Ministry, the work of the Kingdom of God on earth, takes place in places other than a pulpit or regular church services. Ministry opportunities or calling from God takes place where, and in ways, that have nothing to do with a beautiful Sanctuary, clean restrooms, nice sanitized facilities full of polite people knowledgeable in the art of social graces and Divine Worship. Following our Master who died for us all might very well take us into the dirty and the dangerous. We might very well be required to touch and even associate with the pigs in the pig pens where life is dirty, and the mud of the local culture threatens to suck our souls downward; at the least make us so disgusted as to tempt us to walk away from some messy, dirty, obnoxious person who has no idea of the opportunity being offered to them to meet their Creator and enjoy His Holy Presence!

The language is disgusting, the noise which passes for music is offensive, and the attitudes and priorities seem insane at best. I'm not accustomed to listening to someone I am trying to help as they tell the 9-1-1 operator what she can do to herself. I hate the filthy language, the stench of cigarettes, or the whiskey laden breath, and the disgusting values and attitudes. I like things to be more refined, and at least outwardly clean and polite, even if the person I am trying to reach for Christ is suffering from the chains of sin, self and Satan. Truth be known, the dirty, desperate kind with filthy mouths, uncouth & without social graces can sometimes be easier to reach than the urbane, cultured, and polite people. Those that are "no good" and know that they are "no good" are closer to the Kingdom of God, and easier to reach with the Gospel than those satisfied, successful, cultured, polite people who think they must be pleasing to God but whose righteousness is like filthy rags in the sight of God. (Isaiah 64:6)

Let's consider an example or parable to help our understanding: Learning to climb a mountain for one's own sense of accomplishment, successfully crossing the dangerous, death defying ice bridges or avoiding a fall into the terrifying crevices from which there is seemingly no recovery or escape is one thing. But to take those kinds of risks over and over again as part of a "professional" career or "Calling" as the professional mountaineer tries to help the novice climb the mountain to satisfy his own desire to reach the summit is very similar to the work of pastors or missionaries as they try to help the Seeker after God to be acceptable to God. In other words, the trained pastor or religious leader or even an ordinary Christian faces his own spiritual death every day as he works with "those sinners".

The trained mountaineer faces the same dangers all over again with each climb, as does the novice whom he is leading. The dangers are the same to all in the party of mountain climbers. And experience, while extremely helpful, is no guarantee of safety. What am I getting at? Many a Man or Woman of God has fallen to their spiritual (or psychological) death off the mountain of righteous pilgrimage. Bitterness, hurt, lust, self-pity, feelings of betrayal by those who should have been available for emotional and spiritual, sometimes even material, support but just were not "there for them", and these feelings leads to sinful unchristlike words or reactions that can be compared to falling into a crevice, further injury or spiritual, psychological or physical death as the result [105]. But the thrill of success through forgiveness, further teaching and/or the choice to love in obedience to God's Word are all part of what goes into the experience of hearing in eternity that "well done good and faithful servant".

However in the dirty here and now the climb to reach the pinnacles of spiritual maturity and effectiveness in service to God is a very dangerous but spiritually courageous effort. These efforts also bring salvation to some novice who is climbing with the mountaineer and brings Joy beyond compare as together they enjoy the vast expanse of God's Holy Presence and together hear the Lord whisper, "Well done good and faithful servants!" That is the thrill of being a professional mountaineer and guide! And that too is the thrill of being a soul winner or winner of souls, helping them be qualified (through repentance and surrender to God's Sovereignty) for entrance into the Eternal Presence of God in Heaven.

When one reflects seriously on the Love of God in dealing with each of us in our fallen State, one can only stand in awe at His extended Mercy, Compassion and Patience shown forth as a consequence of

---

[105] Numbers 20:7-12; I Samuel 3:11-14; 15:10-28; 51:16-17; Jeremiah 6:29-30; 7:22-23; 26:13; Hosea 6:6; Amos 5:21-24; Matthew 23:23; Judges 16:19-21; Titus 1:16; I Corinthians 9:27; II Corinthians 13:5-6

His Love. The big picture is that during an expanse of more than six thousand years of God seeking to win our love back to Himself He has known both the Joy of acceptance by the human beings He Created and died for, as well as the pain of rejection and unrequited love. Genesis 6:6 speaks of God's heart being filled with pain and regret. Love does that, but it also rewards the Lover with so much more—as with the example of a Mother of a new born baby where the reward far outweighs the pain!

By definition, Love makes the one doing the loving vulnerable to the object of that love. Because you love them, they have the power to hurt you! Also, because you love them, they have the power to fill your life with Joy, Peace and a sense of self-worth. On the other hand, Love is its own reward when the Love is accepted and reciprocated by the object of one's Love. Love, in order to be love, must not resort to force. Love, in order to be genuine Love, will experience pain, patience and pathos (passion). Jesus said to those who would be His Disciples that "the Servant is not greater than his Master" and that necessary to discipleship is the willingness to "take up your cross daily" and follow Him. That Cross can best be defined as whatever pain or inconvenience is necessary to the accomplishment of the Will of God concerning Life, Love and compassionate intercession (involvement) in the lives of others, thus doing God's Work in the Cosmos (often translated in the Bible by the word "world", but actually meaning, "universal order of the created universe" or "human culture" or "society"). [106]

[106] KO/SMOS (from Exegetical Dictionary of the New Testament © 1990 by William B. Eerdmans Publishing Company. All rights reserved.) From Mark 16:15 "world" or, KO/SMON Strong's Concordance NT: 2889; See Colossians 2:20 where "world" is spelled: KOSMOW & means: "human society", (Thayers Greek Lexicon) (my addition =è"culture"; human society IS culture!).

You may be asking yourself about now, "So what good has come out of all this effort put into the life of one bi-polar, schizophrenic potential murderer? Has all the attention to him really paid off?

My answer most definitely is a resounding, "Yes!" I would like to have seen more results by now, but:

(1) David is going to church with me almost every Sunday
(2) and we do pray together; David addresses God as "Jehovah God" and prays from his heart with no effort to be formal or fancy; just a tormented heart reaching out to his God. That, my friend, is progress, even initial, but partial, victory!
(3) and David is much more open with me to discuss his inward, private thoughts, fears and reflections.
(4) Fourthly, I have potentially found someone to replace me as David's mentor/guide, someone he knows, whom he grew up with at school and is amazed that this person is now a pastor in the area; David likes him, even admires him.
(5) I may just have been able to pull David's feet out of the fires of Hell!
(6) And if I can persuade you to remember David in daily prayer that would be an important result of all this effort!

Such is my ongoing experience with David. Please do pray for David and for myself and the pastor I am trying to persuade to take over the challenge of helping David grow in God.

On January 2, 2014 I am back in my home, alive and well, and thankful for God's protection! My good friends, Skip and Gale Bennett provided me safe haven and "top of the line" food and fellowship while I stayed with them for a couple days. David became irritated with me because I had started calling the police every time he rang my door bell in the middle of the night. Usually it would be somewhere between 1 to 3 AM. I had asked David repeatedly not to bother me with ringing my door bell or calling me on the phone in the middle of the night. The Chief of Police had come to see me several times and emphasized how dangerous David really is with his expertise in all forms of weaponry. My life was threatened by David whom I had been working with for several years. The harassment has come and gone periodically over the years, but began with a vengeance . . . shortly before Christmas (2013) (with a short hiatus when I visited my daughter in Seattle) and continued to just before New Year's. The police chief had been coaching me on how to best protect myself (I have no gun) while waiting for the police to arrive in case this guy kicked in the front door. Staying with Skip and Gale and receiving their loving ministry helped me work through the fear and return to a place of peaceful rest in the Lord. I turned down someone's offer to loan me their revolver and decided to trust God. He is the best protection anyone can have! When the Police Chief called me to say he thought he had the situation under control and that it was safe to return home (January 2, 2014) I did so. God does use people, but only His Holy Spirit can give us Peace and help us learn more perfectly how to trust. I have been in a lot of tight spots over the years but this is the first time I ever felt paralyzing fear. Skip and Gale and the Holy Spirit helped me work through the fear and regain that position of Trust. Lord, I repent of my relapse and thank you for that new lesson about your love and the fact that you always know where I am—and that you are faithful! You are faithful both in life and in death!

Chapter Twelve

Insights (Family Issues—Part Two) Coming out of all the Storms along with God's Deliverance and Care for our Family

Insight #2: Telling the Truth
To a world that prefers Euphemisms and Sophistry

So let's start by defining our terms: truth, euphemisms and sophistry.

Truth! There are two kinds of truth: temporal truth and eternal (ultimate) truth. How do I know that as a fact? Because Scripture states that the visible was created by the invisible.[107] The Invisible System of Reality created the Physical or visible universe of matter. From a careful reading of Scripture one will learn that the angelic hosts were created within the invisible system of reality and operate according to truths of which we know little, except that human beings are destined to someday also live in that system of reality with its Ultimate Truth. God was not created, but is the Creator of all that exists. He is Self-existent, has no beginning or end. [108]

---

[107] Hebrews 11:3 and Colossians 1:16-17;

[108] I Timothy 1:17; 6:16; Hebrews 1:8, 11-12; Revelation 1:8, 11; 21:6; 22:13; Daniel 7:14; Matthew 6:13; Romans 1:23; Jeremiah 10:10; Micah 5:2; Psalm 145:13

So there is temporal truth based on facts from a universe that had a beginning through creation and will someday cease to exist. It will be replaced by a new universe and a new earth operating on Truths which are presently to us considered to be supernatural.[109] But the laws of the Invisible System of Reality are perfectly natural within that System. It is important that one always gives higher priority to Ultimate Truth than to Temporal Truth since we will someday live within that System of Reality, i.e., Ultimate Truth. When discussing any kind of Science (medical, physics, astronomy, biology, geology, electricity), or such disciplines such as Psychology, Philosophy, Mechanics, any kind of construction, education, politics, geography, archeology, architecture, the list could go on and on, one is talking about the temporal that will someday cease to exist! Or be superseded by a level of knowledge & reality based on what is now beyond our understanding, an invisible system of reality that is eternal in its very essence & not subject to the laws of nature that make up this present earthly System of Reality. [110]

The tragedy is that we live at a time when discussion of things from the eternal, invisible system of reality is mocked and all sources of eternal truth (Ultimate Truth) are being systematically removed from American culture. Joseph Goebbels, Hitler's propaganda minister is quoted as having said, "A lie said often enough becomes truth." And that is exactly why it is now commonly accepted in America that the US Constitution requires the separation of Church and State. Based on the lie, the US Supreme Court has in affect made laws (an authority the US Constitution does not give them) which eliminate even the

---

[109] Isaiah 66:22; II Peter 3:10-13; Revelation 21:1

[110] II Corinthians 5:1-4; Hebrews 9:11; I Peter 1:3-5; Jesus walking on the water—give that a scientific explanation from the temporal system of reality—Matthew 14:25-29; Or Jesus, vanishing before eyes of the disciples or walking through a locked door—explain Luke 24:30-31, 36-39;

influence of religion from our society. The Constitution does not forbid religious influence it only says that Congress (not the Supreme Court or school districts or any other part of our society) shall not make laws establishing religion. Only Congress has authority to make laws, but laws establishing an authorized religion in the USA are not the same as the influence of religion being allowed at all levels of our national life, including in the government. No ruling of the US Supreme Court is legally binding on the private citizen; the purpose of their rulings being to give guidance to Congress and the President. Only Congress can make laws to which private citizens must obey.

The idea of the Separation of Church and State was first mentioned in a letter by Thomas Jefferson to a Baptist Pastor in which Mr. Jefferson reassured the pastor that there was a wall between the government and the church that would not allow the government to make any decisions that would limit religious freedom in our nation. The concern was that the Federal Government might someday establish a state religion similar to the Church of England by which all other religious expression would be outlawed. That had already been done by one or two of the original colonies in which the Episcopalian Church was the only Church Denomination allowed. The concern by the Baptist Pastor was that the free expression of religion might be limited in our schools, churches and other institutions. Thomas Jefferson assured the pastor that the control or limiting of religious practices in schools, churches and other institutions would never happen.

Much about this issue could be written, but my point is that, based on a lie told often enough to be believed as fact, Ultimate Truth is being systematically removed from American Society so that all we have left is Temporal Truth that will someday be destroyed as God destroys the current universe.

What has captured my imagination for this discussion of Truth is that many Theoretical and Mathematical Physicists are claiming to have discovered that at the basis of all matter is a reality that is invisible, and that this invisible particle is what makes physical matter possible. This final component, necessary for completion of "String Theory Physics", is the foundation of the physical universe. It is this invisible particle that holds matter in beautiful harmony and keeps it from chaos.

Thus my claim that there are two kinds of Truth (Ultimate or Invisible and Temporal or Visible) is not far-fetched, even for those who are agnostic or atheistic toward a belief in a God who created all that exists including the spirit-world and the world of physical matter)! [111]

These ideas have been recognized since the 1960s and studied by theoretical and mathematical physicists around the world. In his article, "A Theory of Everything?", Brian Green, Ph.D. a highly recognized physicist and bestselling author, states, "The Elegant Universe" is an expression of Albert Einstein's dream to discover a way to express "the laws of the universe in one mathematical equation that explains it all" and that this "is the Holy Grail of physics". [112] A number of top physicists [113] claim that String Theory Physics has led them to this invisible particle which is the source and support of all that exists.

---

[111] Physics: The Elegant Universe and Beyond a 4-DVD presentation of Physics narrated by Dr. Brian Green (available from Netflix); accessed by Joseph Meyers on February 28 & March 26, 2014

[112] http://www.pbs.org/wgbh/nova/physics/theory-of-everything.html accessed on March 25, 2014 at 2:19 PM, Pacific Time, by Joseph Meyers

[113] Gabriele Veneziano from CERN (the European Organization for Nuclear Research, one of the world's largest and most respected centers for Nuclear Research), discovered the mathematical equations necessary to support String Theory Physics) & Leonard Susskind, Stanford University. John Henry Schwartz, of Princeton U. & the California Institute of Technology along with Michael Green of the U. of Cambridge discovered the "massless (invisible) particle; S. James Gates, Jr., U. of Maryland and other supporters of String Theory Physics add to our knowledge and understanding.

Their efforts to understand Matter as the multi-component description not only of the billions of galaxies in the starry heavens, but also in the smallest of particles in our human bodies and all else that exists on planet earth, have led them in their studies of these "building blocks of the universe" (gravity, time, electromagnetism, and the strong and weak particles called protons and neutrons) to ultimately develop String Theory Physics. Because the foundational particle is invisible and cannot be proven with current technology, String Theory Physics seems temporarily stymied from proving by testing within the scientific method of verification the mathematical equation which will finally establish this "Theory of Everything" as Ultimate Truth. It does, however, lend scientific support to my comments about the differences between Temporal Truth and Ultimate (eternal) Truth, both important to intelligent Christian Apologetics (proofs).

Euphemism! The term needs definition and explanation. A euphemism describes the act of using a nice, favorable or good sounding word in place of an unfavorable one; i.e., in place of a discouraging, ominous, or adverse word or phrase; the act of choosing a less distasteful word or phrase than the one intended, or the one more accurately descriptive. The word comes from two Greek words, "eu" meaning, "good" and "phemi" meaning, "to speak" or "speaking". Thus, "good speaking".[114] For instance, "a woman's right to choose" (notice the phrase doesn't finish the idea or describe "what" is being chosen) is a euphemistic phrase for the word, "abortion" or "legalized murder of an unborn child". "A woman's right to choose" is hypocritical in that it changes the focus to be on the woman's womb and away from the

---

[114] W.E. Vine's Dictionary of N.T. Words and Strong's Greek/Hebrew Definitions, NT:5350; two examples of how this word is used in the N.T., Acts 4:18 and II Peter 2:16. The first where the Apostles are forbidden to speak about Jesus and the second where a donkey speaks miraculously with a man's voice to rebuke the dishonest prophet.

life of the unborn child. It is a callous turn of words to avoid forcing a woman the necessity of focusing on the murder she has authorized. It has been noted that, "If it is not your body, it is not your decision. The body inside a woman's body is not her body!"

See the footnote, even in the Bible, the second half of the word, euphemism, is used negatively to hinder an unvarnished telling of the truth. Here is some unvarnished truth! A baby's heart begins beating about 18 days after conception. At 21 days its' heart is pumping blood through a closed circulatory system. Brain waves can be detected after six weeks from the time of conception. Fingerprints have formed at 14 weeks from conception. By nine weeks all structures necessary for the sensation of pain are functioning. At four weeks from conception a baby's eye, ear and respiratory systems begin to form. Thumb sucking has been documented after seven weeks, and by nine weeks the baby is able to wrap its fingers around an object. Between 13 and 15 weeks a baby's taste buds are present and functioning. At 20 weeks the baby can hear external noises like music or its' Mother's heartbeat. At 23 weeks babies have been shown to demonstrate rapid eye movements, a typical indication of an active dream state. The baby is dreaming! And yet the lie is often propagated that the baby is nothing more than a membrane, a fetus, attached to the Mother's womb. Sonograms have shown the membrane lie to be just that, a lie! [115]

How does abortion occur? One way is the insertion of a saline solution into the baby's body which produces a muscular reaction showing a slow and painful death that sometimes lasts several days. Another method is the insertion of scissors at the base of the skull in order to open a wound that allows for a suction tube to be inserted and the baby's brains to be sucked out until the skull is collapsed and

---

[115] www.prolifeaction.org/faq/unborn.php#stages accessed at 2:45 PM on March 18, 2014

the infant dies! Often, arms and legs are violently separated from the infant's body allowing the doctor to separate its mangled body from the Mother's body and to make completion of the murderous medical procedure easier for the doctor and/or mother.

As I said earlier, all these insights are based on events from my own life, events that have caused me much mental and emotional anguish.

The American culture and language now, in modern times, has a plethora of euphemistic expressions. For instance, someone's "significant other" is used rather than the words, "adulterous relationship" or "homosexual partner". The fact is, unmarried people don't just "live together", they "fornicate together"! We need to call it what it is! Call it what God calls it! The fact is that American culture has deteriorated to the point that, as a culture, many Americans copulate like dogs in the street! As a result, many children grow up not knowing the identity of their real father (or sometimes, their real mother). It's just whoever sleeps in the house tonight.

Sophistry! So what is Sophistry? According to the dictionary of etymological terms, Sophistry is "a subtle, tricky, superficially plausible, but generally false or error filled method of reasoning." Sophistry is most often used on people who don't take the time to think deeply so as to separate truth from trickery, or truth from error. Here are a couple examples: The first is a quote from President Bill Clinton who said (I personally heard him say this): "I am not pro-abortion; I am just pro-choice." It could be that President Clinton's motive and what he wished to express was his desire to focus on women and their desire to do what they want with their own body. After all, women vote, but unborn children do not vote! This sounds normal for a politician. But what the President actually said was that he was pro-choice, which is a euphemistic term for abortion. Logically, one cannot be pro-choice without also being pro-abortion! What the President said sounded very intellectual, very smart. And to people who don't stop to think before they accept or believe others, that works political advantage and garners votes. Sophistry does that! It tricks people into accepting ideas based on argument that is just plain dishonest and deceptive.

When asked about his opinion as to when life begins, Presidential Candidate, John McCain, was quick to answer, "At conception." Presidential Candidate, Barak Obama, used sophistry when he replied to the same question with the words, "whether you're looking at it from a theological perspective or a scientific perspective, answering that question with any degree of specificity . . . is above my pay grade."[116] That answer sounded very intelligent, but actually it was the opposite. It was dishonest, evasive and provided a prime example of "false wisdom" (Sophistry)! If candidate Barak Obama was so ill-informed as to be unaware of sonograms and their proof about life starting at conception, then Pastor Rick Warren could have done us all a favor by replying that such a deceptive response did not qualify him to be President. Barak Obama was not being asked about his pay grade. He was being asked about his opinion as to when life begins, but he used sophistry to dodge the question and was dishonest with the American people. Many of us believe that Pastor Rick Warren might have saved our country a lot of grief if he had challenged Mr. Obama on that response!

So what is my point? Or maybe, what should be the reader's "take-away" point regarding these three areas: truth, euphemisms and sophistry?

Ask yourself questions when you listen to someone trying to convince you of something. What kind of truth is this? Is it something with only temporal value that will not long endure, or does it have eternal value? Keep your priorities in alignment, putting the eternal over the temporal. Remember, someday you will be old and have the tendency to look

---

[116] http://pjmedia.com/rogerkimball/2008/08/17/above-his-pay-grade-obama-opts-out/ Accessed at 2:11 PM on March 19, 2014

back and wonder if your life really mattered. At least one can hope that you will be inclined to think that deeply. Deep thinking might lead to a mid-life crisis which would be the price of a life lived carelessly or in a self-centered manner, but it might help you make the remainder of your life count for things that really matter, like God, people, relationships. And when you listen to others, insist on unvarnished truth, which will help protect you against the pitfalls of euphemisms and sophistry.

Next, listen for euphemisms! Remember, a euphemism is a statement that varnishes or makes pretty something that really is ugly or difficult to accept (or should be difficult to accept). "A woman's right to choose" is a cleaned up, made to look pretty phrase to cover up the unvarnished (not cleaned up or made to look pretty) truth about abortion as legalized murder! Insist on taking off the varnish and getting down to the truth, the whole truth and nothing but the truth!

Finally, beware, be on guard against sophistry! Remember, sophistry is false wisdom! It is a statement or action that makes something sound or look intelligent, when in reality, it is a cover up for deception and lying. Hitler used sophistry to deceive the German people. He talked about the greatness of the German nation, the German people. This fed their egos and their need for new hope after their awful defeat in World War I. They were hungry to believe in themselves again. Nothing wrong with that! But Hitler fed them the food of lies covered over with a lot of good food for their beaten and battered self-images. Remember, rat poison is about 95% good food. It is the 5% that kills the rat! The way Hitler used partial truth was to convince German people to follow him in his desire to conquer the neighboring nations of France and Poland, and the rest of Europe so that the German Third Reich (Third Kingdom) would last one thousand years. That seemed like a wonderful goal after their humiliating defeat in World War I. He also used sophistry to convince the German people that the Jewish people should be exterminated! That event in recent history is so very similar to what is happening in America right now to convince us that the extermination of millions of unborn children should be a freedom guaranteed by the US Constitution for Mothers across the nation. More than 56 million babies have been slaughtered since the passage of Roe v. Wade in 1973.[117] That figure is nine times greater than the six million Jews slaughtered by the German government during World War II. Does the US Constitution really see legalized murder as a guaranteed freedom? Or do you think maybe America will face judgment by a righteous and just God for our murderous euphemisms and sophistries used to justify the annihilation of so many human beings?

If women have a constitutional right to do with their bodies what they wish, even if it means the taking of a separate human life, shouldn't men have the same right? Shouldn't a man be able to pick up a gun with his hand (part of his body), wrap a finger (part of his body) around something called a trigger and use the same hand (part of his body) to point the gun at another human being? Isn't he simply exercising a constitutional right to use his body as he chooses? Do you see how asinine, how absolutely, awfully, ridiculous this becomes? I wonder how many politicians would continue to be "pro-choice" with a gun pointed at their head by a man using his body in a manner guaranteed as a right by the US Constitution. What is permissible for the women should be permissible for the men, right? What I am advocating, based on truth absent euphemisms and sophistry, is the overturn of the US Supreme Court approval of Roe v. Wade, and the insistence that the Court's future decisions be based on the Original Intent of the Founding Fathers who wrote the US Constitution.

---

[117] http://www.numberofabortions.com/ Accessed at 9:05 AM on March 20, 2014 by Joseph Meyers

Insight #3: The Meaning of Judgmentalism in comparison to: Correction, Reproof or Conviction of Sin

What did Jesus mean when, as recorded in Matthew 7:1, He said, "Judge not" (NLT—"Do not judge others and you will not be judged." What is Jesus saying here? First of all, we need to realize that the Greek (language in which the Holy Spirit inspired the New Testament writings) here has several shades of meaning; the word, KRINETE from KRINO, first, "to distinguish, mentally decide, discernment that allows a wise and good choice; secondly, "to try (as before a tribunal), condemn and punish". And so the word can be translated "Judge" in the sense of condemnation, sentencing and punishment, or it can be translated (and often is) by the words, "to discern, determine" referring to the discernment of good and evil. We are actually encouraged to be discerning in our approach to life and this is the same word in Greek sometimes translated "judge" but in others translated "discern". [118] The context of the Scripture establishes the correct word to be used in translation. The word KRINO is translated "condemn" in John 3:17-18 which makes my point about the proper meaning and usage of the word as differing from "correct, reproof" or, "instruction".

Application: Matthew 7:1 is forbidding us, in our minds, to decide whether a person is or should be condemned [119] and then punished by

---

[118] Matthew 16:3; Luke 12:56; Hebrews 5:14 (discern good & evil); Acts 3:13 (to determine or decide); Acts 16:15; I Peter 1:17; James 2:12; Titus 3:12; II Corinthians 2:1;

[119] John 3:17 where the same word is translated, "condemn"; see also John 5:22 where the word has the same meaning of "condemnation" in the sense of "damnation"; see also, John 7:51; 8:15; 12:47 where the word is used as "condemn to final punishment; also, 2 Thessalonians 2:12 very clearly uses "judge" to speak of final judgment to hell and translates KRINO as "damned"; Hebrews 10:30; 13:4; First Peter 1:17; 4:5-6; Revelation 6:10; 11:18; 18:8; 19:2; 20:12, 13; James 4:11-12 asks who we think we are to do what only God can do; i.e., judge (decide in our minds their eternal destiny) another person. Acts 13:46

Hell-Fire. The term, in Greek, also includes the idea of perceiving a person as worthless, unworthy of loving relationship because of their behavior. To determine a person to be worthless, or of less or no value, because they have disappointed us in some way would be judgmental.

On the other hand, any effort a parent makes to help a child make a course correction in their life and to tell them that they was not living up to her full potential of all that God had intended for their life, nor making their life count for eternity, would be corrective, not judgmental. Nor does it indicate rejection of their person. When, a child and later even as an adult, the adult child behaves badly (contrary to Scripture) for the parent to show their disapproval or administer correction was not judgmental, it was corrective. There is a huge difference between judgmentalism and correction, which the Bible is careful to distinguish in its teaching.

Back to the subject of the important differences between "being judgmental" or offering correction, discipline and instruction: to say that certain behavior is wrong, unwise or not living up to one's full potential is reproof and correction, which is far different than judgmentalism! The passage of Scripture in Matthew 7:1 has nothing at all to do with recognizing right and wrong or good and evil, it has to do with final sentencing or condemnation (in our minds) of a person. To be judgmental is the opposite of unconditional love! And Ruth and I firmly believed in unconditional love, especially toward each other and our children. A child can be well on their way to making there life count for things temporal. Only Judgment Day in Heaven will reveal how much of that also had impact for eternity.

To point out good or righteous behavior as opposed to evil or unrighteous behavior in not being "judgmental" in the sense it is used in Matthew 7:1! Ruth never rejected the kids or thought them unworthy to be our children because of their behavior. She sometimes disapproved of their behavior, but never their person! And she made that point to them repeatedly.

One can say, "Those actions, or the path you are on, will send you to Hell or ruin your life on earth if you do not repent and change your behavior". One can warn of moral, psychological or spiritual danger based on eternal values and do so without judging in the sense of condemnation such as, "you are going to hell!"—or, "you are not worthy to be my child, friend, husband or wife". We never have a right to tell someone that they are going to Hell. Nor should a parent ever refer to their child as "worthless" or "incapable of succeeding" or use such words as, "You are just a loser!" Those definitely are judgmental statements! Only God knows a person's eternal destiny! No one is ever "worthless" in God's eyes, nor should they be in our eyes! We can warn people that the path they are on (their habitual actions) will eventually take them to Hell unless they repent and get on a different path (habit or behavior). To say, "that is wrong" is not the same as telling a person that they are worthless or unlovable. Nor is it being judgmental for a parent to punish a child for certain behavior. The purpose of punishment is to make wrong behavior painful (in this life) so that, hopefully the child will develop different habits of behavior.

It is never wrong to pronounce judgment on evil or sinful actions! See Luke 7:43 where the word "suppose" is translated for the Greek word for "judge/discern"; 12:57 where the same word translated as "judge" is translated "to discern" right from wrong. While in Matthew 7:1 we are told not to judge a person as to whether they are going to hell or not, or are worthless or not, in the same chapter, Matthew 7:20, we are told to discern what kind of person someone is by what comes out of their life as fruit (the fruit of their vocabulary, what comes out of their mouth, their attitudes or their impact on others for good or evil).

But it is wrong to decide whether a person is a "fool" (Matthew 5:22) or "worthless" or "worthy of Eternal Damnation", and that is the kind of "judge not" that Jesus was talking about. Only God has that prerogative! Every person is created by God with a special destiny; i.e., a potential they can strive to achieve; or, if they wish, settle for less than their full potential. But they are still the object of God's Love and should also be the object of their parent's unconditional love. Ruth and I did love our children unconditionally!

Another way of examining this issue: if telling a person that what they are doing is wrong or that they have chosen a path that has an evil direction, or is less than they are gifted for, is in itself being "judgmental" then why does the Bible speak so often of the need for correction (making plain that which is good, righteous or evil/bad behavior)? Or why does the Bible command children to obey their parents? (See Ephesians 6:1 and Colossians 3:20) If the parents are being judgmental to define right and wrong for their children then those commandments of Scripture for children to obey their parents should never have been part of God's Word. Correction and reproof are commanded as part of Christian experience and should never be wrongly interpreted as the one giving the correction or reproof as being judgmental. [120] Such a reaction would be yielding to the deception of Satan, as well as being a form of rebellion. If rebellion has taken root in someone's heart they are very prone to misunderstanding Biblical teaching on this point.

---

[120] Proverbs 5:10-13; 6:20; 12:1; 13:18; 15:5, 10-12; 20:20; 23:13-14, 22; 30:11-12, 17; Deuteronomy 21:18-21; Deuteronomy 27:16; Titus 3:1; I Peter 2:13-17; Ephesians 6:1-4; Colossians 3:20; Exodus 20:12; Leviticus 19:3; Matthew 19:19;

The Amplified Bible translates II Timothy 3:16-17:

---

¹⁶ Every Scripture is God-breathed (given by His inspiration) and profitable for instruction, for reproof *and* conviction of sin, for correction of error *and* discipline in obedience, [and] for training in righteousness (in holy living, in conformity to God's will in thought, purpose, and action),

¹⁷ So that the man of God may be complete *and* proficient, well fitted *and* thoroughly equipped for every good work.

If "instruction, reproof and conviction of sin, correction of error and discipline in obedience" are forms of judgmentalism, someone should have told God about His error before His Holy Spirit inspired the teaching on correction and reproof to be placed in Holy Scripture! But that would be correction, wouldn't it? Which some people would say is a form of judgmentalism. All of a sudden we are going in crazy circles!

Let's take a quick look at the Greek vocabulary of the above verse: **elegcho** (el-eng'-kho) is translated as "reproof" and can additionally mean, "convict (inwardly), confute (refute, disapprove of an action, invalidate, show to be false), admonish, convince, tell a fault, rebuke".

"Correct" comes from the Greek, **epanorthosis** (ep-an-or'-tho-sis) meaning, "a straightening up again of what has shifted from its true position", a repairing and restoring of what is shattered"; "rectification" or, "reformation" (to form again).¹²¹ (Jeremiah 18:1-11) One aspect of a parent's task is definitely that of helping their children "straighten up again" a shattered, shifted or faltering, compromising, or rebellious or sinful character. The pressure on children today to be well thought of at school or among their peers is almost irresistible. Their priority is

---

¹²¹ Strong's Greek/Hebrew Definitions and Kittel's Theological Dictionary of the New Testament

all too often to please their friends than to please God or their parents. The tug-of-war between ungodly values coming from a few ungodly teachers and/or fellow students makes the task of parenting sometimes very unpleasant. Only if a child makes the internal decision to value their relationship with their parents above that of their teachers, and to listen to their parents rather than their teachers whenever there is a conflict in values, can these tensions be eased.

"Instruction" (in righteousness) is the translation of the word, paideia (pahee-di'-ah); and refers to "tutorage, i.e. education or training"; by implication, "disciplinary correction: sometimes translated as: "chastening, chastisement, or nurture". The word contains a root word in Greek meaning, "child".

All of these are used to describe the function of God's Word (Scripture) and cannot be identified with "judgmentalism" which is forbidden activity to Christians (Matthew 7:1). The one is commanded in Scripture (i.e., correction, reproof, instruction) and the second is forbidden; i.e., "judgmentalism". Parents are well advised to put Second Timothy 3:16-17 into active practice in the home. A parent has every right, even duty before God, not only to point out sinful behavior to their children, but also to give them what the parent believes is wise guidance in areas that are not mentioned in Scripture. A parent must occupy themselves with regularly repairing what has been shattered of their child's godly character, whether that shattering comes from the influence of ungodly friends or ungodly teachers at school. A wise child, instead of rebelling against parental authority will submit even if they don't understand or agree with the wisdom behind the restrictions laid down by their parents.

Some (even preachers) have said that we should not use the Scripture as a club. Where does the Bible warn us about that? If the Word of God is powerful and sharper than any two-edged sword and if the highest value should be to give a person the tools they need to be able to find the "narrow path" that leads to Heaven and Eternal Life as opposed to the "Broad path (way) that leads to destruction and Eternal Damnation, then to gently, lovingly mention the teaching of Scripture concerning any matter that identifies good and evil, leaving the choice to the person involved but nevertheless giving them the knowledge they need to make a right choice is an act of love not judgmentalism, nor is it using Scripture as a club (I think I hear the hiss of a spirit-snake in that idea!). Do it lovingly with compassion, leaving their ego intact. Don't humiliate them or condemn them, but use Scripture to correct, rebuke and instruct them! Do it because you care deeply for them!

It is often said, "Don't put me on a guilt trip", but the Word of God clearly teaches that recognition of guilt is necessary so that one will know how to repent and get themselves through the narrow gate that leads to life! [122] And this in place of going backward as in Jeremiah 7:24.

Matthew 7:13-14—New Living Translation

[13] "You can enter God's Kingdom only through the narrow gate. The highway to hell* is broad, and its gate is wide for the many who choose that way. **14** But the gateway to life is very narrow and the road is difficult, and only a few ever find it.

---

[122] Prov. 9:6; Isaiah 55:7; Ezekiel 3:18; 18:20-23, 27-32; 33:8-9; Numbers 15:31; Ezra 9:13-15; Jer. 7:24

Take special note of these Scriptures:

Ezekiel 3:18-19, 21—NKJV

18 When I say to the wicked, 'You shall surely die,' and you give him no warning, nor speak to warn the wicked from his wicked way, to save his life, that same wicked *man* shall die in his iniquity; but his blood I will require at your hand. **19** Yet, if you warn the wicked, and he does not turn from his wickedness, nor from his wicked way, he shall die in his iniquity; but you have delivered your soul. **21** Nevertheless if you warn the righteous *man* that the righteous should not sin, and he does not sin, he shall surely live because he took warning;

Proverbs 19:18—New Living Translation

18 Discipline your children while there is hope. Otherwise you will ruin their lives.

Hebrews 12:7-11—NLT

7 As you endure this divine discipline, remember that God is treating you as his own children. Who ever heard of a child who is never disciplined by its father? **8** If God doesn't discipline you as he does all of his children, it means that you are illegitimate and are not really his children at all. **9** Since we respected our earthly fathers who disciplined us, shouldn't we submit even more to the discipline of the Father of our spirits, and live forever?*

10 For our earthly fathers disciplined us for a few years, doing the best they knew how. But God's discipline is always good for us, so that we might share in his holiness.

By extension of application and based on First Corinthians 7:14 as translated by the Amplified Bible, there is a special dispensation of Grace and Mercy that has been extended to any child of Christian parents, that gives special hope for wayward loved one to be united in Heaven with their godly parents, or for an ungodly spouse of a Believer.

So I believe that my Son, who died of AIDS but who, on his death bed, repented and accepted Jesus as his Savior is, by the Grace of God, already in Heaven. And I believe that my daughter has a special dispensation of God's Grace and Mercy over her life. She is not trash! She is in the process of becoming a beautiful Woman of God, and always has been the object of His unconditional love! She is also the pride and joy of her papa's heart. I have been able to witness the slow turn of her heart toward God and have rejoiced!

Here is I Corinthians 7:14:

> [14] For the unbelieving husband is set apart (separated, withdrawn from heathen contamination, and affiliated with the Christian people) by union with his consecrated (set-apart) wife, and the unbelieving wife is set apart *and* separated through union with her consecrated husband. Otherwise your children would be unclean (unblessed heathen, outside the Christian covenant), but as it is they are prepared for God [pure and clean]. (Amplified Bible)

However, that does not mean that any child or spouse can live in defiance and active, purposeful disobedience to God thereby rejecting the covering provided by their Christian Loved One, and still be saved. Jesus said, "If you love me, keep (guard as precious) my commandments." John 14:15

A girl should remember that a boy who wants to have sex before marriage cannot be trusted! His action is the perfect setup for extramarital sex in years to come because of his basic character flaw. He is dishonest and lacks integrity to be faithful until death breaks the union between husband and wife. If he'll cheat WITH you before marriage, he'll probably cheat ON you when he gets tired of you or is mad at you or the two of you are having adjustment problems after marriage. The problem is a lack of moral values & guidelines, a self-centeredness that will always put his wife second after his own desires and preferences are satisfied! Until that character flaw is corrected, he can't be trusted!

The Bible teaches that a husband is to love and sacrifice his life for the good of his wife, caring for her tenderly and making the provision of her every need spiritually, emotionally, mentally (an intellectual companionship with an open sharing of thoughts, likes and dislikes, studying or reading together, and having a sincere appreciation for her opinions and preferences), financially, as well as physically (a good healthy, mutually satisfying physical intimacy) his highest priority just as Christ sacrificed his life for the Church. (Ephesians 5:25-28, 31) The marriage bond includes a certain sacrifice of individuality to the extent that each prefers the happiness and wellbeing of the other over their own. For the wife, the key word is "submit" while for the husband the key word is "death" (to self). So which is more severe, "submit (N.T. Greek meaning: "be of lower rank than as far as final authority is concerned") or "die" (on the cross of self-denial, no less)? How many men are willing for that one? This is quite a balancing act when actually put into practice in everyday life!

Love as described in First Corinthians 13:4-7 gives the guidelines.

---

1 Corinthians 13:4-7—New International Version

Love is patient and kind. Love is not jealous or boastful or proud or rude. It does not demand its own way. It is not irritable, and it keeps no record of being wronged. It does not rejoice about injustice but rejoices whenever the truth wins out. Love never gives up, never loses faith, is always hopeful, and endures through every circumstance.